THE STORY OF LIBERTY

BY

CHARLES CARLETON COFFIN

AUTHOR OF "THE BOYS OF '76"

Illustrated

The Story of Liberty

Copyright © 1987 by Maranatha Publications

Cover Design: Landers Design, Gainesville, FL
Cover Photograph: The Pilgrim Society, Plymouth, MA

Verses marked KJV are taken from the King James Version of the Bible.

Verses marked NAS are taken from the New American Standard Bible, copyright © 1960, 1962, 1963, 1968, 1971, 1972, 1973, 1975, 1977 by The Lockman Foundation and used by permission.

ISBN 0-938558-20-X

Printed in the United States of America.

Maranatha Publications, Inc.
Post Office Box 1799
Gainesville, Florida 32602

A NOTE FROM THE PUBLISHER

Most Americans are ignorant of the fact that the fruits of civil liberty which they enjoy have their origin in Christianity.

What was at first only a little stone began to strike at the foundations of the religious and civil institutions of Medieval Europe. That which was destined to become a great mountain of refuge for the oppressed and afflicted of the earth, that civil and religious liberty which was destined to make its home in the wilderness of America, would not be established without cost. Over the ensuing centuries, liberty would be purchased by the blood of the martyrs and the testimony of the servants of Jesus. It would encompass over 500 years of struggle as the human race endeavored to climb from slavery to freedom.

The rebuilding of America's Christian foundation and its superstructure of individual freedoms begins in the homes of American Christians, when the adults of this generation put a stop to the ignorance of America's Christian history. The rich heritage of Christian self-sacrifice that was the foundation of America should be set as a "seal upon the heart" of every adult and every boy and girl who want to see their religious and civil liberties preserved.

America's history and the events that preceded her founding pertain to Christ. It is His story of civil freedom and civil government. It is by diligently pondering the divine influence behind America's history that we begin to understand the goodness of God in establishing the nation of America for His gospel purposes.

It was the founders' understanding of history and of the price which liberty cost that called forth the physical bravery and moral courage of men such as George Washington, the signers of the Declaration of Independence, and the mature adults who were able to accomplish the tremendous amount of hard work, both manual and intellectual, that was evident during this period. It produced the citizens of a nation who were willing to lay their all on the altar of sacrifice to purchase freedom and liberty for generations yet unborn.

It was the knowledge of the courage of the martyrs of the past that caused Daniel Webster to proclaim when considering the Declaration of Independence, "We may die colonists...die slaves; die; it may be on the scaffold. Be it so... If it be the pleasure of heaven that my country shall require the poor offering of my life, the victim shall be ready at the appointed hour of sacrifice, come when that hour may. But while I do live, let me have a country, or at least the hope of a country and that a free country. All that I have and all that I am, and all that I hope in this life, I am now ready here to stake upon it... Independence now and independence forever!"

Yet, how many American Christians today would be able to make such courageous statements? How many American Christians would think that their life was a "poor offering"? Perhaps the reason is that the books of today do not prepare children to cope with life or the real world.

Today, most Americans have studied history rewrites which have been designed to separate America from her spiritual roots and to debunk the true character of those who gave their lives to make America great. For too many, history is a boring incomprehensible enigma.

The events of history, however, are not accidents. History is the autobiography of Him "who works all things after the counsel of His will" (Eph. 1:11 NAS), and who is graciously timing all events in the interest of His Christ and the kingdom of God on earth.

As the Bible was preached to the masses and translated into the language of the people, the Reformation arose, awakening men's consciences and intellects and stimulating science, literature, and invention. A free church, free education, free association, the right to speak and to write—these are the consequences of the liberty of conscience proclaimed by the Reformers.

The Bible in the hands of the individual became the root of America's Christian form of civil government—a Christian Republic. The Bible was first the means of transforming the life of the individual, and later the means of transforming not only church government but civil government as well.

The book of Job exhorts: "... Inquire of past generations, and consider the things searched out by their fathers. For we are only of yesterday and know nothing... Will they not teach you and tell you, and bring forth words from their minds?" (Job 8:8-10 NAS).

It is with this in mind that we have endeavored to republish Charles Coffin's *The Story of Liberty*, originally published in 1879. *The Story of Liberty* is not America's story alone. It belongs to all those who are enjoying freedom and liberty in any part of the world. And it belongs to all the nations that will yet serve Him. As we reach back into the records of history to observe the hand of the Great Author of all liberty, we will find direction for the days ahead and discover the keys we need to understand and interpret the future.

As we look at that which preceded our nation's history and led to its founding, we will begin to have an idea of what liberty has cost those who love the truth and how much still is at stake. We cannot neglect the present and hope to enjoy in the future the blessings of the past. Liberty was purchased by Christian courage, self-sacrifice, and unceasing vigilance. Only by these virtues can we hope to keep it. We must, by God's grace, be as determined to protect our liberties as our forefathers were to win them. "Stand fast therefore in the liberty wherewith Christ hath made us free, and be not entangled again with the yoke of bondage." (Gal. 5:1 KJV).

Rose Weiner
Maranatha Publications

INTRODUCTION.

To the Boys and Girls of America :

This "Story of Liberty" is a true narrative. It covers a period of five hundred years, and is an outline of the march of the human race from Slavery to Freedom.

There are some points in this book to which I desire to direct your attention. You will notice that the events which have given direction to the course of history have not always been great battles, for very few of the many conflicts of arms have had any determining force ; but it will be seen that insignificant events have been not unfrequently followed by momentous results. You will see that everything of the present, be it good or bad, may be traced to something in the past; that history is a chain of events. You will also notice that history is like a drama, and that there are but a few principal actors. How few there have been !

The first to appear in this "Story" is King John of England. Out of his signing his name to the Magna Charta have come the Parliament of Great Britain and the Congress of the United States, and representative governments everywhere. The next actors were John Wicklif and Geoffrey Chaucer, who sowed seed that is now ripening in individual liberty. Then came Henry VII., Henry VIII., Katherine of Aragon, Anne Boleyn, Katherine's daughter (Mary Tudor), Cardinal Wolsey, Archbishop Cranmer, Anne Boleyn's daughter (Elizabeth), King James, John Smith, John Robinson, William Brewster, and the men and women of Austerfield and Scrooby.

In Scotland were Mary Stuart and George Buchanan ; in Bohemia, Professor Faulfash and John Huss ; in Germany, the boy who sung for his breakfast (Martin Luther), Duke Frederick, John Tetzel, and John Guttenberg ; in Holland, Laurence Coster, Doctor Erasmus, and William the Silent; in France, Francis I., Catherine de' Medici, the Duke of Guise, Charles IX., and Henry IV.; in Spain, Thomas de Torquemada, Isabella, Ferdinand, Christopher Columbus, Charles V., Philip II., and Loyola; in Italy, Alexander VI. and Leo X. These have taken great parts in the drama: actively or passively, they have been the central figures.

One other thing: you will notice that the one question greater than all others has been in regard to the right of men to think for themselves, especially in matters pertaining to religion. Popes, archbishops, cardinals, bishops, and priests have disputed the right, to secure which hundreds of thousands of men and women have yielded their lives. You will also take special notice that nothing is said against religion—nothing against the Pope because he is Pope; nothing against a Catholic because he is a Catholic; nor against a Protestant because he protests against the authority of the Church of Rome. Facts of history only are given. Catholics and Protestants alike have persecuted, robbed, plundered, maltreated, imprisoned, and burned men and women for not believing as they believed. Through ignorance, superstition, intolerance, and bigotry; through thinking that they alone were right, and that those who differed with them were wrong; forgetting that might never makes right; honestly thinking that they were doing God service in rooting out heretics, they filled the world with woe.

There is still another point to be noticed: that the successes of those who have struggled to keep men in slavery have often proved to be in reality failures; while the defeats of those who were fighting for freedom have often been victories. Emperors, kings, cardinals, priests, and popes have had their own way, and yet their plans have failed in the end. They plucked golden fruit, which changed to apples of Sodom. Mary Tudor resolutely set herself to root out all heretics, and yet there were more heretics in England on the day of her death than when she ascended the throne. Charles V. and Philip II. grasped at universal dominion; but their strength became weakness, their achievements failures. On the other hand, see what has come from disaster! How bitter to John Robinson, William Brewster, and the poor people of Scrooby and Austerfield, to be driven from home, to be exiles! But out of that bitterness has come the Republic of the Western world! Who won—King James, or John Robinson and William Brewster?

There is still one other point : you will notice that while the oppress-
ors have carried out their plans, and had things their own way, there
were other forces silently at work, which in time undermined their plans,
as if a Divine hand were directing the counter-plan. Whoever peruses
the "Story of Liberty" without recognizing this feature will fail of fully
comprehending the meaning of history. There must be a meaning to
history, or else existence is an incomprehensible enigma.

Some men assert that the marvellous events of history are only a series
of coincidences; but was it by chance that the great uprising in Germany
once lay enfolded, as it were, in the beckoning hand of Ursula Cotta?
How happened it that behind the passion of Henry VIII. for Anne Boleyn
should be the separation of England from the Church of Rome, and all
the mighty results to civilization and Christianity that came from that
event? How came it to pass that, when the world was ready for it, and
not before, George Buchanan should teach the doctrine that the people
were the only legitimate source of power? Men act freely in laying and
executing their plans; but behind the turmoil and conflict of human wills
there is an unseen power that shapes destiny—nations rise and fall, generations come and go; yet through the ages there has been an advancement of Justice, Truth, Right, and Liberty. To what end? Is it not
the march of the human race toward an Eden of rest and peace?

If while reading this "Story" you are roused to indignation, or pained
at the recital of wrong and outrage, remember that out of endurance and
sacrifice has come all that you hold most dear; so will you comprehend
what Liberty has cost, and what it is worth.

CHARLES CARLETON COFFIN.

CONTENTS.

12 CONTENTS.

ILLUSTRATIONS.

WINDSOR CASTLE, FROM THE MEADOW AT RUNNYMEDE.

THE STORY OF LIBERTY.

CHAPTER I.

JOHN LACKLAND AND THE BARONS.

AT the time when this story begins there is very little liberty in the world. It is the 15th of June, and the grass is fresh and green in the Runnymede meadow, where the Army of God has set up its encampment. No other army like it was ever seen. All the great men of England are in its ranks—the barons and lords, the owners of castles who ride on noble horses, wear coats of mail, and are armed with swords and lances.

Pavilions and tents dot the meadow; flags and banners wave in the summer air; General Fitzwalter is commander. There is no hostile army near at hand, nor will there be any clashing of arms on this 15th of June, and yet before the sun goes down the Army of God will win a great victory over the King of England, John Lackland, who is in Windsor Castle, which overlooks the meadow from the south side of the river Thames, which comes down from the north-west and sweeps on to London.

The king is called John Lackland because his father did not deed him any land.   His brother was Richard *Cœur de Lion*—the lion-hearted— who was brave, but also wicked and cruel.   He commanded the Crusaders, and fought the Saracens under Saladin, in Palestine.   One day he told his cook to have some fresh pork for dinner, but the cook had no pork, nor did he know where to find a pig.   He was in trouble, for if there was no pork on the table he would stand a chance of having his head chopped off.   He had heard it said, however, that human flesh tasted like pork.   Knowing that no pork was to be had, he killed a Saracen prisoner and cooked some of the flesh and placed it on the table.

The king praised the dinner.   Perhaps, however, he mistrusted that it was not pork, for, said Richard, " Bring in the head of the pig, that I may see it."

The poor cook knew not what to do.   Now he certainly would have his head cut off.   With much trembling he brought in the head of the Saracen.   The king laughed when he saw it.

" We shall not want for pork as long as we have sixty thousand prisoners," he said, not in the least disturbed to know that he had been eating human flesh.   The Saracen general—Saladin—sent thirty ambassadors to

BATTLE OF ACRE.

Richard beseeching him not to put the prisoners to death. Richard gave them an entertainment, and instead of ornamenting the banquet with

RICHARD SLAUGHTERING THE SARACENS.

flowers, he had thirty Saracens killed, and their heads placed on the table. Instead of acceding to the request of Saladin, he had the sixty thousand men, women, and children slaughtered out on the plain east of the city of Acre.

"Tell your master that after such a fashion the Christians wage war against infidels," said Richard to the ambassadors. Kings did as they pleased, but for everybody else there was no liberty.

When Richard died, John seized all his money, jewels, and the throne, pretending that Richard had made a will in his favor. John's older brother, Geoffrey, who was heir to the throne, was dead; but Geoffrey had a son, Arthur, whose right to the throne was as good as John's. Arthur was a boy, while John was thirty-two years old. The uncle seized Arthur, and put him into a dungeon in the Tower in London;

CRUSADERS.

and ordered the keeper, Hubert de Burgh, to put Arthur's eyes out with a red-hot iron.   Shakspeare has pictured the scene when Hubert entered one morning and showed Arthur his uncle's order:

"*Arth.* Must you with hot irons burn out both mine eyes?
Hub. Young boy, I must.
Arth.   And will you?
Hub.   And I will.
Arth. Have you the heart? When your head did but ache
I knit my handkerchief about your brows,
(The best I had, a princess wrought it me),
And I did never ask it you again:
And with my hand at midnight held your head;
And, like the watchful minutes to the hour,
Still and anon cheer'd up the heavy time:
Saying, What lack you? and Where lies your grief?
Or, What good love may I perform for you?
Many a poor man's son would have lain still,
And ne'er have spoke a loving word to you;
But you at your sick service had a prince.
Nay, you may think my love was crafty love,
And call it cunning; Do, an if you will:
If Heaven be pleased that you must use me ill,
Why, then you must.—Will you put out mine eyes?
These eyes that never did, nor never shall,
So much as frown on you?
    Hub.   I have sworn to do it,
And with hot irons must I burn them out."

But he did not.   Arthur was so affectionate and kind that Hubert had not the heart to do it.   It is not certainly known what became of Arthur, but that John had him murdered is most probable.

Before John seized the throne, he married a girl named Avisa, daughter of the Duke of Gloucester; but afterward he saw Isabella, wife of Count La Marche, in Normandy, and deserting Avisa, persuaded the foolish woman to leave her husband and marry him.   When the count and his friends flew to arms, he seized them, took them over to England, thrust them into loathsome dungeons, and starved them to death, while he lived in affluence in the castle at Windsor.

There were rich Jews in London and Bristol, and John coveted their money.   He seized them.

" Give up your money, or I will have your teeth pulled, every one of them," said he.   Most of them gave up their money; but one man resisted.

" Pull a tooth," said the king.   The tooth was pulled.

" Will you give up your money?"

" No."

" Pull another." Out came another tooth.

" Will you comply with the king's demands ?"

" No."

" Pull 'em all out." Out they came.

" Will you hand over your money ?"

" No."

" Then seize it; take all." So the poor man lost his teeth, and his money also.

John commanded the country people to drive their cattle into camp, and supply his soldiers with food. The people in Wales, however, would not obey, whereupon he seized twenty-eight sons of the chief families, and shut them up in prison. That stirred the Welshmen's blood, and they flew to arms; but John, instead of giving up the young men, put them to death. He is a tyrant. The barons and lords have resolved that they will no longer submit to his tyranny. They have organized themselves into an army, calling themselves the "Army of God." A few months ago, they sent a deputation to the king, stating their demands.

KING JOHN.

" I will not grant them liberties which will make me a slave," he said, swearing terrible oaths.

There is no liberty for anybody, except for this wicked and cruel tyrant. But his answer only makes the barons more determined. They resolve that if the king will not grant what they ask, they will secure it by the sword.

John can swear terrible oaths, and make a great bluster; but he is a coward, as all blusterers are, and turns pale when he finds that the Army of God is marching to seize him. He sends word to the barons that he will meet them at Runnymede on the 15th of June, and grant what they desire. The barons have written out their demands on parchment. They will have them in writing, and the agreement shall be the law of the land.

John rides down from the Castle, accompanied by a cavalcade, through Windsor forest, where the deer are feeding, and where pheasants are building their nests, and meets the barons on an island in the river. He is so frightened that he does not ask the barons to make any modification of their demands, but grants what they desire. A great piece of beeswax, as large as a saucer, and an inch thick, is stamped with John's seal, and attached to the parchment; then the king rides back to the Castle, moody and gloomy; but as soon as he gets inside the fortress, he rages like a madman, walks the hall, smiting his fists, rolling his eyes, gnashing his teeth, biting sticks and chewing straws, cursing the barons, and swearing that he will have his revenge. What is this document to which the king's seal has been attached? It is a paper establishing a Great Council, composed of the barons, the archbishops, bishops, and earls, whom the king is

ROUND TOWER OF WINDSOR CASTLE.

to summon from time to time by name, and the lesser barons, who are to be summoned by the sheriffs of the counties. Together, they are to be a Parliament. Hereafter the king shall not levy any taxes that he may please, or compel people to drive their cattle into camp; but Parliament shall say what taxes shall be levied. The barons may choose twenty-five

WINDSOR CASTLE (SOUTH VIEW).

of their number, who shall see that the provisions of the agreement are carried out. Another agreement is that no freeman shall be punished till after he has had a trial by his equals. There are other stipulations, but these are the most important. The agreement is called the *Magna Charta*, or Great Charter.

John Lackland plans his revenge. There is a powerful man in Rome, the most powerful man on earth, who will aid him—Pope Innocent III. He claims to be, and the barons and everybody else regard him as God's representative on earth. He has all power. The people have been taught to believe that he is the only individual in the world who has the right to say what men shall believe and what they shall do, and that he can do no wrong; that what he says is right *is* right. He is superior to all kings and emperors. Just after the great battle of Hastings, which was fought in October, 1066, Pope Gregory VII. made these declarations:

"*To the Pope belongs the right of making new laws.*
"*All the princes of the earth shall kiss his feet.*
"*He has the right of deposing emperors.*

"*The sentence of the Pope can be revoked by none.*

"*He can be judged by none.*

"*None may dare to pronounce sentence upon any one who appeals to the Pope.*

"*He never has erred, nor can he ever err.*

"*He can loose subjects from the oath of fealty.*

"*The Pope is holy.   He can do no wrong.*"

John has already humiliated himself before the Pope, and acknowledged him as his superior in everything.   He sends a copy of the Charter, that the Pope may read it, begging to be released from keeping his oath.

The Pope is very angry when he reads the Charter, for he sees that it encroaches upon his authority, taking political affairs out of his hands. He swears a terrible oath that the barons shall be punished for daring to take such liberties.   He releases John from his oath, and sends word to the barons that if they do not renounce the Charter he will excommunicate them.   The barons are not frightened, however, and send back this reply :

"It is not the Pope's business to meddle with the political affairs or the rights and liberties of Englishmen."

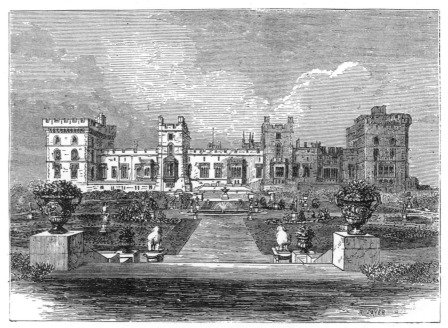

WINDSOR CASTLE (EAST VIEW).

The Pope excommunicates them, and aids John in stirring up the people to fight the barons.   He excommunicates the Archbishop of Canterbury, the highest prelate in England, who officiates in Canterbury Cathedral, and who sides with them.   The barons, seeing that the Pope and John together are too strong for them, offer the crown to Lewis, son of the King of France.   The French king is quite willing to send an army to help them.   John marches along the sea-coast to prevent the landing of the French, and comes to a low place when the tide is out; but the tide comes in suddenly with a rush and roar, and he loses all his carriages, treasure, baggage, regalia, and many of his soldiers, and is obliged to flee.

THE PLACE WHERE THE MAGNA CHARTA WAS SIGNED.

A few months later, broken down by fever, by disappointment, and rage, he dies at Norwich, and his son, Henry III., comes to the throne.

There are two classes of people in England—the upper and the lower class—the barons and the villains.   A villain in the nineteenth century is a swindler, a cheat; but six hundred years ago a villain was a poor man who worked for his living.   He was a serf, and owed allegiance to the barons.   The villains could not own any land, nor could they own themselves.   They had no rights nor liberties.

The barons are a few hundreds, the villains several millions.   The barons, while demanding their own liberties, are not thinking of obtaining any liberties for the villains.   It does not occur to them that a villain has

"HE HAS THE RIGHT OF DEPOSING EMPERORS."

any rights or liberties. Little do they know, however, of what will grow out of that parchment.

Six centuries and a half have passed since that 15th of June, in 1215, at Runnymede; the meadows are as fresh and green as then; the river winds as peacefully as it has through all the years. England and Amer-

"ALL THE PRINCES OF THE EARTH SHALL KISS HIS FEET."

ica have become great and powerful nations; but would they have been what they are if the Army of God had not won that victory over John Lackland? No; for out of that Charter have come the Parliament of Great Britain and the Congress of the United States, and many other things. It was the first great step of the English people toward freedom.

Not far from that verdant meadow where the army set up its encampment is a little old stone church, with ivy creeping over its walls and climbing its crumbling tower. One hundred and fifty years ago, Thomas Gray, a poet, who lived in a little hamlet near by, used to wander out in the evening to meditate in the old church-yard, and here he wrote a sweet poem, beginning,

"The curfew tolls the knell of parting day;
  The lowing herd winds slowly o'er the lea;
  The ploughman homeward plods his weary
      way,
  And leaves the world to darkness and to me."

THE CHURCH.

A few years after he wrote it, in 1759, one night a great fleet of English war-ships was moored in the river St. Lawrence, and an army in boats with muffled oars was silently moving along the stream.   The general commanding it was James Wolfe, a young man only thirty years of age. In his army were soldiers from New Hampshire, Massachusetts, Rhode Isl-

CANTERBURY CATHEDRAL.

and, Connecticut, and New York.   One of General Wolfe's officers was Colonel Israel Putnam, of Connecticut; another was Richard Montgomery, of New York.   As the boats moved along the stream, the brave young general from England recited this verse of the poem:

> "The boast of heraldry, the pomp of power,
>   And all that beauty, all that wealth, e'er gave,
>   Await, alike, th' inevitable hour;
>   The paths of glory lead but to the grave."

"I would rather be the author of that poem than take Quebec to-morrow," said he.

But would the poem ever have been written if the Army of God had not set up its banners?   Quite likely not.

In the darkness the army under General Wolfe climbed the steep bank of the St. Lawrence—so steep and so narrow the path that only one man at a time could climb it; and in the morning the whole army stood on the Plains of Abraham, behind Quebec.   Before another sunset a great battle had been fought, a great victory won. Wolfe was victor, Montcalm the vanquished; but both were dead. The flag of France, which had floated above the citadel of Quebec, the emblem of French power, disappeared forever, and the flag of England appeared in its place. From that time on there was to be another language, another literature, another religion, another civilization, in the Western World. But would the battle ever have been fought, would things in America be as they are, if the barons had not obtained that agreement in writing from John Lackland? No. That parchment, crumpled and worn and yellow with time, with the great round seal attached to it, lies in a glass case in the British Museum, London. The parchment is but a piece of sheepskin; the wax was made by the bees which hummed amidst the hawthorn hedges of old England six hundred years ago. The parchment and the wax are of very little account in themselves, but what has come from them is of infinite value. As this story goes on, it will be seen that the assembling of the Army of God in the meadow of Runnymede was the beginning of the liberty which we now enjoy.

GRAY'S MONUMENT.

CHAPTER II.

THE MAN WHO PREACHED AFTER HE WAS DEAD.

DOCTOR JOHN WICKLIF has been dead these forty years, and his bones have been lying the while in Lutterworth Church-yard; but it has been decreed by the great Council of Constance that they shall lie there no longer. A party of monks, with pick and spade, have dug them up, and now they kindle a fire, burn them to powder, and shovel the ashes into

LUTTERWORTH CHURCH.

a brook which sweeps past the church-yard; and the brook bears them on to the Avon, which, after winding through Stratford meadows, falls into the Severn, and the Severn bears them to the sea. But why are the monks so intent upon annihilating the doctor's bones? Because the doctor, who was a preacher, though he has been dead so long, still continues to preach! The monks will have no more of it; and they think that by getting rid of his bones they will put an end to his preaching. They forget that there are some things which the fire will not burn—such as liberty, truth, justice. Little do they think that the doctor will keep on preaching; that his parish will be the world, his followers citizens of every land; that his preaching, together with that parchment and the great piece of beeswax attached to it, which the barons obtained from John Lackland, will bring about a new order of things in human affairs; that thrones will be overturned; that sovereigns will become subjects, and subjects sovereigns.

A century has passed since the Magna Charta was obtained, but not much liberty has come from that document as yet. The people are still

STRATFORD.

THE MONKS.

villains. The king and the barons plunder them; the monks, friars, bishops, and archbishops—a swarm of men live upon them. They must pay taxes to the king, to the barons, and to the priests; and they have no voice in saying what or how much the taxes shall be. They are ignorant. They have no books. Not one man in a thousand can read. The priests and the parish clerks, the bishops, rich men, and their children are the only ones who have an opportunity of obtaining an education. There are no schools for the poor.

CARMELITE MONK.

The priests look sharply after their dues. Be it a wedding, a funeral, the saying of mass for the dead, baptizing a child, granting absolution for sin, or any other service, the priest must have his fee. The country is overrun with monks and friars—Carmelites, who wear white gowns; Franciscans, dressed in gray; Augustinians and Dominicans, who wear black. They live in monasteries and abbeys, shave their crowns, and go barefoot. They have taken solemn vows to have nothing to do with the world, to spend their time in fasting and praying; but, notwithstanding their vows, none of the people—none but the rich men—can spread such bountiful tables as they, for the monasteries, abbeys, nunneries, convents, and bishoprics hold half the land in England, and their revenues are greater than the king's. In the monastery larders are shoulders of the mutton, quarters of juicy beef, haunches of choice venison. In the cellars

GOOD OLD WINE.

are casks of good old wine from the vineyards of Spain and the banks
of the Rhine, and yet the friars are the greatest beggars in the country.
They go from house to house, leading a donkey, with panniers lashed to

THE WAY ST. DUNSTAN SERVED THE DEVIL.

the animal's sides, or else carry a sack on their backs, begging money,
butter, eggs, cheeses, receiving anything which the people may give; and
in return invoking the blessings of the saints upon their benefactors, and
cursing those who refuse to give. They have relics for sale: shreds of
clothing which they declare was worn by the Virgin Mary; pieces of the
true cross; bones of saints—all very holy.

They have a marvellous story to relate of St. Dunstan, who was a
blacksmith, and very wicked, but afterward became a good man, and was
made Archbishop of Canterbury. One day the devil came and looked

into the window where the saint was at work, trying to tempt him, whereupon St. Dunstan seized his red-hot tongs and clapped them upon the devil's nose, which made the fiend roar with pain; but the saint held him fast till he promised to tempt him no more.

The people are very ignorant. There are no schools; there are none to teach them except the priests, monks, and friars, who have no desire to see the people gaining knowledge, for knowledge is power, and ignorance weakness. The people are superstitious, as ignorant people generally are. They believe in hobgoblins and ghosts. They have startling stories to relate of battles between brave knights and dragons that spit fire, and are terrible to behold. St. George, the patron saint of England, had a fierce encounter with a dragon, and came off victorious. The peasants relate the stories by their kitchen fires; the nobles narrate them in their castles; the poets rehearse the exploits of the brave knights in verses, which the minstrels sing from door to door. Although no one ever has seen a dragon, yet everybody believes that such creatures exist, and may make their appearance at any moment.

A KNIGHT FIGHTING A DRAGON.

The people believe in witches. Old women who are wrinkled and bent with age are supposed to sell themselves to the devil, and he gives them power to come and go through the air at will, riding a broomstick, at night, bent on mischief; with pow-

MISCHIEF IN THE AIR.

er to fly into people's houses through the keyholes, to bewitch men, women, children, horses, dogs, cattle, and everything. If a horse is contrary, the people say old Goody So-and-so has bewitched it; if the butter will not come in the churn, the cream is bewitched; if anything happens out of the usual course, the witches are the mischief.

"There is mischief in the air."

King, priest, nor people will not suffer witches to live, for the Bible commands their destruction, say the prelates of the Church, who alone have the Bible; and many a poor, innocent woman is put to death.

The monks and friars having been recognized by the Pope, and holding their authority directly from him, assert their right to preach in the churches, crowding out the parish priests.

Little good does their preaching do. It is mostly marvellous stories about the saints, and what happened to people who did not feed them; or about the wonderful miracles performed by relics. They sell pardons for sins committed or to be committed; and they have indulgences absolving men from all penalties in this life, as well as after death. The monks drive a thrifty trade in the sale of relics. The good people who believe all the stories of their wonderful power to cure diseases, to preserve them from harm, bow down before the bits of bone, and pieces of wood, and rusty nails, and rags which they exhibit; but there are so many relics that some of the people begin to see the tricks which the monks are playing upon them, for it is discovered that John the Baptist had four shoulder-blades, eight arms, eleven fingers, besides twelve complete hands, thirteen skulls, and seven whole bodies—enough almost for a regiment! It is discovered that some of St. Andrew's bones once belonged to a cow; that St. Patrick had two heads—one small, preserved when he was a boy, and the other large, the one he wore when he became a man!

Some of the monks spend their time in writing books—printing the letters with a pen; but many of them are lazy. The abbots and bishops are fond of hunting foxes, and ride with the country gentlemen after the hounds, and sit down to good dinners in the barons' halls. The parish priests, for the most part, are ignorant. Their sermons on Sunday are narratives of monkish traditions, stories of the saints, with commands to attend mass. They get up spectacles called "miracle plays," acting them as dramas. They ask the women and girls indecent questions when they come to confession, and their lives are very far from being pure. They are so debased that they drink themselves drunk in the village ale-house.

If the monks, or priests, or bishops commit a crime, even though it be murder, the king cannot arrest them, for the bishops have their court, and a man who enters the priesthood is not amenable to civil law. They are let off with a light penance, and then may go on saying mass, and absolv-ing the people from their sins. But if one of the peo-ple commits murder, he will have his head chopped off by one of the king's execu-tioners.

The priests, however, are not all of them wicked. There are some who, instead of spending their time in the ale-houses, or in plunder-ing their parishioners, look kindly after their welfare. Some are learned men, edu-cated at Oxford or Cam-bridge, who exhort the peo-ple to lead honest lives. The man whose bones the monks are burning was a good priest, a learned man. We may think of him as attend-ing school, when a boy, at Oxford, graduating from one of the colleges; and, after graduating, he studies theol-ogy, and becomes a priest,

A MONK PREACHING.

and preaches in the Oxford churches.   He is so learned and eloquent that the people come in crowds to hear him.   There are students at Oxford from all over Europe—from France, Holland, Switzerland, Germany, and Bohemia—thirty thousand or more—who listen to his preaching.   His fame reaches London ; the king (Edward III.) sends for him, and he preaches to the court.

A girl, who is as good as she is beautiful—Anne, the daughter of the King of Bohemia—comes to England to be the wife of the Prince of

ADORATION OF RELICS.

Wales, Richard II.   She listens to Doctor Wicklif, and becomes his friend. With her come many of the nobles of Bohemia, and learned men.   One of them is Professor Faulfash, who has been to the universities of Heidelberg, in Bavaria ; Cologne, on the banks of the Rhine ; and to Paris. He listens with great pleasure to the eloquent young preacher, and, when he goes back to Bohemia, carries with him some of the books which Doctor Wicklif has written.

Let us not forget Professor Faulfash, for we shall see him again by-and-by.

Doctor Wicklif is a good man, and preaches against the immoral practices of the monks and friars. He does not arraign them before the Bishops' Court for their extortion, drunkenness, or infamous living; but he arraigns them at the bar of public opinion, and that is a great offence in the eyes of the monks, who say that the people have no right to have an opinion. The Pope decrees that men must believe in religion as he believes. There is no appeal from his decree. If a man believes differently, he shall be thrown into prison, tortured till he makes confession, and then he is burned to death, and all his

THE INTERIOR OF CHRIST CHURCH, OXFORD.

property confiscated. Who gave the popes this authority? No one; they took it, and, having taken it, they intend to keep it.

FRONT OF BALIOL COLLEGE, OXFORD.

The Pope commissions a set of men to hunt for heretics. They are Inquisitors, or men who ask questions, and have power to put men to death, to torture, to confiscate property. We shall fall in with them farther along in the story.

Notwithstanding the Pope professes to be holy and incapable of doing wrong, Doctor Wicklif informs the people that the priests, the monks, the bishops, and the Pope himself, are sinful, like other men. They belong to a holy office, but that alone does not make them holy men. To be holy they must lead righteous lives. It is not right for them to extort a living from the people, by threatening them with the loss of their souls if they do not supply their wants. Doctor Wicklif denounces them as a set of robbers who live upon the fat of the land, while the people are in poverty and wretchedness. They take from the people, and give nothing in return. They are ignorant; many of them cannot read, and can only mumble a few prayers. They manifest no desire to acquire knowledge, and would like to keep the people in ignorance. He maintains that the king is superior to the Pope in his own realm, and that he has a right to put a stop to all the swindling and extortions of the monks, and to punish men who commit crime. They cannot tolerate such preaching, for it makes the king greater than the Pope. It is the exercise of an individual opinion, the beginning of individual liberty. "Doctor Wicklif is a heretic!" they cry. That is a terrible accusation. A heretic is a fellow who does not believe as they believe. A man who does not believe that the Pope can do no wrong, that he is not superior to kings, is worthy of death. He ought to be burned. It is the duty of the Pope, the bishops, and the priests to prevent the spread of such opinions. If a man is afflicted with a cancer, is it not the duty of the physicians to cut it out, to burn it with fire? The Pope and the bishops are God's physicians, and they must destroy all heretics: so they reason. But who gave them this authority over the beliefs of men? No one. *They took it*, and have exercised it so long that they honestly believe that they truly are God's agents, and that it is their duty to exercise it, and to exterminate all who do not believe as they do. They believe that they will be doing God service if they put to death all who do not believe what the Pope decrees, or who does not obey all his commands. Men have no right to any opinions of their own. So at this period the intellects and consciences of men are in slavery.

Doctor Wicklif is summoned to appear before the Bishops' Court, in the palace of the Archbishop of Canterbury, a great building which stands on the banks of the Thames, in Lambeth Parish, London. On a day in January, 1378, the bishops, in their flowing robes, sit in the Council Chambers to try the man who has preached such obnoxious doctrines. All London is astir. People come in boats and on foot, filling the streets. Nobles and great men are there; one is the powerful Duke of Lancaster, John of Gaunt. Many of the people and the duke alike are determined that no harm shall come to the man who has preached so fearlessly, and whom they love.   Anne of Bohemia sends word that he must be protected.   The bishops do not dare to put him in prison ; but they report him to the Pope, and the Pope sends a *bull*—not an animal with four legs and two horns, and ferocious, but a piece of parchment, with a ribbon and a round piece of lead attached to it, which is called a *bulla*.   The Pope's

LAMBETH PALACE.

seal is stamped upon the lead, ordering Wicklif to make his appearance in Rome to answer the charges preferred against him.   The Pope cannot allow a parish priest to set up his opinions unchallenged, for to permit

Doctor Wicklif to go on will be the subversion of all the authority and power of the Pope, bishops, and priests, and in time the whole fabric of ecclesiastical government will tumble to the ground.

Although the Pope sends his summons, Doctor Wicklif does not obey it, for he is getting to be an old man, and, besides, there are two popes just now—one in Rome, and one at Avignon, in France. There is a great division in the Church. The people compare the two popes to the dog Cerberus, which, according to the old Greeks, sat at the gate leading to the infernal regions. The popes are fighting each other. The King of

READING THE BULL.

Castile recognizes the French Pope, whereupon the Roman Pope sends word to the people of Castile that if they do not obey him they will be forever accursed. The Roman head, to obtain money, sells the offices of the Church. Anybody can be a bishop, archbishop, or cardinal by paying for it. He sells the offices over and over; and if those whom he has cheated complain, he can laugh in their faces: he has their money, and they may help themselves if they can. He suspects that some of the cardinals are corresponding with the other Pope: that is a terrible offence, in his eyes. He puts them to torture to wring a confession from them, and then puts them to death. He curses all who oppose him, swears fearful oaths, and takes his revenge upon some priests who offend him by sewing them up in sacks, taking them out to sea, and pitching them overboard!

Doctor Wicklif reasons wisely that it will not do for him to make his appearance in Rome before such a Pope, and he is more than ever of the opinion that the Pope commits sin, as well as other

PREACHING-PLACE, LONDON.

men. He remains in England, preaching to the good people of Lutterworth. Sometimes he preaches in London, at the preaching-place erected in the streets. He has great crowds to hear him on Sunday, and works hard through the weeks, translating a book from the Latin into the English language—the Bible. The only

JOHN WICKLIF TRANSLATING THE BIBLE.

Bibles in England are in the libraries of Oxford, Cambridge, abbeys and monasteries, and some of the churches. They are all in Latin or Hebrew, written on parchment. Scarcely one person in ten thousand has ever read a Bible. Doctor Wicklif believes that the people have a right to read it, although the Pope has forbidden its reading by any except the priests, monks, and bishops, and other prelates of the Church. But into what dialect shall he translate it? for there is no uniform language in England. In the Eastern counties—the East Midland section, as it is called, where the Saxons first landed and obtained a foothold—the language is almost wholly Saxon; in the Southern counties—all along the South shore, where

the Normans landed—the language is largely Norman.   In the Western
and Northern counties are other dialects, so unlike that of the East or
South that a man from the old town of Boston, on the East coast, or a

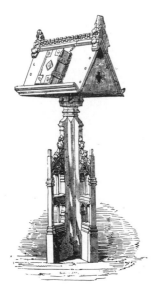

man from Plymouth, on the South coast, would
hardly be able to make himself understood by a
countryman from York or Lancaster.

Doctor Wicklif selects the East Midland—his
own native dialect—which is spoken by a majority of the people; besides, it is strong, vigorous,
and expressive.   Many other preachers believe
that the people have a right to read the Bible,
and clerks are set to work making copies of
the translation, which are placed on desks in the
churches, and chained, so that no one can take
them away.

The people listen to the reading with wonder
and delight.   They begin to think; and when
men begin to think, they take a step toward freedom.   They see that the Bible gives them rights
which hitherto have been denied them—the right
to read, to acquire knowledge.   Schools are start-

BIBLE CHAINED TO A DESK.

ed.   Men and women, who till now have not known a letter of the alphabet, learn to read: children teach their parents.   It is the beginning of
a new life—a new order of things in the community—the beginning of
liberty.

One of Doctor Wicklif's friends is Geoffrey Chaucer, a poet, who helps
on the cause of freedom mightily in another way.   He is a learned man,
and has been to Genoa and Florence on an embassy for the king, and has
made the acquaintance of many renowned men.   He is a short, thick-set
man, with a pleasant countenance, and laughing eyes.   He is witty and
humorous.   The king thinks so much of him that he directs his butler to
send the poet a pipe of his best wine every year.   The Princess of Wales
(Anne, from Bohemia) is pleased to call him her friend, and the poet dedi-
cates a poem to her, entitled "The Legend of a Good Woman."   He sets
himself also to write some stories in verse, which he calls "The Canterbury Tales;" but while he is writing them, let us see what is going on in
England.

In 1377, Richard II. is made king.   The barons complain to him that
the villains — the people who owe them service — do not give it; that
they are banding themselves to throw off the service altogether, claim-

ing that freedom is their right. Doctor Wicklif's books and preaching have set them to thinking, and preachers are going here and there telling the people that the barons have no claim upon them. One of the agitators is a fellow named John Ball, who sings sarcastic ballads. In one of them he rehearses this couplet :

> "When Adam delved and Eve span,
> Who was then the gentleman ?"

The people ask the question over and over, and make up their minds that they, as well as the men who live in castles, have some natural rights.

One day a baron arrests a burgher, and imprisons him in Rochester Castle, claiming that he is his slave, whereupon the people seize their arms, surround the castle, and set the prisoner at liberty.

Every individual in the kingdom is taxed—every child, every man and woman. A child must pay so much, a grown person more. A tax-col-

FLORENCE.

lector comes to John Walter's house. Walter earns a living by laying tiles on the roofs of houses. The people call him the Tiler, or Tyler, and instead of pronouncing his full name—John Walter, the tiler—call him Wat Tyler. He has a daughter, just growing to womanhood.

"She must pay a full tax," says the collector.

"No ; she is not a woman yet," the mother replies.

"I'll soon find out whether she is a woman or not," the tax-collector answers, and rudely insults the girl.

"Help! help!" The mother shouts the words, and her husband comes in with a club.

"What do you mean by insulting my daughter?"

The collector is a ruffian; having insulted the daughter, he lifts his hand to give the father a blow, when down comes the cudgel upon

CANTERBURY.

the fellow's head, crashing the skull, and scattering his brains about the room. The news spreads. The people join the Tyler. They are ready for insurrection. They seize their swords, bows and arrows, and clubs.

"Let us march to London and see the king," they shout. From all the towns of Kent they come, one hundred thousand or more. They attack the houses of the knights, lords, and nobles. They swarm into Canterbury, and pillage the palace of the archbishop, who lives in great state, and to whom a large portion of the taxes are paid. There is great excitement in London. The young king, his mother, and many of the nobles take refuge in the Tower, for the news has reached them that the insurgents are arresting all the high-born men and women they can find. They seize Sir John Newton, threaten him with death if he will not do as they command, and send him to the king, desiring Richard to meet them at Blackheath, just out of London. The king is brave. He will go and see them. He leaves the Tower in his barge, with the barons.   The boatmen pull at the oars, and in a short time they reach the multitude, who, upon seeing the barge, set up a great shout.

"I have come at your request.   What do you desire?" the king asks.

There is a great outcry—all speaking at once; and the barons, fearing an archer may draw his bow and shoot the king, advise him to return to the Tower.   This angers the crowd.   "To London! to London!" they shout; and the multitude, barefooted, bareheaded, armed with clubs, surge on toward Southwark.   They are on the south side of the river, while the largest part of the city is on the north side, and there is only one bridge. The citizens raise the draw, and the excited rabble cannot cross the Thames.   The rich merchants of London own beautiful villas on the south side, and the hungry, ragged, excited multitudes ransack the houses, destroying property, and committing great havoc.   The people of London sympathize with the people of Kent, for they, too, are groaning under the taxes.

"We will let down the drawbridge, and permit them to come into the city.   We will show them that we are their friends, and then they will be quiet," the Londoners say to each other.

The drawbridge is lowered, and the great black crowd pours across the bridge.   The people give bread and wine and liquor, which excite the insurrectionists all the more. They rush to the Palace of Savoy, owned by the Duke of Lancaster, bring out all the furniture—the tables, chairs,

THE WESTGATE, CANTERBURY.

the silver plate—heap all in a pile, and set it on fire.   They do not steal the silver.   One man undertakes to secrete a silver cup, but the others pitch him upon the fire.

"We are here in the cause of truth and righteousness, not as thieves," they say.

What shall the king do ?   He cannot fight the insurgents, for he has only four thousand troops.   This is what his councillors advise him :

" It is better to appease them by making a show of granting what they desire than to oppose them ; for if you oppose them, all the common people of England will join them, and we shall be swept away."

The next morning the king meets Wat Tyler and some of the leaders at Mile End, in a meadow, and grants what they desire.   He sets his clerks

SAVOY PALACE.

to making out charters for the towns, abolishing taxes, and granting privileges never before enjoyed.   Most of the people are satisfied, and return to their homes ; but some, still thirsting for revenge against the Archbishop of Canterbury, make their way to the Tower, seize the archbishop and some of the priests, drag them into the Tower yard, and chop off their heads, which they place upon poles, and carry them, dripping with blood, through the streets.

Richard hears of what is going on, mounts his horse, and rides out to meet the rioters.   He rides boldly up to Wat Tyler, who draws a knife ; but before he can use it, the Mayor of London whips out his sword and runs it through Wat's body, and the rioter tumbles to the ground.   Wat's followers rush up, but Richard looks them calmly in the face.

" Come, my friends, I will be your leader," he says.

It is a brave speech for a boy of fifteen to make; but the men of Kent like Richard's pluck, and lower their spears. The king's troops come galloping upon the field, ready to draw their swords.

"You must not harm them. Let them go peacefully to their homes," says Richard; and the people, feeling that the young king is their friend, return to their homes.

But the barons are determined that the people shall not have their freedom. The bishops are angry over the death of the archbishop, and demand that punishment shall be meted out, not to those who were instrumental in putting him to death, but upon all the people—in the revoking of the charters which Richard has just granted. What can the boy do? Are not the barons, lords, bishops, and great men wiser than himself? He cannot stand alone against them; he complies with their demands, but recommends Parliament to give the people their freedom.

"Give them their freedom!" the barons exclaim. "Never will we be deprived of the service which they owe us."

"Doctor Wicklif's pernicious doctrines are at the bottom of all this," the bishops, the monks, and friars exclaim.

The Lords pass a law, which the bishops think will put an end to the mischief, in which the sheriffs are ordered to put all heretics in prison until they justify themselves before the bishops. The only appeal from the Bishops' Court is to the Pope, who is sewing men up in sacks and casting them into the sea. The Commons will not consent to such a law, and so the Magna Charta begins to protect the people.

The Pope sells a fat office to an Italian. The office is an abbot's position in the bishopric of Wells; but the bishop of that diocese does not relish it, nor do the other bish-

A BISHOP.

ops, for the next ship may bring other Italian vagabonds to plunder the people. They join in declaring that the right of appointment belongs to

the king, and not to the Pope, whereupon the Pontiff, who pitches of-
fending priests into the sea, excommunicates them; that is, he threatens to shut them out of heaven if they do not ask his pardon. Perhaps
the bishops think that a man who tortures cardinals to death because
he suspects that they are working against him, who sells offices in the
Church to the highest bidder, even though he be Pope, may not, after
all, hold the keys of heaven, for they persuade Parliament to pass this
law:

"*All persons who recognize the Pope at Rome as being in authority
superior to the king shall forfeit their lands and all their property, and
have no protection from the king.*"

The bishops are members of Parliament, and by obtaining the passage
of such a law array the nation on their side. Little do they dream of

THE PILGRIMS STARTING FROM THE TABARD TAVERN.

what will come from this action of theirs. They do not mistrust that
when a century has rolled away, a king, Henry VIII., will pick up this
act, and use it as a sword against the Pope, and strike a blow which
will split the Church in twain. We shall see by-and-by how it came
about.

The people are fast becoming heretics, or Lollards, as the monks and
friars call them—comparing them to tares, or *lolium*, in a field of wheat.
The poet Geoffrey Chaucer is sowing tares very effectively in a quiet way.
He has completed his story in verse, and the people are reading it. He
has written it in the East Midland dialect, adding some Norman words to

give it grace and beauty. It describes a party of pilgrims who meet at the Tabard Tavern, in London, on their way to the shrine of Thomas Becket, in Canterbury Cathedral. Becket was a priest, arrogant, self-willed, who refused to acknowledge the superior authority of the king, Henry II., and who was put to death by some of the king's friends; but the Pope humbled the monarch, who was obliged to kneel naked before Becket's tomb, while the monks lashed his bare back with a bundle of sticks. He found that the Pope was more powerful than himself.

To make a pilgrimage to somebody's tomb, to say Pater-nosters and Ave-Marias over the bones of a dead monk or nun, is supposed to be a meritorious act, and so all over England—over Europe—men and women are

THE MONKS HUMBLING THE KING.
(From an Old Print.)

making pilgrimages. Among the pilgrims who travel from London to Canterbury are a priest, a monk, a friar, a pardoner, and a summoner. The pardoner has pardons for sale; the summoner is the sheriff, who brings offenders before the Bishops' Court. Although the monks and friars have vowed to wear coarse clothes and live on mean fare, none are better dressed than they, none live so luxuriously. The poet is one of the pilgrims, and describes his fellow-travellers:

"A monk there was of skill and mastery proud,
A manly man—to be an abbot able—
And many a noble horse had he in stable.
I saw his large sleeves trimmed above the hand
With fur—the finest in the land.
His head was bald, and shone like polished glass,
And so his face, as it had been anoint,
While he was very fat and in good point.

Shining his boots; his horse right proud to see,
A prelate proud, majestic, grand was he;
He was not pale, as a poor pining ghost;
A fat goose loved he best of any roast.

*   *   *   *   *   *   *

A friar there was, a wanton and a merry,
Licensed to beg, a wondrous solemn man,
His pockets large—he stuffed them full of knives,
And pins, or presents meant for handsome wives.
The biggest beggar he among the brothers.
He took a certain district as his grant,
Nor would he let another come within his haunt.

CHAUCER'S MONUMENT.

" A summoner there was, riding on apace,
Who had a fire-red cherubim's large face;
Pimpled and wrinkled were his flabby cheeks,
Garlic he much loved, onions too, and leeks.
Strong wine he loved to drink—as red as blood;
Then would he shout and jest as he were mad.
Oft down his throat large draughts he poured;
Then, save in Latin, he would not speak a word.
Some sentences he knew—some two or three
Which he had gathered out of some degree.
No wonder, for he heard it all the day;
And surely, as you know, a popinjay
Can call out 'Wat !' as well as any pope.

"You could not such another pardoner trace.
For in his pack he had a pillow-case,
Which, as he said, was once the Virgin's veil.
He also had a fragment of the sail
St. Peter had when, as his heart misgave him
Upon the sea, he sought the Lord to save him.
He had a golden cross—one set with precious stones;
And in a case—what carried he? Pig's bones!
He, in a single day, more money got
Than the poor parson in a year, I wot.
And thus with flattery, feints, and knavish japes
He made the parson and the people apes."

So the poet holds these pilgrims up to ridicule. The monks and friars are very angry, and lay a plan to kill Chaucer, who is obliged to flee to Holland, the land of the windmills; but, after a time, he returns to find that the people are fast becoming Lollards. The reading of the Bible in English has set the people to thinking about the monks, while the "Canterbury Tales" have set the community to laughing at them. From thinking

THE LAND OF THE WINDMILLS.

and laughing the people begin to act, refusing to give to the beggars, who are so angry with the poet that he has to flee a second time; but he returns once more to London, where he dies a peaceful death in the year 1400, having done a great deal to advance human freedom.

When Doctor Wicklif selected the Midland dialect for his translation of the Bible, and when Geoffrey Chaucer used it in writing his Canterbury stories, they little knew that they were laying the foundations, as it were, of the strongest and most vigorous language ever used by human beings for the expression of their thoughts; but it has become the English language of the nineteenth century — the one aggressive language of the world—the language of Liberty.

It was in 1385 that Doctor Wicklif died. The grass grows over his grave. Forty-one years pass, pilgrims come from afar to visit the spot where he is buried; they break off pieces of his tombstone, and carry them away as relics. The monks and friars will have no more of that. They will not have a man who has been dead nearly half a century keep on preaching if they can prevent it, for the doctor has a great following; half of England, and nearly all of Bohemia, have accepted his teachings. The Great Council of Constance, which we shall read about in the next chapter, has ordered that the doctor's bones shall be dug up and burned; and the monks, as we have seen, execute the order. They cast the ashes into the river, and the river bears them to the sea. They have got rid of Doctor Wicklif. Have they? Not quite.

CHAPTER III.

THE FIRE THAT WAS KINDLED IN BOHEMIA.

THE young man who had studied at Heidelberg, Cologne, and Paris, Professor Faulfash, of Bohemia, who came to England with the Princess Anne when she came to marry Richard II., and who heard Doctor Wicklif, and who carried some of the doctor's books to Bohemia,

RECEIVING ABSOLUTION.

is a lecturer in the University at Prague. He has discovered that the monks and friars of Bohemia are as lazy and shameless as those of England. He preaches against them. He wants a reformation in the Church. He preaches that men and women, priests and bishops—all must lead pure lives. He believes that men and women should confess their sins to God, and not to a priest; that forgiveness for sin means something more than words spoken by the priests; that absolution is something more than kneeling before a confessor's box, and having a few drops of holy-water sprinkled on the head, from a sponge tied upon the end of a rod, in the hands

RUINS OF THE PAPAL PALACE AT AVIGNON.

of the priest. He does not believe that sins can be forgiven, nor that blessings can be conferred by any such mummery.

The priests denounce his preaching as blasphemous. "Professor Faulfash is a heretic," they say.

It is the one word—more terrible than all others—but the professor is not disturbed by it. Instead of becoming silent, he grows more bold.

One of the priests who cry out against him is the queen's confessor, a man—John Huss—who undertakes to prove that such doctrines are heretical. He does not succeed very well, for as he studies the question he discovers that the monks and friars are leading shameful lives. More than that, he begins to read Doctor Wicklif's books, and the more he reads, the more he sees that Professor Faulfash and Doctor Wicklif are in the right, and himself, the monks and friars, the bishops and the Pope, in the wrong. He sees that the people ought to be permitted to read the Bible. He preaches as he thinks. He is eloquent, learned, sincere, and earnest, and people flock in crowds to hear him. The monks and friars hasten to Archbishop Sbinco with a woful story—that the queen's confessor is a heretic.

The archbishop is an ignorant man. Archbishops and bishops are not always appointed because they are learned or eloquent, but for other reasons. The people call the archbishop a dunce, and say he is an A B C archbishop, indicating that he knows little more than the alphabet. The archbishop determines that the young priest, although he is confessor to the empress, shall be disciplined; but the king protects him, and appoints him elector of the University of Prague.

The archbishop, in great wrath at being thus interfered with, sends word to the Pope at Rome, for these are the days when the Church has two heads—one at Rome, one at Avignon. The Pope sends back word that the rebellious priest must not be permitted to go on. Especially is he commanded not to preach in a language which the people can understand; he may preach in Latin, but not in Bohemian.

It is not so easy to stop John Huss, however, for the king is his friend, and cares not for priest or Pope. The archbishop contents himself with gathering up all the books of Doctor Wicklif that he can lay his hands upon which have been translated into the Bohemian language—all that Professor Faulfash and John Huss have written— and burning them. If the books are burned, that will stop the spread of heresy, the archbishop imagines. The king compels the archbishop to pay for the books. This in turn makes the Pope angry, and he issues orders to the archbishop to stop all preaching in Prague—to

THE POPE ON HIS THRONE.

inform the people that they can no longer have absolution granted them by the priests. The Pope will let the people know that he is supreme. The king, however, is not disturbed by the order, but directs the priests to go on with their preaching. The action of the king emboldens Professor Faulfash and John Huss, who send letters to the mayors of cities all

CASTLE OF ST. ANGELO.

through Bohemia to resist the demands of a corrupt and wicked priesthood.   This makes the Pope exceedingly angry, and he orders the two
men to appear at Rome and give an account of their doings; but they do
not obey, for they know that there is a strong prison in Rome for such
heretics as they—the Castle of St. Angelo.

Sigismund is Emperor of Germany.   He wants a council of the cardinals and other prelates of the Church called to see if the Church cannot
be united under one Pope.   The two heads are tearing each other fear-
fully.   When the cardinals meet in council, they double up their fists,
take one another by the throat, and have just such rows as the common
people indulge in upon the streets and in the beer-shops.

The popes have stirred up wars, and armies are marching, and battles
are fought, for no one knows what.   The Emperor of Germany desires

a settlement of the troubles, and through his influence a great council assembles in the old city of Constance, in Switzerland, where all questions in dispute are to be discussed.

Never before was there such a gathering. The emperor comes in great state. The Pope of Rome is there, but not in state, for he is fearful that the council may depose him. There are seven patriarchs, twenty archbishops, twenty cardinals in their red cloaks, twenty-six princes, ninety-one bishops, one hundred and forty counts, hundreds of doctors of divinity, and many priests—four thousand or more in all. Multitudes of people come, filling the old town to overflowing, and making the dull streets alive as never before. Peddlers, hucksters, tricksters, mountebanks, charlatans, tramps, monks, friars, beggars—all flock to Constance.

The princes and counts have their wire-pullers to influence the cardinals and bishops. All are hoping to make something out of the council—to gain power, or money, or position. The council sits month after month, to the great profit of all the shopkeepers and grocers in the town.

During these months while the council is in session, one man who came to attend it, instead of taking part in its deliberations, is in prison—John Huss. He came of his own free-will—because the emperor wished

THE HOLY MEN SETTLING A DISPUTE.

THE OLD TOWN.

him to attend. He might have stayed away, but the emperor sent him a paper promising him protection—that he should be at liberty to come and go without molestation—that no harm should come to him while in Constance, and yet he is in prison. All through the months while the cardi-

JOHN HUSS IN PRISON.

nals and prelates have been there— marching in procession to and from the council — living riotously, and some of them scandalously, the man who has been preaching that they should lead pure lives, and that the people have the right to confess their sins to God, has been languishing in prison. How happened it, when he had the emperor's promise written out on parchment ? Because the Pope claims to be superior to the emperor. *"He has the right of deposing emperors.*" If he has the right of deposing emperors, then he has the right to disregard the promise which the emperor has made to John Huss. *No faith is to be kept with heretics.* So, finding John Huss in their power, the Pope and cardinals have thrust him into a dungeon, and now he is to pay the penalty for being a heretic.

It is July 6th, 1415. All Constance is astir. The people from the country flock into the town, for the heretic is to be roasted to death, and they must be early on the ground to see the procession which will escort the fellow from the prison to the cathedral. It comes, the cross-bearer at the head, carrying a gilded crucifix. Then comes the Bishop of Riga in his gorgeous robes; then a company of soldiers armed with swords and lances, guarding the heretic, so that he shall not escape. The streets are thronged with people. The women look down from the quaint old windows to catch a glimpse of the wicked man, as they suppose him to be. They see a man forty years of age. The procession winds through the streets, and enters a great hall. The emperor is there, wearing his golden crown, and seated in a royal chair. At his right hand stands the Duke of Bavaria, holding a cross; at his left hand is the governor of the Castle of Nuremberg, with a drawn sword. Around are cardinals and archbishops, bishops, priests, monks, and friars, and a great multitude of people.

It is not to the emperor that all eyes are turned to-day, but to John Huss, who ascends the platform, and mounts a table, where all can see him. He does not return the gaze, but kneels, and clasps his hands, and looks up to Heaven. The soldiers file away; the bishops, cardinals, and prelates take their seats in the council. Bishop Landinus ascends the pulpit to preach a sermon from the text, " Shall we continue in sin ?" Heresy, he says, is a great sin—one of the greatest a man can commit. It destroys the Church. It is right for the secular magistrate to destroy those with whom it originates. Turning to the emperor, the bishop thus addresses him :

" It will be a just act, and it is the duty of your Imperial Majesty, most invincible Emperor, to execute this stiff-necked heretic, since he is in our hands, and thus shall your Majesty attain an immortal name, with old and young, so long as the world shall stand, for performing a deed so glorious and so pleasing to God."

The bishop comes down from the pulpit, and orator Henricus takes his place.

" You are to weigh this matter well," he says to the council. " You are not to rest till you have burned such a sturdy heretic—one so stiff-necked in his damnable error."

Then a bishop reads the charge against Huss.

"You have disobeyed the Archbishop of Prague. You teach that there is a holy catholic church other than that of which the Pope is the head—a community of all the faithful ordained of God to eternal life—which is heretical."

THE COUNCIL.

"I do not doubt," Huss replies, "that there is a holy Christian church which is a community of the elect, both in this and in the other world."

"Hold your tongue! After we get through, you may answer," says Cardinal Von Cammerach.

"I shall not be able to remember all the charges."

"Silence!" The Archbishop of Florence shouts it.

John Huss drops upon his knees, and lifts his hands toward Heaven. If they will not hear him, there is One above who will.

" O God, I commend my cause to thee."

The reading goes on.

" He has taught that after the words of consecration have been pronounced over the bread it is still natural bread, which is heretical."

" I have not so preached."

" Silence, heretic !"

" He has taught that a priest polluted with deadly sins cannot administer the sacrament of the altar, which is heretical."

" I still say that every act of a priest laden with deadly sins is an abomination in the sight of God."

Ah ! that is a home-thrust. Bishops, archbishops, cardinals, and priests, who are living with women to whom they have not been married, never will forgive the heretic for saying that.

The last charge is read.

" He has contemned the Pope's excommunication."

" I have not. I appealed to him—sent messengers to plead my cause before him, who were thrown into prison. I came to this council of my own free-will, with a safe-conduct from the emperor."

John Huss turns toward Sigismund, and gazes calmly and steadily upon him.

" I came in the full confidence that no violence should be done me, and that I might prove my innocence."

The emperor grows red in the face, for he knows that John Huss came of his free-will. He knows that the safe-conduct which he gave has been taken away from him. He knows that ten thousand swords would leap from their scabbards, and a thousand spears would gleam in the sunlight, in Bohemia, to protect the man who is gazing so calmly in his face. With shame and confusion he sits there with downcast eyes. Everybody can see the reddening of his cheeks. Huss has had no trial ; but an old bishop stands up and reads his sentence. He is to be burned to death. Once more the prisoner kneels and prays :

" Lord God, pardon my enemies. Thou knowest that I have been falsely accused, and unfairly sentenced. I pray thee, in thine unspeakable mercy, not to lay it to their charge."

The bishops smile scornfully. The heretic is praying God to forgive them ! As if they had done, or could do, anything wrong ! As if his prayers were of any account ! They degrade him from the priesthood. A bishop's robe is thrown over his shoulders. This in derision.

" Confess your errors, and retract them, before it is too late," says one of the archbishops.

THE PROCESSION.

He makes no reply to them, but turns to the people :

"The bishops want me to retract ; but if I were to do so, I should be a liar before God."

"Silence, you stiff-necked and wicked heretic !"

They place a chalice in his hands, and then take it away.

"O thou cursed Judas! we take from thee this chalice, in which the blood of Christ is offered for the remission of sins," they say.

There is no blanching of his cheeks.

"Confiding in my God and Saviour, I indulge the hope that he will not take from me the cup of salvation, and I trust that I shall drink of it this day in his kingdom," Huss replies.

Greater than emperor, pope, or archbishop is John Huss, standing there beneath the vaulted roof of the old hall. None so calm, so quiet, so peaceful of heart, as he—soon to be one of Liberty's great sons. None so shame-faced, so insignificant, as Sigismund, Emperor of Germany. One word from his lips would set the prisoner free; but his craven heart has yielded to the demand of those who are thirsting for the blood of Huss. They have made him believe that he is not obliged to keep faith with a heretic; yet he knows that he is committing an act which, ever as he recalls it, will redden his cheeks with shame.

"Let him be accursed of God and man eternally."

In all the assembly of prelates there is not a kindly face, no look of pity.

"I am willing thus to suffer for the truth in the name of Christ."

They place a paper cap upon his head a mock crown—with figures of devils upon it, and this inscription:

> ## "THIS IS A HERETIC."

"Give him over to the beadle." The emperor speaks the words, which one day will come back to trouble him. Sooner or later retribution follows crime. It may not be to-day nor to-morrow, but it will come; and this emperor, the greatest potentate in Europe, will see his empire drenched in blood, towns and cities in flames, and the land a desolation, for uttering those words.

Out from the hall moves the procession once more. Out through the door stream the people. A fire is burning in the street, and the priests are heaping upon it the books written by Huss and by Doctor Wicklif.

Huss smiles when he sees the parchment volumes curling in the flames. They can burn the books, but truth and liberty will still live. He walks with firm and steady steps. None of all the thousands around are so happy as he. The bishops are astonished.

BURNING OF JOHN HUSS.

"He goes as if on his way to a banquet," says Bishop Silvius.

Through the streets, where the people throng the sidewalks and look down from the windows of the lofty buildings, moves the procession—out to the place where he is to be burned. What is it that Huss is saying?

"I will extol thee, O Lord; for thou hast lifted me up, and hast not made my foes to rejoice over me." It is the thirtieth Psalm. They can burn his body, but what of that? His body is not *him*.

"Do not believe," he says to the people, "that I have taught anything but the truth."

No trembling of the lips—no whitening of his cheeks. He is going to testify to the truth. Why should he fear? Truth and liberty are eternal, and will live when emperor and pope have passed away. Truth makes men free, and it will be glorious to die for freedom. The fagots are piled around him—bundles of dry sticks. The executioner stands with his torch.

"Renounce your error," shouts the Duke of Bavaria.

"I have taught no error. The truths I have taught I will seal with my blood."

"Burn him."

The executioner holds his torch to the fagots. What is it that the people hear coming from that sheet of flame?

"Glory be to God on high, and on earth peace, good will toward men."

It is the song which the angels sung above the pastures of Bethlehem. And this:

"We praise thee, we bless thee, we worship thee, we glorify thee, we give thanks to thee for thy great glory." It is the *Gloria in Excelsis*.

The smoke blinds him, the flames are circling above his head. Yet the voice goes on:

"Thou that takest away the sins of the world, have mercy on me."

The flames wrap him round, his head falls upon his breast. The fire does its work, and a heap of ashes is all that remains. The executioner gathers them up, and casts them into the river. The winds and waves bear them away. The particles sink to the bottom, or are wafted on to the great falls at Schaffhausen, where the water foams over the granite ledges, and from thence are borne down the Rhine to the sea, as Wicklif's dust was borne on the current of the Avon and Severn to the ocean.

The priests and bishops and Pope have got rid of John Huss. Have they? By no means. It is only the beginning of their troubles with him, for the people of Bohemia resent his death. It is the beginning of a terrible war, which lasts many years, and drenches the land with blood.

The cardinals and archbishops do not forget that the man whom they have burned to death was made a heretic through reading Doctor Wicklif's books. The doctor has been dead a long while, so they cannot burn him, but it will be some satisfaction to let the world know what they would do to the doctor if he were only in the flesh, and they issue an order to dig up the bones and burn them.   We have seen how it was done.

Though the monks have burned John Huss and the bones of Doctor Wicklif, they have not put a stop to their preaching.   Do words spoken in behalf of truth, justice, and liberty ever die?   We shall see by-and-by,

THE FALLS OF SCHAFFHAUSEN.

after a hundred years have rolled away, how a poor boy—so poor that he will wander through the streets and sing for his breakfast, which the kind-hearted people will give him—how he will hear Doctor Wicklif and John Huss speaking to him across the centuries.   We shall see what a mighty work he will do for truth and liberty.

CHAPTER IV.

WHAT LAURENCE COSTER AND JOHN GUTTENBERG DID FOR LIBERTY.

LAURENCE COSTER is a Dutchman, and lives in the old town of Haerlem, in the land of the windmills, where the people have built great dikes enclosing portions of the Zuyder-Zee, set the windmills to pumping out the water, and laid out the lands into farms. The whole country is intersected with canals, where the boats come and go, bringing cabbages, cheeses, hay, and wood to market. The Dutchmen are very industrious. The boys and girls, as well as the men and women, work in

HAERLEM.

the fields and gardens, or tug at the canal-boats. They harness their dogs into teams, and make them tug at the ropes.

Haerlem is a sleepy old town. The boats lie at the quays, and now and then a cart rumbles along the streets. The housewives rub and scrub their pots and pans in the canals before the doors. They keep their houses neat and clean, and wash the pavements every morning.

Laurence Coster lives in Haerlem with his family. He resolves to have a day with them in the country. He goes out on one of the canal-boats with the children, and sits beneath the trees, to hear the birds sing and to breathe the fresh air; and while the children are playing he carves their names in the bark of the trees with his knife! An idea comes to him, and this is what he says to himself:

"I might carve the letters of the alphabet, each letter on a separate block, ink them over, and then I could stamp any word in the language."

This is in 1423. He goes home, prepares his blocks, carves the letters, ties them up with strings, and prints a pamphlet. Up to this time all the

CANAL IN HOLLAND.

books in the world have been written with a pen on parchment. How slow! Men have spent a lifetime in writing one book, beginning when they were young, working till they were old, and dying with their work unfinished. The Egyptians and Chinese, hundreds of years ago, carved letters on blocks and printed from the blocks; but this Dutchman of Haerlem is the first one to tie letters into words, and print from them. Laurence Coster succeeds so well that he employs John Guttenberg, a young man from Mentz, to help him. Laurence keeps his secret well. The people see pamphlets for sale; little do they imagine, however, that they were not written with a pen.

Coster dies, but his secret does not die with him. The apprentice, John Guttenberg, is not a boy to forget what he has been doing. He goes up the Rhine. We may think of him as being on a boat that

STREET IN HOLLAND.

slowly makes its way up the stream, past the old towns and castles. Rheinstein, with its battlements and towers and strongholds, secure from all attacks, looms far above the stream. He gazes upon the vineyards, sloping from the river up the steep hill-sides. In the autumn the peasants gather the purpling grapes, and sing their songs as they bear the baskets to the wine-press. He comes to Bingen, where the little old church with bells in its steeple looks down upon the peaceful river; but, not stopping there, he passes on to Strasburg, whose cathedral spire rises almost to the clouds, as it were. In that old city John Guttenberg begins to set up type on his own account. He thinks night and day, turning over a perplexing question. Wood wears out, and the types will not bear the pressure of the printing-press. They must be of metal. How shall he make them? To cut each type separately by hand is too expensive and too slow a process. He must make a mould and cast them, and, of course, must have a mould for each letter. That is expensive; but once getting the moulds, he can cast thousands of types. Of what material shall they be cast? Lead is too soft. He must experiment with different metals. Very soon his money is gone. He would like to keep his secret and his plans to himself, but that he cannot do. He must have money. There is a rich man in Strasburg—John Faust,

RHEINSTEIN.

a goldsmith, who knows about metals. He will go to him. The goldsmith sees the value of the invention, and supplies John with money, and the printer goes on engraving the letters for his moulds, experimenting with metals, meeting difficulties at every step, taking so much of John Faust's money that the goldsmith begins to think that he never will see it again.   But perseverance surmounts all difficulties.   One day Guttenberg shows the goldsmith his

BINGEN.

first proof.   There it is—each letter as perfect as if done by a pen.   It is in 1450 that they begin to print their first book, in an out-of-the-way chamber, where no one will be likely to find out what they are about.

Sixty-six years have passed since Doctor Wicklif died, and twenty-five since the monks dug up his bones. There is not much more liberty now than there was when he was alive, for kings do pretty much as they please, and the people are taxed as heavily as ever.

Charles VII. is King of France.   He is a suspicious man.   He is afraid that somebody will put poison in his food, and so makes his ser-

vants taste of it before touching it himself, and he eats so little that he
will die of starvation by-and-by.   One day a traveller, who has a valuable
book which he would like to sell to the king, comes to the royal palace.
It is the Bible on vellum, and contains six hundred and seven leaves.   It
is such a beautiful book that the king buys it, and pays seven hundred and
fifty crowns for it.   The man takes his money and goes away ; the king

The true Effigies of Laurenz Ians. Koster, Delineated
from his Monumentall Stone Statue Erected at
Harlem .

LAURENCE COSTER.

puts the book in the royal library, and is greatly delighted to know that
he has such a magnificent copy.

A traveller knocks at the archbishop's palace with a book which he
would like to show his lordship—a beautiful copy of the Bible.   The archbishop is delighted.   He never saw a more perfect book.   The letters are
even.   What a steady hand the writer must have had !   How clear and
distinct—not a blot, not an error, anywhere !   It must have taken the
writer a lifetime to write it.   He pays the price.   Now he will have some-

GUTTENBERG'S FIRST PROOF.

thing to show his friends which will astonish them.   The archbishop calls upon the king.

"I have something to show you—the most magnificent book in the world," says the king.

"Indeed!"   The archbishop is thinking of his own book.

"Yes; a copy of the Bible.   It is a marvel.   The letters are so even that you cannot discover a shade of difference."

"I have a splendid copy, and if yours is any more beautiful than mine, I should like to see it."

"Here is mine.   Just look at it;" and the king shows his copy.

The archbishop turns the leaves.   "This is remarkable.   I don't see

Poſt obitum Caxton vvlnit te viuere cura
Willelmi. Chaucer clare poeta tuj
Nam tua non ſolum compreſſit opuſcula t
Has quoqʒ laudes.iuſſit hic eſſe tuas

SPECIMEN OF TYPE.

but that it is exactly like mine." The pages are the same, the letters the same. Can one man have written both? Impossible. Yet they are alike. There is not a particle of difference between them. "How long have you had this?" the archbishop asks.

"I bought it the other day of a man who came to the palace."

The true Effigies of Iohn Guttemberg *Delineated from the Original Painting* at Mentz *in Germanie.*

JOHN GUTTENBERG.

"Singular! I bought mine of a man who came to my palace."

Neither the king nor the archbishop knows what to think of it. They place the two Bibles side by side, and find them precisely alike. There are the same number of pages; each page begins with the same word; there is not a shadow of variation. Wonderful! But the archbishop,

in a few days, is still more per-
plexed. He discovers that some
of the rich citizens of Paris have
copies of Bibles exactly like the
king's and his own. More: he
discovers that copies are for sale
here and there.

"Where did you get them?"

"We bought them of a man
who came along."

"Who was he?"

"We don't know."

"This is the work of the
devil."

The archbishop can arrive at
no other conclusion. The Bible
is a dangerous book. None but
the priests should be permitted to
read it. But here is the Evil One

WILLIAM CAXTON.

selling it everywhere; or, if not himself in person, some man has sold himself to Satan for that purpose. He soon discovers that it is Doctor John
Faust, of Strasburg.

"You have sold yourself to the Evil One, and must be burned to
death."

Till this moment the great invention has been a secret; but Doctor
Faust must divulge it, or be burned. He shows the archbishop how the
Bibles are printed; and John Guttenberg has printed so many of them
that the price has been reduced one-half. The archbishop, the king, and

ILLUMINATED LETTER.

everybody else is astonished. So Faust
saves his life; but the idea of his selling himself to the devil has gone into
story and song. It was the translation of
the Bible into English by Doctor Wicklif that gave the first uplift to liberty;
and, singularly enough, the Bible was the
first book printed by Guttenberg.

Laurence Coster, when he cut the letters of the alphabet in wooden blocks
and tied them into words, had no con-
ception as to what would come of it;

but the idea was like the bursting-forth of a fountain in a desert. The
stream that issued from it has refreshed all the earth. With the setting-
up of the printing-press
began the diffusion of
knowledge. Knowledge
leads to liberty. Men
begin to comprehend
that they have natural
rights, which other men
—nobles, barons, kings,
emperors, bishops, arch-
bishops, and popes—are
bound to respect.

PRESENTING A BIBLE TO THE KING.
(From an Old Print.)

One day William Cax-
ton, a merchant of Lon-
don, comes over to Hol-
land to buy cloth. He
sees some of the new
books, and goes into a
printing-office to see how
they are made. He is greatly interested, buys some of the types, and sets
up a printing-press in London, in a chapel in Westminster Abbey. Quite
likely the printer's workmen do not have a very high regard for the
monks and friars that swarm around Westminster, for if there is a blot
on the page, they call it a "monk;" and if there is a blank, they call it
a "friar." And the boy who brings the ink up from the cellar, and gets
his face and hands black from handling it, they call the "devil"—words
which are in use to-day in printing-offices.

The first book printed in England was entitled "The Game of Chess,"
in 1474. The type used was very coarse. Printers then took great delight in having large illuminated capital letters at the beginning of a
book or chapter. They were printed in blue, green, and gold, and made
the page very beautiful. Caxton printed a Bible, which he presented to
the king.

The setting-up of the printing-press soon put an end to all the writing in the cloisters of the monasteries. The monks lay aside their pens.
The printing-press turns out thousands of copies of a book almost while
they are sharpening their pens and getting their parchment ready. People begin to read, and from reading comes thinking, and from thinking
comes something else.

Four hundred and fifty years have passed since Laurence Coster carved the names of his children in the bark of the trees in the gardens of Haerlem—since John Guttenberg printed his first book in that out-of-the-way chamber; but through all the years that discovery of using types to express ideas has been, like the flowing of a river, widening and deepening. Through the energizing influence of the printing-press, emperors, kings, and despots have seen their power gradually waning, and the people becoming their masters.

MONUMENT TO GUTTENBERG.

CHAPTER V.

THE MEN WHO ASK QUESTIONS.

ON an evening in October, six gentlemen and a servant ride out from the old city of Saragossa, in Spain, taking a road which leads westward. They are starting at this hour of the day for Valladolid; they do not expect, however, to reach it at once, for it is two hundred miles distant. They do not care to have everybody know that they are making the journey, for there are bands of armed men on the lookout for them; especially are they on the watch for the servant of the party—Ferdinand

VALLADOLID CATHEDRAL.

—a young man seventeen years old. Although a servant, he has a well-filled purse in his pocket, for he is going all the way to Valladolid—to get married — and has taken a liberal amount of money. Not many servants can show so large a sum. The travellers ride till daybreak, and then stop at an out-of-the-way town to rest through the day, at night travelling once more. They take by-roads and pass through obscure towns, and halt again when morning comes. Ferdinand never has seen the young lady whom he is about to marry; but some of the gentlemen whom he serves say that she is very fair; that her features are regular; her hair a light chestnut; that she has a mild blue eye, and is modest and charming in all her ways. "She is the handsomest lady I ever beheld, and the most gracious in her manners," says one. Perhaps he thinks it will please Ferdinand thus to set forth the charms of the lady. At any rate, the praise or something else so abstracts his thoughts that, when he pays the landlord the reckoning at one of the taverns, he leaves his purse

behind, and discovers, when he reaches Valladolid, that he has not a cent
in his pocket! Here is a dilemma for a young man on the eve of his
marriage!

Ferdinand has served his fellow-travellers faithfully. He has cared
for their horses, waited upon them at table, filling their glasses with wine,
and he has done it in a courtly way. The landlords, quite likely, have
noticed that he is the prince of servants; but not one of them, probably,

ISABELLA.

has mistrusted that he is indeed a prince — son of the King of Aragon;
nor do they mistrust that he is travelling in disguise to be married to
Isabella, Princess of Castile; that he has taken this way to escape those
who are opposed to the match, and who would lay hands upon him if
possible.

Isabella never has seen Ferdinand, who is a year younger than herself;
but of all the suitors for her hand she has selected him, and is greatly

pleased to find him all that her fancy has pictured. She is very religious, says her prayers, and goes regularly to confession.

On the 19th of October, 1469, the marriage is consummated, for,

CORONATION OF ISABELLA.

though Ferdinand has left his purse behind, his credit is good. There is a great gathering of grandees, nobles, and ladies—two thousand or more—wearing rich dresses; and by the marriage the kingdoms of Aragon and Castile are united, making the Spain of these later years.

After her marriage she has another confessor, Thomas de Torquemada, a Dominican monk, who wears a black cowl.

"I want you to make a promise," he says to Isabella.

"What is it?"

"That when you come to the throne, you will exterminate heresy."

Isabella promises to do as he desires.

DOMINICAN MONK.

The years go by, and after the death of her brother Henry, in 1476, Isabella is queen. There are heretics in Spain, men who dare to think for themselves. That is a terrible crime in the eyes of Thomas de Torquemada, and it must be stopped. The Pope has an institution already organized by which heretics can be rooted out — the Holy Office, as it is called. The men connected with it are Inquisitors, or men who ask questions. Thomas de Torquemada is chief questioner. The men who ask questions do it in private. If they have a suspicion that a man is an unbeliever, they may arrest him, and bring him to their secret chamber and question him. These are their rules: Any one may witness against an accused person. The Holy Office may take the evidence of one heretic *against* another; but a heretic's evidence in *favor* of a person is good for *nothing*. If two witnesses testify one in *favor* and the other *against* a person, the testimony of the first is to be rejected, while the last shall be accepted. A wife may testify *against* a husband, and it shall be received; but if she testifies in his *favor*, it shall be rejected; and so with the husband against the wife, or children against parents, or parents against children. If a witness does not testify all that the questioner desires, they may put *him* to the torture.

The questioning takes place in an out-of-the-way chamber, in a building that has thick stone-walls — so thick that no moan or wail will reach

the ears of the passer-by. There is the thumb-screw — a little vise in which the accused must put his thumb, and then the screw is turned a little. It begins to bite. Another turn; it bites harder. More turning, a little at a time, till the end of the thumb is as thin almost as a wafer

A THUMB-SCREW.

—mashed to a jelly, and the blood oozes from every pore.

There is a ring-bolt in the floor, a pulley overhead. The questioners tie the feet of the prisoners to the ring, their hands to the pulley; then tug at the rope till the arms of the accused are almost pulled from the shoulders, and their legs from the body.

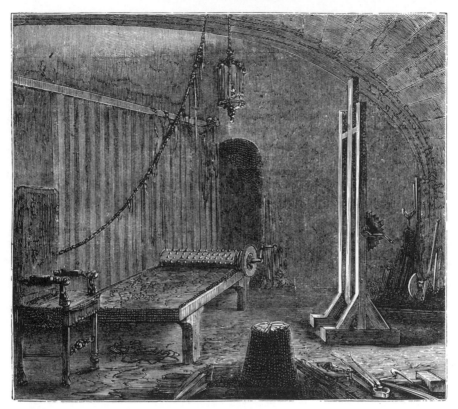

TORTURE CHAMBER.

Another instrument is the rack. The prisoner is thrown upon a ladder and his feet tied to iron bolts in the wall, and his arms to a windlass, and men with levers work it till the knees and arms are pulled from their sockets. Another instrument is the rolling bench—a table studded with projecting knobs of oak. The accused are stripped to the skin, thrown upon the table, tied hands and feet, and a heavy roller filled with knobs rolled over them, grinding the flesh to jelly.

There are punches for punching holes in the ears and tongues of the heretics, and skewers to run through them, and pincers for pulling their tongues out by the roots, knotted whips, iron collars set with sharp teeth, chains, balls, manacles.

They fasten the heads of the accused in a frame, put a gag in their mouth, propping the jaws apart. Above them is a dish filled with water, which drips into their throat. Drip, drip, drip, it falls hour after hour. Swallow they must till they are filled to suffocation.

Men and women, maidens in their youth and beauty, have the clothes torn from their backs, and they must stand exposed before these questioners. The Holy Office is amenable to no law. From the decision of Thomas de Torquemada there is no appeal. No one is exempt from his jurisdiction. Rich as well as poor are arrested. It is easy to accuse men, and those who never have dreamed of being heretics find themselves in the clutches of Torquemada. Men who are their enemies swear that they are heretics, to cause their arrest, torture, confiscation of property, and death by burning—so taking revenge.

Isabella and Ferdinand urge the men who ask questions to do their work thoroughly—to let no heretic escape, especially if they have money, for by confiscating their property the king and queen and the Pope will replenish their purses. Thomas de Torquemada is not the man to let the grass grow under his feet, especially when his share of the plunder will be a goodly portion.

The Holy Office is not a new institution. Pope Innocent VIII., who has appointed Thomas de Torquemada to superintend it in Spain, did not inaugurate it, for other popes have used it to exterminate heresy. Innocent has set it in operation in Spain to bring money into his pocket. All the world regards the Pope as being God's agent on earth, with power to pass them into heaven, consign them to purgatory, or send them to everlasting torments. All power is given him; he has the keys of heaven and hell. No one disputes his authority, none dare to protest against it. His agents —the men whom he appoints—are to be obeyed. When men have absolute power, they do as they please. If they are greedy for money, they will seize whatever they can lay their hands on. If they are hard-hearted, they will find pleasure in witnessing the sufferings of those on whom they exercise their power. It is an age in which pity and tenderness are unknown. To be tender-hearted is to be weak. It is an age of brute force. Might makes right. Men have no individual rights. There are no courts of law to protect them.

Thomas de Torquemada is cruel. It is a pleasure to him to see men put to the torture—to hear their bones crack, to see them writhe in pain, while being roasted to death over slow fires. He sends men through Spain to discover who there may be that he can accuse of heresy. If a man has a spite against his neighbor, and wishes to ruin him, he has but to whisper to the Inquisitors that his neighbor is a heretic. The Inquisitors are quick to hurry him to prison, put him to torture, sentence him to death; and then, when the fire has done its work, they seize his property, keeping a portion for themselves, and sending the rest to Pope Innocent. He is

BURNING A HERETIC IN PRESENCE OF THE POPE.

greedy for wealth. He puts it in operation in Rome. If a man in Rome commits murder, or any other crime, he can go clear of punishment by paying a good sum to the Pope. He puts money into his pockets by licensing priests to keep taverns, play-houses, and other establishments disreputable for priests or anybody else to keep. Being a priest, the Pope cannot marry; but he has children, nevertheless, and appoints them to lucrative positions. He sells indulgences and pardons for any crime.

One of the persons accused by Torquemada is Señor Pecho, who is worth a great deal of money. Torquemada seizes it all, and puts the owner to death. The widow and children are beggars in the street; but Isabella, as a special favor, graciously gives them a trifle, but appropriates the remainder of the estate to her own use. Not only does she appropriate this, but many other estates, till the Pope, seeing that she is getting more than her share of the spoils, sends a legate to look after his portion. But Isabella knows how to manage the legate. She gives him a liberal share of the plunder, and he reports that the expenses of the Office use up pretty much all of the property of the accused.

Thousands are cast into prison. More than two thousand men and women are burned — thrown into furnaces. Other thousands flee from the country.

"Do not take such harsh measures," is the advice of some of her friends.

"It is better for the service of God that the country should be depopulated than that it should be polluted with heresy," Isabella replies.

The queen is so devoted to her religion that she would rather see her country a desert than that men should question the authority of the Pope, or disregard the teachings of the bishops and priests. Pity has no place in her heart. She has all power in her realm. Men and women must believe as she believes and as the Church teaches, or she will exterminate them. Day by day the terrible work goes on. The Inquisitors march in solemn procession through the streets of the cities, conducting their victims to the place of execution. Without doubt the queen, Torquemada, and the Inquisitors sincerely believe that they are doing that which will be acceptable to God. And no doubt they are also pleased to divide up the estates of those whom they have put to death; at any rate, they can make themselves more comfortable in life; and it is gratifying to know that, while adding to their own possessions, they have been zealous for the faith and the welfare of the Church. By promoting the interests of the Church, they are laying up treasures in heaven. Will not the good done here be remembered there? Will not God reward them for the service, by giving them good things through all eternity? The more zealous they are for him on earth the greater will be their pleasures in paradise. It is their duty and privilege to eradicate heresy. They have no right to be pitiful or tender-hearted when the interests of the Church and the glory of God are at stake.

Among others burned is the good Bishop of Tarragona. Many widows are condemned, especially widows of rich men. Is it that they are greater heretics than others? Or is it that Isabella and Torquemada can

BURNING THE BISHOP OF TARRAGONA.

secure their estates? They are working zealously to bring all the world to one way of thinking—their way. Theirs is the right way, and if any one doubts it, he is to be put to death. Liberty of conscience, liberty of thought, speech, or action, are all unknown. The Pope has decreed that no one shall dissent from his decree or authority, or, if doing so, death shall be his portion.

If a witness shall swear falsely, or cause a heretic, or one who is not a heretic, to be put to death, he shall not be put to death in turn, though the Holy Office may, if it see fit, put him in prison.

If a man be accused, he must pay the men who ask questions for their time and trouble of accusing him!

If a man be condemned and put to death, infamy shall forever be heaped upon his children, on the ground that children are partakers of the sins of their parents. But the Pope is merciful, and the Holy Office may sell the children into slavery.

If a man be condemned and his property confiscated, though he may be innocent, the Holy Office is under no obligation to return it, on the ground that to be poor will make men humble!

If a man blaspheme, this is his punishment: he must stand outside of the church on Sundays when mass is said. But if he say anything against the Pope, the Church, the Virgin, or if he read the Bible, or do not confess to the priest, he shall be put to death! If a priest swear profanely, he may be fined, but the public shall know nothing of it.

If a man be a heretic, his wife must leave him. A man must leave his wife if she be an unbeliever. Children must forsake parents, and parents children.

Persons condemned by the men who ask questions are burned to death. The burning is called an *auto-da-fé*—the act of faith. It is a great occasion. Ferdinand and Isabella, all the grandees and ladies, the cardinals, archbishops, bishops, priests, and multitudes of people, assemble to witness the burning. There is a grand procession. The school children; the priests, in companies, wearing their robes, carrying crowns, banners, and candles, escort the condemned to death. The victims wear yellow gowns, upon which are embroidered black devils with hoofs, horns, and tails. Gags are thrust into the victims' mouths, so that they may not speak to the people.

Following the condemned are the magistrates, nobles, bishops, cardinals, the king and queen, the men who ask questions carrying a blood-red flag. A great crowd surges along the streets.

The procession reaches the place of burning, where a bishop or priest preaches a sermon praising the Pope, heaping upon the condemned the insulting epithets. They are dogs, vipers, wild beasts, enemies of God and man, fit only to be given over to the flames—to burn eternally. The sheriff reads their sentence; the bishop and priests chant a psalm.

"Deal with them gently," says the judge to the executioner, who chains them to the stakes, heaps the wood around them, and sets it on fire ; and

"FRIENDS THEY HAD NONE."

so the men and women, whose only crime has been dissent from believing as the Pope believes, are put to death.   Ferdinand, Isabella, Torquemada, and the Pope take possession of their estates, and the children are reduced to beggary.   In a short time the country is filled with beggars, who wander through the streets in rags, homeless and friendless.   It is a crime to give charity to children of condemned heretics.   They are outcasts, shut out from all human sympathy.

While Ferdinand and Isabella are thus rooting out heresy, they are trying to drive the Moors from the country.   Armies are marshalled, battles fought, cities besieged.   The Moors are compelled to leave their beautiful palaces, where they have enjoyed quiet and peace for centuries; but Ferdinand and Isabella are strongest, and they are driven from the homes where the fountains are ever flowing amidst the palm-trees in the spacious courts.   The king and queen accompany the armies and animate the soldiers by their presence.

One day a middle-aged man, a sailor, comes into camp, bringing a letter for Fernando de Talavera, Isabella's old confessor — a letter written by Talavera's friend, the good prior Father Perez, of the Convent of

Rabiada, near Palos, introducing the sailor, who has an idea that the earth is round, and that if he were to sail west he might reach the east. The sailor wants to lay the project before Ferdinand and Isabella.

A MOOR'S PALACE.

COURT OF THE ALHAMBRA.

Father Talavera receives the sailor courteously, and introduces him to Ferdinand and Isabella, who listen with interest to his project; but they have other things on hand, and cannot aid him in fitting out an expedition to explore unknown seas. The sailor, however, is not a man to be discouraged by trifles. He will wait, years will go by, and his beard will turn to gray; but let him not be forgotten, for we shall see him again.

The war against the Moors goes on. When Ferdinand and Isabella are in need of money to pay the troops, the rich Jews supply them, for there are many Jews in the country. They are thrifty and industrious, carry on trade, attend to their own affairs, care for their poor, and are peacefully disposed. In all Spain there are no better subjects than they. Through their aid, Ferdinand and Isabella keep their armies in the field, winning battle after battle, taking town after town, driving the Moors at last to their last stronghold, the old city of Granada, in which is the Alhambra, the gorgeous palace, one from which for centuries the Moorish flag has waved in triumph; but on the 2d of January, 1492, the banner with the crescent moon upon its folds gives place to the flag bearing the cross, and Ferdinand and Isabella take possession of the Alhambra.

In all the wide world there is no palace like this, with its massive walls, spacious halls, marble floors, elaborately chiselled columns and arabesque roofs; its gardens, where the roses are always in bloom, where fountains are ever playing. For six hundred years the Moors have ruled in Granada, but to-day they surrender all to Ferdinand and Isabella.

ALONG THE CORRIDORS OF THE PALACE.

" You shall still be a free people ; you shall be treated with respect ; shall have your own customs, and shall not be molested in your religion. No Moor shall be compelled to become a Christian." It is Ferdinand's promise.

The Spanish troops march into the city, the Moors lay down their arms, the crescent flag comes down, and the cross takes its place. In the courts of the Alhambra a *Te Deum* is chanted, and Father Fernando de Talavera, Isabella's old confessor, is appointed archbishop in a city in which till now there has not been a Christian. All are Moors or Jews. Ferdinand and Isabella are masters of all Spain. All Christian heretics have been rooted out. The fires have blazed, thousands have been burned, other thousands have fled, and from the confiscated estates the king and queen, Torquemada and the Pope, have reaped rich harvests. But there are the Jews. Their ancestors crucified the Saviour. They will not eat pork, and they will persist in eating meat on Fridays. They read the Old Testament and the Talmud. They are sharp at a bargain, and are getting rich. But what rights has a Jew? Not any. They must become Christians, or they shall be turned over to be dealt with by Torquemada.

On the 30th of March, 1492, Ferdinand and Isabella issue this proclamation :

" If after July 31st a Jew is found in the country, he shall be put to death. No one shall give shelter to a Jew. Any one doing so shall forfeit all his property. The Jews may sell their houses and farms, but no one shall be permitted to carry any gold or silver out of the country."

That is the order which Ferdinand and Isabella issue on the last day of March. If the Jews cannot carry gold or silver, what can they carry? Who will buy their farms? Who pay a tithe of the value of the property?

Rabbi Abarbanal is an old man who has been of great service to the king and queen. When they wanted money to carry on the war against the Moors, he supplied them, paid the troops, and so enabled them to conquer. He enters the Alhambra, and kneels before them on the marble pavement.

" Have mercy, O king ! Use us not so cruelly. I will pay six hundred thousand crowns of gold for the ransom of my people."

" Do not take it." Isabella speaks the words. Thomas de Torquemada is her confessor, and now he rushes into the audience-chamber, with a crucifix in his hand.

" Judas sold the son of God once for thirty pieces of silver, and you are going to sell him again. Do it ! Here he is. Sell Jesus !"

He throws the crucifix upon the table, and runs out of the hall. The

GIBRALTAR.

good old rabbi turns away, for Ferdinand has a deaf ear to his entreaty.
Perhaps an idea has dawned upon him. Will he not, by the confiscation
of all the property of the Jews, get more than six hundred thousand
crowns ?

From the ports of Carthagena, Valencia, Cadiz, Gibraltar, ships are
sailing away, carrying the fugitives to Africa, Italy, and the East. Some
are shipwrecked, some murdered; many die of disease, more by famine.
Some are sold into slavery. Remorselessly the edict is carried out. Their
property is seized, and Ferdinand grows rich upon the spoils.

Through the waning summer months the stricken Jews take their departure : five hundred thousand are driven from the country ! With them
go the thrift and industry of Spain. Isabella, Ferdinand, and the Pope,
through the Holy Office, have possession of the property; but estates without tenants bring no income to the treasury. In driving them out, Ferdinand and Isabella kill the goose that laid the golden egg.

Besides the five hundred thousand Jews driven out, more than one hundred thousand heretics are burned to death, or are thrown into prison, or lose their property by confiscation. The records of the Holy Office show how zealously Torquemada worked to exterminate heretics.

This is the record:

Burned at the stake	10,220
Died in prison	6,880
Punished by confiscation of property, perpetual imprisonment, or loss of all civil rights	97,321
Total	114,421

Torquemada dies; but Diego Deza steps into his place as chief questioner, and the terrible machine of the Holy Office goes on night and day grinding men and women, humanity, liberty, justice, right, and truth into the dust.

"The Moors must become Christians, or be banished," says the new chief questioner to Ferdinand.

"The treaty stipulates that they shall have peaceable enjoyment of their religion," Ferdinand replies.

"Their religion is an abomination in the sight of God. It is right to break faith with infidels."

Ferdinand sees an opportunity to fill his treasury. The Holy Office urges him to show his zeal for the Church, and he makes his decision:

"The Moors must become Christians, or leave the country."

The expulsion begins, and year after year goes on. The conquered Moslems, since their surrender, have

STREET SCENE IN SPAIN.

been dutiful subjects. Many of them are wealthy. They offer to buy their ransom, but they appeal to deaf ears and to stony hearts. Pity has

MOORS.

fled, and humanity is dead. Into the treasury of the Church and the king flows the accumulated wealth of six hundred years. Some of the Moors have professedly become Christians; but they will eat no pork, and they will eat meat on Friday, as the Holy Office discovers, and they are hurried to the stake to pay the penalty with their lives. Fires blaze. Men, women, and children are burned to death. Weeping and wailing is heard on every hand; dismay and despair are seen in the face of every Moor. On the side of Ferdinand, Isabella, and the Pope there is power; but for the Moors there is no comforter. So Ferdinand and Isabella rear the foundations of their united thrones on the graves of hundreds of thousands of the victims of their broken faith; while the Pope joins them in exterminating the last vestige of liberty, honor, justice, and right.

The king, queen, and the Pope take possession of the estates; and the country is filled with beggars, who wander homeless, friendless, through the land, holding out their hands to the passers-by, in the streets of the cities, for a morsel of bread.

CHAPTER VI.

HOW A MAN TRIED TO REACH THE EAST BY SAILING WEST.

IT is the month of February, 1492.   The skies are mild, the flowers in bloom, and the birds are singing in the orange gardens of the Alhambra, in the old town of Granada.   Notwithstanding this joy and gladness in nature, there is one man in Granada who has no heart to enjoy it, for he has just seen a great hope, one which he has cherished many years, go down, never to rise again, so far as he can see.   He comes out from the Alhambra—leaving its magnificent colonnades, its bubbling fountains, its beautiful gardens, never expecting again to behold them—mounts a mule, rides out through the narrow streets, through the city gate, with

THE ALHAMBRA.

his head bowed upon his breast. He is a gray-bearded man, and time is deepening the furrows in his forehead, and on this day they are deeper than ever. He has a proud spirit, and it is hard to bear the great disappointment that has come to him. In bitterness of spirit, he rides away.

He is a sailor, and has conceived the idea that by sailing west he can reach the east. He believes that the earth is round, although nearly everybody else says that it is flat. The sailor was born in Genoa, where, when

COLUMBUS.

he was a boy, he helped his father comb wool. He went to school in Pavia, and studied Latin, geometry, astronomy, and navigation. When he was only fourteen years old, he went to sea with his uncle, and was in a battle with some Venetian ships. Then he sailed through the Straits of Gibraltar, coasted along Africa as far south as Guiana. Once, off the coast of Portugal, he had a terrible fight with a Venetian ship. He was a captain then. Both of the ships were set on fire, and he saved himself by swimming two miles to the shore. It was a fortunate escape, however,

for an old sea captain, who had a
beautiful daughter, befriended him,
and the daughter became his wife.

Those were delightful days. Lisbon was a royal city. It had a strong
old castle, built of stone—the Castle
of Belem — and a castle on a hill
overlooking the town. Every day
there were processions of priests in
the streets, carrying banners and
crosses.

The old captain had made many
voyages to the Canary Islands. He
did not believe the stories told about
the unknown sea far away to the
west of the islands—that it was boiling-hot, nor that the great continent
Atlantis which Plato wrote about

WOOL-COMBER.

had disappeared beneath the waves. It was from talking with his wife's
father that the gray-bearded man had come to believe that by sailing west
he could reach the Indies. He remembered that the old Carthaginians

HE BELIEVES THAT THE EARTH IS ROUND.

maintained that there were green islands in the west. He had read that
St. Brandon, a priest of Scotland, eight hundred years before, had been
swept by a storm far away to the west, and had landed in a strange country. He was informed that Martin Vincent, a sailor of Lisbon, when he
was four hundred miles from land, on a voyage to the Canary Islands,
once picked up a piece of wood curiously carved, which the winds had
drifted from the west. Reeds like those brought from India had floated
to the shores of Portugal, and the bodies of two men unlike any other
human beings had been seen in the water by sailors when far from land.
From whence came they?

Fired with enthusiasm, the sailor went to the king, John of Portugal,
with his project, and made it so plain that the earth was round, that China
(which Marco Polo had visited) could be reached by sailing west, that the
king in part believed it. But would not great glory, honor, and advantage
come from such a discovery? Certainly; and the king determined to
secure whatever benefit might come from it. He was not a high-minded

THE OLD CASTLE.

man, and, after getting all the information he could from the sailor, sent out a ship secretly to make discoveries; but the sailors, after a few days,

MARCO POLO.

became frightened at finding themselves so far from land, and returned, saying that there was no land in that direction. "You can't reach the east by sailing west," they said.

Those were dark days to the brave sailor. The king had acted perfidiously, and now his wife died. He could no longer stay in Lisbon, but

GENOA.

took his little boy, Diego, and went home to his native city (Genoa), for
he thought perhaps his townsmen would help him; but they laughed at
him instead.

"Reach the Indies by sailing west?"

"Yes."

"You are crazy."

So he can get no help from those who know him best. He has a
brother in Spain; he will go and visit him. He lands with his son Diego
at Palos. His brother lives in the country. He is too poor to hire a mule,
and the sailor, with his pack on his back, leading Diego, goes out over the
dusty road on foot. He comes to the convent La Rabiada. Diego is
hungry, for he has had little to eat. Surely the good fathers will give
him a crust of bread and a drink of water. He knocks at the gate. The
porter answers the knock, and goes to get a bit of bread, and while he
is gone Father Perez, the prior of the convent, who has been out for a
walk, comes up. He wears a broad-brimmed hat, and has a red cross embroidered on his robe. He is a good man, and hears the sailor's story.

"Reach India by sailing west?"

"Yes."

"That is an idea worth thinking about.   You must spend the night with me.   I have a learned friend, Doctor Fernandez.   I will ask him to come in and spend the evening."

So the sailor and Diego got a good supper; and Father Perez and Doctor Fernandez listen to the sailor's story, and are greatly pleased with what he has to say.   Father Perez gives him a letter of introduction, as we have already seen, to Father Talavera, who is Queen Isabella's confessor, and who has great influence at court.   He is one of the men who ask questions.   The sailor must go and see him, and he will introduce him to the king and queen.   Meanwhile, Diego can stay at the convent and attend school.   This is in 1486.

The sailor leaves Diego with his good friend, and hastens to Cordova, where King Ferdinand is commanding a great army.   All the nobles of Spain are there, and squadrons are marching to drive the Moors out of the country.   The sailor delivers his letter to Father Talavera; but the queen's confessor cannot stop to notice a poor sailor, even though he comes with a

"A MORSEL OF BREAD FOR DIEGO, IF YOU PLEASE."

letter from his friend, Father Perez; nor has the king any time to listen to his story.   The army moves away, and the sailor, to keep himself from starvation, draws maps and charts, which he sells in Cordova.

The days are very dark now.   No money, and starvation before him. But he finds another friend (Cardinal Mendoza), who has great influence with the king.   Having married Isabella, and made Castile and Aragon a united country, Ferdinand is planning new enterprises.   He covets the

"BY SAILING WEST, I SHALL BE ABLE TO REACH THE INDIES."

kingdom of Navarre, in the Pyrenees.   He will seize that by-and-by, and so rob Catherine de Foix of her dominion.   But just now he is sitting by the gurgling fountains.   The cardinal goes to the king.

"I have made the acquaintance of a sailor who has a grand project to lay before your Majesty."

"What is it ?"

"To reach the east by sailing west."

"Oh yes, I remember Father Talavera said something about it some time ago."

"He is no ordinary man.   I have listened to his story with great interest : his project seems reasonable."

"I will direct Father Talavera to call a council of learned men to investigate the matter."

The council meets in the Convent of St. Stephen, in Salamanca.   There are bishops, archbishops, and learned doctors from the universities, in the assembly, who hear what the sailor has to say.

"Do you mean to say that you can reach the east by going west ?"

"Yes."

"It is a preposterous idea."

"But the ancient geographer Ptolemy, and the learned men of his time, maintained that the earth was round; and if it is round, does it not stand to reason that we can reach India by sailing west?"

"No. To say that the earth is round is contrary to the Bible, which says, in the Psalms, that the heavens are stretched out like a tent. Of course it must be flat."

"The sun and moon are round, as we see; why not the earth?" the sailor replies.

"If the earth is a ball, what holds it up?" the cardinal inquires.

"We might ask what holds the sun and moon up," is the sailor's answer.

"The idea that the earth is round is absurd. How can men walk with their heads hanging down and their feet upward, like flies on a ceiling?" asks a learned doctor.

"How can trees grow with their roots in the air?" interposes another.

"The water would all run out of the ponds, and we should all fall off," says still another.

So the wise doctors reason.

"The idea is based on a false philosophy, and to say that the earth is round is heresy," says one.

COLUMBUS EXPLAINING HIS PLAN BEFORE FERDINAND AND ISABELLA.

That is their decision. Heresy! It is an ominous word. The men who ask questions make short work with heretics. The sailor must be careful about his belief. If he maintains that the world is round, when the doctors say it is flat, it will be worse for him.

Seven years pass. The sailor is growing old, but he has not given up his belief that he can reach India by sailing west. He has waited for Ferdinand and Isabella to drive the Moors from Spain. They have succeeded—have taken the last stronghold, Granada, and are now in the grand and beautiful Alhambra, with their little girl Katherine, who is four

RETURNING TO THE ALHAMBRA.

years old. They sit by the gurgling fountains, walk amidst the orange-groves, and stroll along the corridors where the Moorish kings have lived in luxuriance and pride. The sailor has thought, now that the war is over, Ferdinand and Isabella would aid him. Vain hope; he has had his last interview with them. The queen was almost persuaded to help him, but has at last declined. Never again will he trouble her. He is riding away, turning his back forever on Spain.

"Have you seen a man on a mule—a gray-bearded man—pass out of the gate?"

A horseman asks the question of the soldier guarding the entrance to the city.

"Yes; there he is, away on the plain," says the sentinel, pointing to the retreating form.

The horseman sees a little speck far away, strikes the spurs into the sides of the horse, and flies like the wind along the road.

"Halloo!"

The sailor reins in his mule.

"The queen has sent me to ask you to return."

Christopher Columbus turns once more to the city, and with him turns the world. It was Luis St. Angel, one of Columbus's friends, who saw him ride away so downhearted, who hastened to the queen to persuade her to call him back.

"Think how great the gain may be, at a trifling expense, if what the sailor believes should prove true," said the earnest man.

"It shall be done. I will undertake. I will pledge my jewels to raise the money. Call him back."

So the horseman rides after him. He goes back to the grand palace to hold one more interview with the king and queen. Perhaps, while they are turning over the project, he plays with the little girl Katherine, taking her in his arms, maybe, and telling her a story. Let us keep Katherine in remembrance, for we shall see her by-and-by.

All things are arranged. It is the 3d of August. Three little ships lie at anchor in the harbor of Palos. They are little larger than fishing-boats, and only the largest has a deck in the centre. The other two are built high, with decks at stem and stern, but open in the centre. There is a commotion on shipboard and on the shore. A great crowd has assembled, for the ships are about to sail away where ships never yet have sailed, over unknown seas—over that sea where the waves are boiling-hot. The sailors are loath to go. No one knows what dangers await them—what storms, what whirlpools, what mysterious agencies may destroy them. The admiral of the little fleet (the gray-bearded sailor, Christopher Columbus) says that the world is round; if so, how will they ever be able to return? Can a ship sail up-hill? The sailors have not volunteered to go, but have been forced into service by the king. On the shore their friends are weeping and lamenting their departure. Never again will they behold them. The vessels are the *Santa María*, with the admiral's flag flying above it; the *Pinta*, commanded by Alonzo Pinzon; and the *Niña*, commanded by Yanez Pinzon.

Columbus's ever-faithful friend, the good prior of La Rabiada, stands upon the deck of the *Santa María* to bestow his blessing.   The last good-bye is spoken, the anchors are raised, the sails spread, and the vessels sail away, shaping their course toward the Canaries.

On the third day the *Pinta's* signal of distress is flying; her rudder is unhung and broken, but Captain Alonzo Pinzon is an able seaman, and

THE SHIPS.

secures it with ropes until the Canary Islands are reached, when a new rudder is obtained.

On Saturday, the 6th of September, the three vessels turn their prows westward.   On Sunday morning they are still within sight of land; but a fresh breeze springs up, and soon the last glimpse fades away.

The sailors would be brave in a battle, but now they give way to their fears.   The apprehension of experiencing something which no man has ever experienced—something strange and terrible—causes their cheeks to whiten and their eyes to fill with tears.

The admiral calms them by his description of India—a land abounding with gold and silver and precious stones, which they will surely visit.

Monday morning comes, and they discover the mast of a vessel floating in the sea, which is covered with sea-weed, and has been a long time in the water. The sailors give way to their lamentations. They too, surely, will be shipwrecked.

On the 13th of September the ships are two hundred miles west of the Canaries. Columbus notices, in the evening, that the compass no longer points to the north star, but has changed five degrees to the west. What is the meaning of it? Is the guide to which they have always trusted to fail them now? He knows that the sun and moon are globes; he believes that the earth also is a globe; but he does not know that the earth turns on its axis every twenty-four hours—so bringing day and night. Such an idea has not yet dawned upon the mind of any man. There is a young man, however, up in Poland, Nikolaus Kopernik, nineteen years old, who is studying astronomy, and who a few years hence will propound the

THE CANARY ISLANDS.

startling theory that the apparent movement of the sun around the earth is in reality the earth turning on its axis every twenty-four hours.

There is also a man in Pisa—the city in which there is a wonderful leaning tower—Galileo, who is studying the heavens. He is twenty-seven years old; and a few years hence he will construct a tube with glasses in it which will bring the stars and planets so near to the earth that he will see that several moons are clustered around Jupiter—that they change their positions from day to day.

GALILEO.

But Christopher Columbus knows nothing of this; he sees only that his compass is failing him. The sailors behold it with terror; but he quiets their fears by saying that the north star is not exactly north.

On, day after day, they sail. Birds hover around the ships. The water is full of sea-weed. By the 1st of October they have sailed twenty-three hundred miles—though the reckoning which Columbus shows to the sailors makes it only seventeen hundred miles.

The wind blows steadily from the east; but the sailors, seeing how far they have come, fear that with the wind blowing steadily in one direction they never will be able to return. They are all but ready to mutiny; but Columbus quiets them, and offers to give twenty-five dollars to the man who first discovers land. Now all eyes are turned toward the west.

"Land!"

A sailor shouts it. All hearts beat more quickly, but the sailor is mistaken: no land is to be seen, and the enthusiasm is followed by despondency. They murmur once more.

"We are not far from land. We shall soon discover it," says Columbus. "See! there is a bush with berries on it."

They pick up a shrub floating in the sea. Sure enough there are berries on it. That did not grow in the sea.

"These are land birds," says Columbus, pointing to birds that hover around the vessels.

"Look there! A piece of wood. That did not grow in the sea."

They pick up the wood. "What! it is carved. These are marks of tools. It is not part of a vessel. It did not come from a ship. No ship ever sailed here. There must be land ahead."

At sunset the crew kneel upon the deck, and chant the vesper-hymn.

SEA-WEED.

It is sixty-seven days since they left Palos. Columbus has calculated that it is three thousand miles from Spain to China, and he has sailed almost that far. He knows from the birds around him, by the change in the temperature of the atmosphere, that he cannot be far from land. Once only has he changed his course, and that to the south-west, following the birds which fly in that direction. Ten o'clock. What is that? A light! There it is—far away. A moment he sees it. It is gone. There it is again.

Two o'clock in the morning, October 12th—hour most memorable! Roderigo de Friana is on the lookout at the mast-head of the *Pinta.* What is that? It cannot be a bank of cloud, for the stars are brightly shining.

"Land! Land! Land!"

There is a commotion on shipboard.

"Where?"

"There—there. Don't you see it?"

"Land! Land! Land!"

The cannon are fired. No echoes like those ever before were awakened along the shores of the Bahama Isles. Day dawns.

There it is, a green and sunny isle—an earthly paradise—green trees, fragrant flowers, myriads of birds, groups of men, women, and children, gazing in wonder upon the ships.

The sailors who have been so faint-hearted, so ready to mutiny, throw themselves upon the deck and beg Columbus to forgive them. The anchors are dropped and the boats lowered. The banner of Spain is unfurled, and Columbus, in a scarlet robe, wearing his sword, approaches the shore. He steps from the boat, kneels, and with clasped hands gives

THE NEW WORLD.

thanks to God, and then with imposing ceremonies takes possession of the land in the name of the king and queen, and names it San Salvador. The natives gather around, wondering at what they see. From whence came

these beings? From the clouds? Or did they rise from the sea? They
accept with delight the trinkets which Columbus gives them. They throw
themselves into the water and swim out to the ships, climb the sides, and
gaze in astonishment at what they behold. When the cannon are fired,

THE LANDING.

they fall on their faces. To them it is lightning and thunder. They bring
fruits (bananas and yams and oranges), and birds of bright plumage (parrots and other birds), and give them to the sailors. They wear pieces of
gold attached to their ears, which they give in exchange for little tinkling
bells. The Spaniards are eager to obtain gold.

"Where did you get it?" they ask, by signs, and the Indians point
toward the west. The sailors can see other islands lying along the horizon, and they enter the ships and sail away, carrying seven of the Indians,
who willingly go with them.

They visit island after island, gazing in wonder and delight at the ever-
changing but beautiful panorama. The mountains are clothed with trop-
ical verdure. There are myriads of bright-hued flowers, climbing vines,
groves of palm and cocoa. The sea breaks on pebbled beaches, the skies

ALONG THE SHORE.

are mild, the air balmy and resonant with the songs of birds such as they never before have seen. They have found paradise.

They come to an island larger than the others, where rivers of sweet waters descend from the mountains. They go up a placid stream in their boats, beholding everywhere new beauties.

"I could live here forever," says Columbus. The natives call this island Cuba. He returns to the ship and coasts for three days along the shores, believing that he has reached India.

The Indians bring them a fruit which grows in the ground, which they roast in a bed of hot ashes, and which is sweet and nutritious.

"What do you call it?" the sailors ask, by signs.

"Batatoes."

This is the first eating of potatoes by Europeans.

The Indians roll up a dry leaf of a plant which bears a beautiful pink flower, light one end and inhale the smoke at the other end, puffing it from their mouth and nostrils.

"To-bac-co," say they.

The sailors try it, and are made sick at first, but soon enjoy it. From Cuba the vessels sail to an island which the Indians call Hayti, but which Columbus calls Hispaniola. He lands, and beneath the giant forest trees rears a cross and plants the standard of Spain. Thousands of parrots chatter around them, humming-birds dart swiftly through the air, and flamingoes stalk along the shore.

The sailors capture an Indian girl, but Columbus treats her kindly, and she is delighted with the necklace of little bells which he gives her. One of the vessels strikes upon a rock and is wrecked, but the sailors take the goods on shore. Through the Indian girl, Columbus induces the natives to return from the forest into which they have fled. They are simple-hearted, kind, and honest; nor do they steal any of the goods. "They love their neighbors as themselves," writes Columbus in his journal.

The chief gets up a grand banquet of fish, fruits, and potatoes; and, after the feast, the natives have a dance. Columbus, in turn, orders the sailors to go through military evolutions. The Indians gaze in admiration upon the bright swords gleaming in the sunshine, but fall to the ground in

REARING THE CROSS.

terror when a cannon is fired. Columbus builds a fort, and leaves a garrison to hold it, and sails for Spain. He reaches the Azores, but, soon after leaving those islands, a great storm comes on, and the ships are separated. He fears that all will be lost; but, on the 4th of March, he drops anchor at the mouth of the river Tagus, ten miles from Lisbon; and on the 15th of March he sails into the harbor of Palos.

What a commotion there is!

" Christopher Columbus has come!"

The cry runs over the town. Every boat is launched, and the rowers pull with all their might, to be the first to reach the ship.

"A new world is discovered!" The bells ring, cannon thunder, bonfires blaze. It is not a fiction, for there are the Indians—six of them—and

RETURNING TO SPAIN.

parrots, flamingoes, rolls of Indian cloth, bananas, potatoes, gold! The news goes from house to house. Everybody rejoices over the wonderful intelligence.

It is a triumphal march which Columbus makes to Barcelona — six hundred miles—to pay his respects to Ferdinand and Isabella. He goes as a conqueror, noblemen accompanying him. People come from afar to see him, to gaze upon the Indians and the parrots.

The king and queen receive Columbus in great state, and take delight in honoring him. And why should they not? Has he not given them a new empire? But the doctors who ridiculed him at Salamanca are envious. It is not pleasant to have all their fine theories upset, and to feel that they have made fools of themselves. Besides, this adventurer is an

THE KING AND QUEEN RECEIVE HIM IN GREAT STATE.

Italian; and they do not like to think that an Italian, and not a Spaniard, is the discoverer of a new world. The Grand Cardinal invites Columbus to a dinner. The great doctors are there. One is so envious that he cannot restrain himself from giving Columbus a little stab.

THAT IS THE WAY TO DO IT.

" Do you think that there is no man in Spain capable of making the discovery ?" he asks.

Columbus replies by asking a question :

" Is there any one at the table who can make an egg stand on end ?"

They try, but all fail.

" Can you do it ?"

" Certainly."

He breaks the shell at the end, and the egg stands.

" That is the way to do it."

"Anybody can do that."

" So anybody can go to the new land, now that I have discovered it."

Very soon Columbus is sailing west again, this time with twelve ships and twelve hundred men. Thousands want to go. They take horses, pigs, cattle, and dogs, for these animals are not found in the new world. Twelve priests go to convert the Indians to the Catholic faith. He comes to the colony, but no one is there. They find skulls, bones, decayed bodies,

ALL HAVE PERISHED.

ruins. Those whom he left quarrelled among themselves, then separated and lived with the Indians. A powerful tribe came down one day from the mountains and killed every Spaniard, and a great many of the coast Indians. He leaves a second colony, and sails away to the west in search

of new lands, and discovers the island of Jamaica. He finds no mountains of gold, and the adventurers are disappointed. Sickness breaks out;
their provisions fail. Some of the ships turn back to Spain. Many of
those who are with him are young noblemen, who, because they do not

IN CHAINS.

find gold, denounce Columbus as a deceiver; but he sails on, discovers new
lands, and then returns to Spain. The nobles are so jealous of him that
two years pass before he can get ready for another voyage. He sails once
more, steering farther south, and, after sailing thirty-eight days, discovers
an island with three mountain peaks, which he calls "The Trinity;" and
just beyond he beholds the main-land, South America, and sails many
miles along the coast. This is in 1498.

He is Governor of the New World. The only settlement is that in
Hayti; but the grandees are so jealous that they cannot bear to have an
Italian over them. They accuse him to the king falsely, invent lies, till
the king is persuaded to supersede him, and send out a vain, pompous,
cruel man—Bobadilla—to be governor, who arrests Columbus, puts him in
prison, rivets fetters upon his ankles, and sends him to Spain.

The captain of the ship is indignant at such treatment of the noble-
hearted sailor.

"I will strike off the irons," he says.

"No; the king commanded me to submit to whatever Bobadilla should order in his name. I will not remove them. I will wear them, and keep them as memorials of my reward !"

In irons he is taken to Cadiz.

"Shame ! shame !"

The people shout it, and the king strikes off the fetters.

Once more Columbus sails. He is an old man now; his beard is white, and he is not so strong as he was. He stops at Hayti, and then sails

A DRAGON EATING IT UP.

west through the Caribbean Sea, skirting the main-land, seeking ever to find a passage to India. He lands at a place where there is a delicious spring of water, and which to this day is called Columbus's Spring. His vessels are driven ashore in a storm. He is taken sick. The Indians are hostile. He needs provisions, but cannot get them from the Indians, who are planning to attack the strangers. He must make them supply him with food. He understands astronomy, and knows that the moon will soon be eclipsed. The Indians are superstitious, and he sends this word to the chiefs :

"The Great Spirit is offended with you, because you will not supply me with provisions."

The Indians laugh at the message.

"You will see the moon fade away. The Great Spirit will cover it up and make it all dark."

They laugh again. Night comes, and the full moon rises, round and red; but soon the Indians see a shadow creeping over it, beginning at one side.

"A dragon is eating it up!" they cry, and throw themselves upon the ground in terror.

"The Great Spirit will pardon you, and give you back the moon, if you bring me provisions."

"We will bring them."

They come with baskets filled with yams and potatoes and fruits. So he obtains provisions, but his vessels are driven ashore in a storm, and he must die there unless a vessel shall perchance sail along the coast.

One day the sailors see two specks far away, and soon discover that they are two vessels. A fire is kindled, and those on board the ships, attracted by the smoke, sail along the shore and discover those whom they are seeking. So Columbus and his fellow-sailors are rescued from death.

Twelve years have passed since Columbus discovered San Salvador. The islands which then were a paradise, the abode of simple-hearted people, are drenched in blood. The Spaniards have had but one thought—

THE RESCUE.

to get gold and to gratify passion. Thousands of the Indians have been killed, other thousands carried into slavery. The Indians had no rights which the cruel men felt bound to respect.

On the 20th of May, 1506, at Valladolid, Christopher Columbus, old, in poverty, begging his bread, lies down to die. No one cares for him, but he dies calmly and peacefully. So closes the life of the man who led the way for the discovery of the future home of Liberty.

COLUMBUS'S MONUMENT, GENOA.

CHAPTER VII.

THE NEW HOME OF LIBERTY.

THE news that Christopher Columbus has discovered wonderful lands in the West reaches the old town of Bristol, in England. It was down past this town that the dust of Doctor Wicklif floated to the sea. It was a Bristol trader whose teeth were pulled out by John Lackland for refusing to give up his money. The merchants of Bristol were enterprising men, and were sending their ships to France, to the Mediterranean, and the North Sea.

Two of the sea-captains employed by the merchants were a father and son, John and Sebastian Cabot. The father was born in Venice, a city that stands in the sea, where the people, instead of riding in carriages, glide along the water-ways in gon-

SEBASTIAN CABOT.

dolas. They were brave, adventurous men, and, hearing of Columbus's discoveries, persuaded the Bristol men to fit out a fleet for the purpose of discovering a new route to the Indies. The merchants can do nothing without first obtaining permission from the king, Henry VII. There is not much liberty in England or anywhere else. The king is supreme. Henry loves money, and when the citizens of Bristol come before him with their petition, he sees an opportunity to impose conditions which possibly may bring money into his pockets at their expense.

"If you discover any countries, they shall be mine," he says.

He is possessed with the idea that he alone can lay claim to all countries discovered, no matter who may be living upon the land.   The people
of England have few rights which he is bound to respect; much less will
the Indians have any rights.

"That we promise," the merchants reply.

"If you make any money, I must have one-fifth of it."

This is a hard condition.   Not a dollar will he contribute toward fit·

THE SEA SWARMS WITH FISH.

ting out the expedition.   The merchants must be at all the expense.
They may lose every cent of their investment, their vessels may be
wrecked; the king will not share in any loss.   But on no other condition will he permit the fleet to sail.   Hard as the terms are, the merchants accept them.

In the month of May, 1497, John Cabot commanding one vessel, Sebastian another, with a third to keep them company, set sail from Bristol. The tide wafts them down the Severn River, just as it wafted John Wicklif's dust. They steer westward—out upon a stormy sea, to sail where vessels never have sailed before.

By the middle of June they find themselves on soundings, and the sea is swarming with fish. They catch all they want. Never before have they seen such myriads of fish.

On the 24th of June they discover land. It is not India, for they are only sixteen hundred miles west of Ireland. They name it *Prima Vista.* It is *new found land.* They behold dense forests of pine and cedar, but no sign that it is inhabited.

They sail north-west, and discover a bleak and rocky shore, where the surf is breaking on cavern ledges—the coast of Labrador. Since the days

AMONG THE ICEBERGS.

THE ROCKY SHORE.

of the old Northmen, no European eye has seen the Western continent.
Columbus has as yet only discovered the West India Islands.   Onward
the vessels glide, sailing north-west, till at midnight, on the July days, the
sun only disappears for a few moments beneath the horizon.   They are in
the frozen sea, with icebergs around them.   Their provisions begin to fail;

the ice blocks their farther progress; and the brave sailors, disappointed in not being able to find a way to India, but happy in the thought that they have discovered new lands, return to Bristol.

Although the merchants have spent much money, they resolve to fit out a second expedition. John Cabot is getting to be an old man; but Sebastian is in the full vigor of manhood, and a skilful navigator, and they give the command to him. He sails west to the New-found land, but, instead of steering north after sighting its wooded shores, turns south, enters the Bay of Fundy, where the tide rushes in with a roar like distant thunder, rising sixty feet. Sailing still farther, he comes to Frenchman's Bay, and gazes upon Mount Desert, at whose base the sea breaks upon granite ledges, tossing the spray high in air.

Day after day the vessel glides along, past bluffs and headlands, where the waves have eaten their way into rocky caverns, then past sandy beaches glowing in the summer sun. If a storm comes on, Captain Cabot finds shelter behind some island.

Southward the vessel sails, past Cape Ann, past Cape Cod; then turning westward, skirts the shores of Long Island, and then the coast of New Jersey, and the low beaches of Delaware and Virginia—sailing till provisions fail, when the hardy

THE CAVERNS.

captain turns about, and reaches England, informing the king that he has discovered a fair and virgin land in the west, which he may claim as his own.

As this story unfolds, we shall see that through the enterprise of the Bristol merchants, through the discoveries of Sebastian Cabot, and through the claims of the king to the ownership of all lands discovered by him, the new home of liberty became the heritage of the people of England.

The King of Spain could not at that moment claim possession of the New World by priority of discovery; for while Sebastian Cabot was sailing along the coast of Virginia, Columbus was starting on his third voyage, during which he discovered South America, as we have seen.

Would the United States have been the nation that it is if Spain had first discovered North America, and established its colonies and planted its civilization on the shores of Virginia? Far from it; for the king, who could violate his most solemn promises, as Ferdinand violated his with the

AMERIGO VESPUCCI.

Moors — the queen, Isabella, who could sit complacently by while heretics were being roasted to death —the people who could drive out the Jews and Moors, and seize their estates, were not the sovereigns nor the people to establish liberty in the Western World. We shall see that it required such men as those who compelled John Lackland to sign the Magna Charta; such men as John Wicklif, who dared to brave the Pope's authority; such men as Geoffrey Chaucer, who dared to ridicule the monks—men who were strong-hearted enough to resist tyranny, who were ready to sacrifice everything they held dear rather than yield their natural rights — that it required such men to plant the seeds of a new civilization in the western hemisphere.

It was not till two years after Cabot's voyage that Amerigo Vespucci sailed on his voyage of discovery; and although the continent of America bears his name, he was far from being the first to discover it.

The intelligence that the sea off Newfoundland is alive with fish is good news to the fishermen of Northern France, for the Pope has decreed that everybody must eat fish on Friday. The fishermen of Honfleur and otner towns set sail in their little vessels for the New-found-land, and drop their anchors in a bay, which they call St. John's. They dress their fish,

DRESSING THEIR FISH.

and dry them on the rocks and ledges. They build hurdles of brush, and lay the fish upon them to dry, pack them in the hold, and go back to France with their vessels loaded to the water's edge.

While the fishermen of France are making these voyages to Newfoundland, the Spaniards are establishing colonies in the West Indies, for they now know that the islands are not the East Indies. They make the Indians slaves, treat them cruelly, making themselves rich on the unrequited labor of the simple-hearted natives.

Adventurers are sailing here and there, establishing colonies and seeking for gold. One of the adventurers is Martin Encisco. He is at Hayti, ready to sail into the unexplored regions of the west. Just before the anchor is hoisted, two men bring a cask on board the ship. The sails are hoisted, and the vessel speeds away over the waters. The sailors hear a pounding inside of the cask; then the head falls out, and, to their amazement, a young man stands before them. It is Vasco Balboa, a young Spanish nobleman, who has led a dissolute life in Spain, who has been try-

9

ing to recover his fortune at Hayti, but who has been getting deeper in debt.   He has taken this method to escape from his creditors.

"Who are you?" Captain Encisco asks.

"Vasco Nuñez de Balboa."

He is young, noble-looking, fearless, and well-dressed.

"I will leave you on the first island I come to," says the captain, in a rage ; but he soon sees that Balboa is a man who can be of great use to him.

This man from the cask has already been down to a place called Darien—a rich country, where the Indians have gold in abundance.

"I will pilot you there ; we shall find gold," says Balboa.

They reach Darien, make an attack upon an Indian village, and collect gold ornaments worth fifty thousand dollars.   Encisco makes a settle-

TWO MEN BRING A CASK ON BOARD.

ment ; but he forbids the sailors to trade with the Indians.   The sailors do not like that ; so they mutiny, and elect Balboa to be their leader.   The man from the cask sends Encisco back to Hayti a prisoner ; but he is careful to send a large amount of gold to the royal treasurer there, who is a great favorite of the King of Spain.   He has among his followers a brave but cruel man, Pizarro, who by-and-by will be heard of in Peru.

One day Balboa is surprised to see two men come into his camp dressed in skins of wild beasts. They are Spaniards, deserters from a colony on the coast, and they have been living with an Indian chief, who has treated them with much kindness. The chief is rich; and the men offer to conduct Balboa to his capital. With one hundred and thirty men he marches to the town. The chief receives them courteously; and Balboa, after seeing how much gold the chief has in his possession, takes his departure, but in the night stealthily returns, falls upon the village, capt-

THE HEAD OF THE CASK FALLS OUT, AND A YOUNG MAN STANDS BEFORE THEM.

ures the chief and all his family, and plunders the place.   The chief com-
plains bitterly of the perfidy.   He wishes to be a friend to the Spaniards,
and offers his daughter to Balboa in marriage.   The commander of the

THE CHIEF OFFERS HIS DAUGHTER IN MARRIAGE.

Spaniards sees that it will be better to have the good-will rather than the
enmity of the chief, and accepts the girl as his wife, and becomes very
fond of her, and she of him.   In company with the chief, he visits another chief, who lives in a great palace four hundred and fifty feet long,
and two hundred and fifty broad, built of heavy timber.   The Spaniards
are surprised to find an immense store of provisions, and spirituous liquors
distilled from palm-juice and corn.   In another building are the bodies
of the dead, which have been dried by fires and wrapped in cloths, and
adorned with jewels and precious stones.

The chief's eldest son makes a present to Balboa of four thousand ounces of gold, which the commander distributes among his followers. In the division a quarrel arises between two men, who draw their swords to fight. The young chief steps between them, and kicks the gold-dust contemptuously about, scattering it upon the ground.

"Do you quarrel about such stuff? Is it for this that you make slaves of us, and burn our towns? Beyond those mountains is a great sea, and the rivers that run into it are filled with gold, and the people who live there drink from golden vessels," says the young chief.

After many adventures, Balboa determines to cross the high mountains which rise in the west, and see if the stories he has heard are true. One hundred and ninety men volunteer to go with him. They are all armed, and he has a pack of ferocious blood-hounds.

On the 6th of September, 1513, leaving half of his men in care of the boats—about twenty miles from the mouth of Caledonia River—with In-

"DO YOU QUARREL ABOUT SUCH STUFF?"

dians to guide him, he begins to climb the mountains. They march through dark woods, where in some places the palms are so thick and tall that they shut out the sunlight, and where thick vines run from tree

to tree. Monkeys chatter at them. They see venomous snakes. It is
a toilsome journey. They march beneath the burning sun. The men

CLIMBING THE MOUNTAINS.

are ready to drop by the way, but the adventurous commander sends
the weak ones back to the boats, and the rest move on. They come to
a tribe of Indians, who dispute their way, armed with slings and war-
clubs; but the soldiers fire upon them, and Balboa lets slip the blood-
hounds, which rush upon the Indians, leaping at their throats. The flash,

the rattle, the smoke of the guns, fill the Indians with astonishment, and they flee to the woods; but the Spaniards pursue them, and do not cease the slaughter till six hundred have been cut in pieces. They move rapidly on, and at noon the next day Balboa and the sixty men with him are at the base of a tall mountain peak.

"From there you will see the Great Water," says the Indian guide.

The Great Water! The explorer has heard of it; now he is to see it.

SLAUGHTER OF THE INDIANS.

The men stop while Balboa goes on. He will be the first to behold the great sea.

There it is! The mightiest ocean of the globe — ten thousand miles

DISCOVERY OF THE PACIFIC.

wide—its waves rolling upon the shore, fringing it with white foam. Balboa sinks on his knees, and gives thanks to God.

The rest climb the peak and gaze upon it, and fall prostrate upon the ground. A priest chants *Te Deum Laudamus*, and the whole company join in the thanksgiving. They cut down a tree and rear a cross upon the spot, pile a heap of stones around it, and descend the western slope.

Another tribe of Indians oppose them, but the muskets and the bloodhounds quickly win the victory. The chief sues for peace, and gives Balboa four hundred pounds of gold in exchange for some little tinkling bells, and thinks that he has the best of the bargain.

They reach the ocean, taste the water to see if it is salt, and then Balboa, with the flag of Spain in one hand, and his sword in the other, wades in and takes possession of the ocean for his master, the King of Spain.

So the Pacific Ocean, which laves the western shore of the continent where Liberty is to have its future abiding-place, is first beheld by a European; and so Balboa takes possession of it for the monarch who is driving the Jews out of his realm, and roasting heretics by the thousand.

Great hardships are endured by the Spaniards before they get back to the little band on the eastern shore. They have many encounters with

BALBOA TAKING POSSESSION OF THE PACIFIC.

the Indians.   One of the chiefs captured offends Balboa, and he is torn to
pieces by the blood-hounds.   The Spaniards find gold very abundant, and
obtain so much that it becomes a burden.   The soldiers cannot carry it.
They are forced to climb mountains, wade through swamps, endure terrible hardships.   Balboa is taken sick, but his devoted followers carry him
on a blanket.   After months of toil they reach their boats, astonishing

THE HOUNDS TEAR HIM TO PIECES.

their comrades with the immense amount of gold in their possession—
gold in dust, in scales, in nuggets, golden ornaments, cups, and drinking
vessels, worth hundreds of thousands of dollars.

Balboa hears of lands rich in gold southward on the Pacific coast, and
resolves to visit them.   He cuts down trees, hews the timbers and plank,
compels the Indians to transport the materials across the mountains.   He

and his followers endure incredible hardships. One day a new governor arrives from Spain, who hates Balboa, and accuses him of treason, arrests him, and has him executed. Columbus is rewarded for discovering a new world by being sent home in chains; and the man who discovered the Pacific Ocean is executed. That is the gratitude of Spain to her illustrious men.

EXECUTION OF BALBOA.

CHAPTER VIII.

A BOY WHO OBJECTED TO MARRYING HIS BROTHER'S WIDOW.

NEARLY one hundred years have passed since the monks dug up the bones of Doctor Wicklif. There are not many followers of the doctor in England, for the bishops have been weeding the Lollards out. So many have been imprisoned in the Tower, in London, that one section of the edifice is called the Lollards' Prison. In one of the chambers the bishops sit in council for the condemnation of heretics,

LOLLARDS' PRISON.

not that they have committed murder or theft, or for any other crime against society, but for reading Doctor Wicklif's translation of the Bible, which is a crime, in their estimation, to be punished by imprisonment or death.

In Bohemia there has been a terrible war lasting many years. Thousands have been killed, and multitudes have died of starvation; cities have been burned, and the land made desolate; and all because the Emperor Sigismund violated his word, and allowed John Huss to be put to death. Men have little more freedom than they had one hundred years ago. The heretics have been subdued everywhere. Men must think, speak, and act just as they are told. The Pope is superior to the State

THE COUNCIL CHAMBER, TOWER OF LONDON.

The bishops have their own court. A priest may commit murder, and the king cannot touch him. The bishops never put a priest to death, even if he commits murder; but let a man who is not a priest be caught reading the Bible, and they will soon have him roasting in the fire. The Church has a "Sanctuary," a safe place. If a man has committed a crime, and makes his escape to the sanctuary, the sheriff cannot touch him for forty days; and if he wishes to escape to another country, by taking a crucifix in his hand he can go without molestation to the sea-shore, wade into the sea up to his neck, call three times for a ship to come and take him, and then no one can arrest him. Such a privilege enables men to commit crime with impunity. Justice is defeated. But it brings a great deal of money into the bishops' pockets, for when a rich man seeks refuge in the sanctuary they make him pay roundly for the privilege of being there.

Although Doctor Wicklif preached against indulgences, the sale is go-ing on more briskly than ever before. A great scholar from Holland,

THE SANCTUARY.

Doctor Erasmus, makes a visit to England. He goes to Walsingham Ab-bey, with his friend the Dean of St. Paul's; and the guide shows them the precious relics which are kept in a chest, before which thousands of pil-grims reverently kneel and worship, leaving purses filled with money for the priests.

The guide shows them something white, which looks like powdered chalk.

"What is that?" Doctor Erasmus asks.

"Some of the Virgin Mary's milk," says the guide.

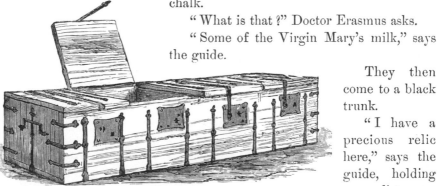

THE CHEST.

They then come to a black trunk.

"I have a precious relic here," says the guide, holding up a dirty rag.

" What is it ?"

" It is a fragment of St. Thomas's shirt."

The pilgrims kneel and worship the holy relic. Doctor Erasmus does not follow their example, but turns away disgusted, rather. Supposing it was a part of Thomas's shirt, does that make it holy? Is it of any more value than any other rag? He returns to Holland, and writes a book

ERASMUS.

about fools, which sets people to laughing. Here and there a man sees that the people are fools, and that the priests are making money out of their simplicity.

The king, Henry VII., who would not let the merchants of Bristol fit out the expedition under John and Sebastian Cabot till they had promised to give him one-fifth of all the money they made, thinks of a way whereby he can extort money from whomsoever he will.   He establishes a court, which is called the Court of the Star-chamber, not only because the ceil-

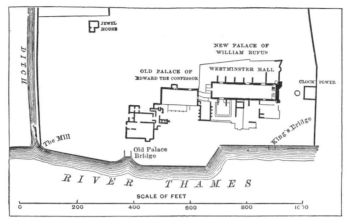

WESTMINSTER ABBEY AND ITS PRECINCT, ABOUT A.D. 1735.

ing of the chamber in which it is held is spangled with stars, but because the *Starra*—a class of state papers—are deposited there.   It is a secret court.   He establishes it in the year 1486.   A man brought before it cannot have any witnesses to testify in his behalf, nor can he have any counsel to defend him.   He cannot make an appeal to any other tribunal.   The court is a direct violation of the Magna Charta.

The avaricious king has two London lawyers in his employ—Richard Empson and Edmund Dudley—who, in turn, employ a set of ruffians called "promoters," who promote the king's cause by swearing to any and every thing which the lawyers wish them to.

Many years ago a law was passed forbidding the nobles to keep any retainers or private soldiers in uniform.   But the nobles have many household servants.   The Earl of Northumberland has a treasurer, a chamberlain, chaplain, constables, and others — one hundred and sixty-six in all. The Earl of Oxford has a great many dependants, who live on his estates. One day the king pays the earl a visit.   It is a grand occasion.   The earl provides a magnificent banquet, and summons all the people who live on his estates to come and honor the king.   He dresses them in uniform. The king notices it.

"Ah, here is a chance to make some money," is the thought that comes to the king.

"These are your menial servants, I suppose ?" he says to the earl.

"Most of them are my retainers, who have come to do you honor."

"By my faith, I thank you for your good cheer; but I cannot allow you to break the law. My lawyers must speak to you."

The lawyers do speak to him, and the earl is compelled to pay an immense sum, or be cast into prison. He feasts the king, and is robbed besides.

Lord Bergavenny has some servants whom the Star-chamber declare are retainers, and he has to pay three hundred and fifty thousand dollars to the king.

Henry is a friend to the Pope. He loves money, but gives liberally to the Church. Out west of London is Westminster Abbey, founded by Edward the Confessor, as long ago as 1060. The place where it stands was once a swamp in the woods; but years before Edward's time, no one knows when, the monks reared a building there, and adopted Peter as their patron saint. There was a clear spring of water near by. They could catch fish in the Thames. They were near enough to London to go out with their bread-bags, to beg their living in the town.

On the Sunday night before the day which had been fixed upon by the bishop for the dedication of the monastery, a fisherman by the name of Edric was out on the Thames, when he saw a light and heard an old man calling to him, wanting to know if he could ferry him across the stream. It was Sunday, but Edric was ready to do the stranger a favor, and rowed him across. The venerable man

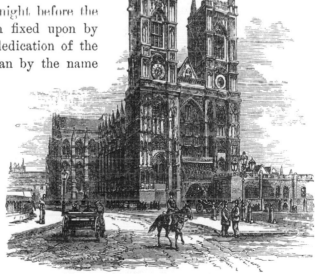

WESTMINSTER ABBEY.

went on to the monastery, when suddenly a host of angels made their appearance. The church was instantly as bright within as if a thousand candles had been lighted, and the stranger and the angels dedicated it with imposing ceremonies.

SHRINE OF EDWARD THE CONFESSOR.

The fisherman was greatly astonished, but soon the stranger came back.

"Can you give me something to eat?" he asked of the fisherman.

"I have been fishing all night, but have caught nothing."

Then the stranger told who he was.

"I am St. Peter, and have control of the keys of heaven. When the bishop comes to consecrate the church, tell him what you have seen, and as for yourself, go out into the river, and you will catch all the fish you want. I have granted this on the conditions that you never again fish on Sunday, and that you always give a portion of what you catch to the monks."

The next day the bishop came to dedicate the monastery, but there, at the door, stands the fisherman with a salmon—a present from St. Peter to the bishop, who heard Edric's story, and was satisfied that St. Peter had already dedicated the building, and there was no need that he should do it. So from that time on the fisherman supplied the monks with fish.

Edward the Confessor, King of England, was very religious. He was ever ready to do something for the Church, to secure an entrance into heaven, and selected this little monastery as one which should have his special patronage. He contributed a large sum of money, and set architects and masons to work to rear an abbey. It was the beginning of the most beautiful edifice in England.

One king after another added to Edward's building, till there arose a great pile—almost a city by itself—Westminster Abbey, Chapter-house, St. Margaret's Church, Hall Palace, clock-towers, infirmary, cloisters, ab-

bot's house, prior's house, sanctuary, granary, and other buildings. The
kings spent their money freely, employing architects and masons, who ham-
mered away at the stones, making elaborate adornments, spending such
enormous sums of money that the House of Commons protested against
expenditures so lavish. That did not stop the work from going on, however, and year by year additions were made, not only to Westminster, but
to other abbeys, till, through the exactions of the kings, and the extortions
of the priests, monks, and friars, a large part of the earnings of the people
was swallowed up by the Church, either in the erection of buildings or the
support of the great swarm of prelates.

Of all the abbeys and monasteries in England, Westminster is the most
renowned. Gracefully the Gothic arches rise, springing from the massive
pillars bending like the interlacing branches of the forest trees. The mel-
low sunlight streams in through gorgeously painted windows, throwing a
flood of golden, purple, and crimson light upon the long-drawn aisles, the

NORTH AMBULATORY AND CHANTRY.

oaken seats, the elaborately carved work of the choir, where the priests
chant the service, robed in white; figures of saints and angels — carved
in the enduring stone—entwined with vines and flowers. Beneath the

abbey is the crypt, where, in niches, the kings and queens of England are entombed. Along the walls of the abbey are tablets and shrines erected to the memory of men who were mightier than kings—the poets, the men who have reigned in the realm of mind.

Upon the stony pavement of the cloisters the monks of Westminster knelt and said their prayers, for religion in those days consisted mainly

THE CLOISTER.

in counting beads and saying Pater-nosters—going over the same prayer again and again. It did not much affect the heart. It did not recognize the rights of man. It consisted in fasting, praying, doing penance, and observing all the requirements of the Church.

The kings of England delighted to add to the attractions of Westminster. Quite likely the abbots and priors were ever ready to make suggestions to the kings in regard to the endowments; be that as it may, it is

HENRY VII.'S CHAPEL.

certain that the kings, one after another, made liberal contributions for the
support of the abbey, and for the addition of something new and attrac-
tive in or about the building. Henry VII. plundered his subjects to obtain money to give to the Church. He decided to build a chapel which
should be the most magnificent of any in England.   An army of masons
were employed to hammer the stone, and the skilful builders to lay them
in the walls.   But it was the people, and not the king, who paid the bills
for quarrying the stone, hammering the blocks, chiselling the beautiful

SCULPTURE ON THE WALL IN THE ABBEY.

and intricate scroll-work and tracery of vines, leaves, and flowers.   Quite
likely the idea never occurred to the king that the building, by good
rights, belonged to the people, from whom he wrenched the money by
taxation and by the tyranny of the Star-chamber; and the monks, the
bishops, and prelates of the Church would have lifted their hands in horror
had any one suggested such an idea.   But the time was approaching when
people would begin to entertain the idea that the king's property was in
reality their own property; and there was a little boy—Henry's son—then
playing around the king's palace at Hampton Court and at Windsor, who
would unwittingly help on such an idea. By-and-by we shall see the

boy; but for the present we will make the acquaintance of the boy's older brother, Arthur.

When Arthur is only three years of age, the king looks around to see whom the boy shall marry, and selects the little girl who was playing in the Alhambra on that day when Columbus stood there, making his last earnest plea to Ferdinand and Isabella for aid to enable him to reach

the east by sailing west. He is good at driving a bargain, and persuades Ferdinand to give his daughter a handsome dowry. Arthur is three and Katherine five when the betrothal is made.

On the 2d of October, 1501, when Katherine is sixteen and Arthur fourteen, Katherine comes to England, and they are married. Ferdinand pays two hundred thousand ducats in gold as a part of her dowry. But in the next April, Arthur suddenly dies. What shall be done now? Henry VII. loves money. If Katherine goes back to Spain, he will have to give up the two hundred thousand ducats. There is his

KATHERINE.

younger son, Henry, twelve years old; he will betroth him to Katherine, and so hold on to the money. But the Bible says, in Leviticus, that a man must not marry his brother's widow. The Archbishop of Canterbury says that such a marriage would be wrong; but the Bishop of Winchester says it was a law binding on the Jews, and not on Christians. Henry will see what the head of the Church of Rome says. The Pope is at war with Louis XII., King of France, and would like to have the King of England for an ally, and grants the desired permission. Being the head of the Church, no one can object to his decision; and as he is infallible, the decision is right, no matter what command there may be in Leviticus to the contrary.

The betrothal between Henry and Katherine takes place at the house of the Archbishop of Salisbury, in Fleet Street, June 3d, 1503. The boy Henry objects to being betrothed—not because Katherine is eight years older than himself, not because she is his sister-in-law, but because he has not been consulted, and because he is under age. Let us not forget it,

SCROOBY.

for we shall see great events come to pass through this objection.   Henry does not make the objection because he does not love Katherine, for he does like her, and is willing, notwithstanding his objection, to have the betrothal go on.   It is not the boy, but the selfish, money-making, prudent king, who, though he has obtained the Pope's permission for the marriage, thinks it worth while to provide a loop-hole through which he can crawl, if it shall be for his interest so to do by-and-by.   Henry will not be of age these six years, and no one knows what may happen in that time.   If the boy objects to the betrothal, he can make that an excuse, if need be, for not consummating the marriage when he becomes of age.

The king has a daughter, Margaret, older than Henry, who is married to King James of Scotland.   It is a long journey which the young lady has to make on horseback from London to Edinburgh.   She does not go alone, however, but is accompanied by a party of high-born ladies and gentlemen.

One night the royal cavalcade stops at a house owned by the Archbishop of York, near the little old town of Scrooby, where the river Idle winds

MARGARET.

through the meadows, turning and winding as if trying to tie itself in a knot.   Myriads of ducks rear their young in the reeds along the river-banks.   The archbishop has built a manor-house, in which he can reside, and enjoy himself while hunting, fowling, and fishing.   It is an old building, partly of wood, partly of brick, with a great hall, and kitchen with a wide-mouthed fireplace, where the cook gets up grand dinners for the archbishop and his friends.   In the old house, Margaret and her maids, the lords and ladies, rest and refresh themselves and spend the night.

The old Scrooby church rears its tower aloft near at hand.   Let us take a good look at the manor-house—at the spacious kitchen, at the dining-hall with its massive table, the stag-horns nailed upon the oaken beams; for we shall come back to the mansion again and again as the years roll by.   We shall see gathered around the hearth-stone some men and women who have done great things for liberty.

Margaret, after a night's entertainment, rides on to become Queen of Scotland, holding her court in Holyrood. We shall see her granddaughter (Mary by name) in that palace, leading a life filled with many vicissitudes, Queen of Scotland, of France, yet meeting with a sad and mournful fate—having her head chopped off by the daughter of this boy who objects to being married to Katherine. It will not be Katherine's daughter, however, who will do the bloody act; but we shall see Katherine's daughter kindling fires all over England, burning heretics, just as Isabella, Katherine's mother, with the aid of Thomas de Torquemada, is roasting them in Spain; all of which are events inseparably connected with the Story of Liberty.

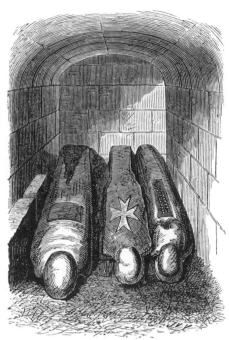

COFFINS OF JAMES I., ELIZABETH OF YORK, AND HENRY VII., AS SEEN ON OPENING THE VAULT IN 1869.

Six years pass. The king, who compelled the merchants of Bristol to promise to give him one-fifth of the money they might make, the man who did so much to beautify and adorn Westminster, is dead, and his body, encased in a stone coffin, is laid away beneath the pavement of the abbey; and his son, Henry VIII., is crowned king in the magnificent edifice, seated in the coronation chair. He is eighteen years of age, tall and stout. He has a round face, a fresh countenance. Although he objected to being betrothed to Katherine, he is ready to fulfil his obligations; for Katherine, a true-hearted and loving lady, has been waiting for him through all the years. The marriage ceremony is performed by the Archbishop of Canterbury, who, six years ago, said that such a marriage would be contrary to the Bible, but who now eats his own words, because the Pope has granted permission. In the next chapter we shall make the acquaintance of the man who gave permission for the marriage to take place.

Although Katherine is twenty-six years old, she is a beautiful bride, and does not seem to be much older than Henry as she stands before the archbishop in Westminster, her dark hair hanging loose and flowing upon her shoulders. She looks lovingly upon the round-faced young man who stands by her side.

Henry has a sister Mary who is only fourteen, and she is in love with her cousin, Charles Brandon; but Henry will not have any such love-match, when the King of France wants her for a wife. The King of France is the same Louis XII. who was divorced from his first wife that he might marry Anne of Bretagne, who is now dead; he is old enough to be Mary's grandfather—weak and feeble, and afflicted with dropsy—and yet the poor girl must give up her true-love and marry him, because Henry wants to make an alliance with France to strengthen his kingdom.

Girls who are born princesses are not often permitted to marry those whom they love. Mary never has seen Louis. She goes on board a ship in the Thames. Henry and Katherine and the noblemen come to bid her farewell. There is a great display of rich dresses and costly jewels. It is a gala-day in London. The shops are closed; the king gives a feast; and everybody is happy, except the young girl who is bidding good-bye to England, good-bye to her lover, to go to France and be the wife of a man just ready to drop into the grave. But she does not bid farewell to her lover, for Charles Brandon goes with her to France, an officer of the court; and, though in love with Mary, he conducts himself discreetly.

HENRY VIII.

Mary does not go alone. It would be cruel to send her away with no one to keep her company. Twelve English maidens accompany her. One is a pretty, sprightly girl, seven years old, Anne Boleyn, who can speak French. Her father is of French descent.

Little does the young king mistrust, as he sees the beautiful girl Anne on the deck of the ship, as to what lies before them both in the unseen future. Little does the light-hearted girl dream of what time will bring to them. If she could but lift the veil that hides the coming years, in-stead of being so joyful on this gala-day, she would stand pale and wan

CORONATION CHAIR.

as a ghost amidst the happy throng. What would she discover? We will wait and see what time will unfold.

The ships sail down the Thames and out upon the sea. The waves are contrary. They dash over the vessels, which dance like cockle-shells before the tempest. Mary and Anne and all the other girls are drenched by the waves. They fear that the ship will go to the bottom, and have a narrow escape from shipwreck. Their trunks are on another ship, which is lost; and though they reach the shore in safety, they have no dry clothes, and are forced to put on such garments as the peasants can lend them. It is a sorry journey for Mary, this going to be the wife of an old man whom she has never seen. What all this had to do with the Story of Liberty we shall see before long.

CHAPTER IX.

THE MAN WHO CAN DO NO WRONG.

THE Pope who granted permission for Katherine and Henry to marry is in his palace in Rome. His papal name is Alexander VI. His father's name was Langolo. He lived in Valencia, Spain, where the Pope was born, and where he was christened Roderick. During his boyhood, his father moves to Venice—the city in the midst of the sea—where he changes his name to Borgia.

He educated Roderick to be a lawyer; but the boy's uncle is a bishop, and can help him on in the Church, and so Roderick, at the age of nineteen, becomes a priest. Being in the priesthood, he ought to be a good man ; but he leads a very wicked life.

In the course of time the uncle is elected Pope. He does not forget the nephew, whom he appoints a cardinal, with a large income—not less than twenty-eight thousand ducats per annum. From whence does the money come ? From the people, who must pay their money into the Church, or be regarded as heretics.

The young cardinal lays his plans for the future. His uncle is an old man, and Roderick is determined, at his death, to step into his shoes as Pope. With so much wealth he can give grand dinners, and win the favor of the cardinals, who elect a new Pope whenever there is a vacancy.

It is only three years that he has to wait for his uncle to die. He has little difficulty in persuading a majority of the cardinals to vote for him. Does he not make great promises as to what he will do for them ? Twenty-two vote for him, while only five oppose him.

On August 11th, 1492, at the time Christopher Columbus is sailing westward over an unknown sea, Roderick Langolo Borgia is carried into the papal palace on the shoulders of the people, followed by the cardinals who have elected him.

" He is a bad man, as you will find out," say the cardinals to those who have given Cardinal Borgia their votes.

THE POPE IN HIS PALACE.

" He will hand over all Christendom to the devil," remarks Ferdinand of Spain, who knows the family.

The new Pope loves display. He puts on costly robes, adorned with precious jewels, and is borne into St. Peter's in great state, seated in a golden chair, on a litter resting on the shoulders of his obedient subjects.

Now that Roderick is Pope, having all power on earth, incapable of doing anything wrong, he brings his children and their mother into the papal palace. He is a priest, and it is not lawful for a priest to marry; but though no marriage ceremony has been performed, the woman lives with him as if she were his wife.

THE POPE GOING TO ST. PETER'S.

The cardinals whom he promised to reward come to receive their gifts, but the Pope laughs in their faces; he does not remember of ever having promised them anything. Some of them are pertinacious in their demands, and he imprisons them in St. Angelo. Two of the prisoners are especially obnoxious to the Pope; they are suddenly seized with a terrible sickness that results in death, and the physicians who attend them,

CÆSAR BORGIA.

when questioned in regard to their sickness, whisper an ominous word— poison! People say that the Pope knows who put poison in the cardinals food.

People all over the world are contributing their money to the Church. It is flowing into the papal treasury from England, Germany, France, Spain, and Italy; and the Pope, the woman who lives with him, and their children, help themselves liberally from the bountiful supply.

THE CARDINALS.

But the Pope wants something besides money for his children; he desires to have them numbered among princes. Frederick is the eldest, and the Pope persuades Ferdinand of Spain to make the young man a duke. The second son, Cæsar, the Pope appoints Archbishop of Valencia —the richest bishopric in Spain. We shall presently see what sort of a man he is, to occupy such a position in the Church.

The third son is Ludovico, who is created a cardinal, and who receives a fortune from the papal treasury.

The youngest son, Godfrey, is created a baron, and is provided with a fortune.

The Pope has one daughter, Lucretia, a beautiful girl, who is already married to a Spanish nobleman; but the father wishes to advance her to a higher position, and divorces her from her husband, and gives her in marriage to Lord Sforza.

The wedding is celebrated with much pomp in the papal palace. The cardinals, archbishops, and bishops are there in their gorgeous robes, and a banquet is served of the choicest viands and wines.

Some of the rich and old families of Rome, who claim to be descended from the nobles of the time of Julius Cæsar, show their contempt for such a Pope. One of the families is the Colonna. One of the noblest and best women

VITTORIA COLONNA.

of the time is Vittoria Colonna, who will not attend the Pope's banquets, nor recognize the Pope in any way, asserting her individual independence and liberty.

The Pope resolves to be revenged. He will let the noble families know that he has all power on earth. He confiscates their estates, appropriates them to his own use, or bestows them upon his children. To Frederick, the eldest, he gives a large sum, which arouses the anger and jealousy of Archbishop Cæsar Borgia.

One morning some fishermen find the body of Duke Frederick floating in the Tiber, with nine wounds in the breast.

" This is your work," the Pope says to Archbishop Cæsar.

" No, I did not kill him," the archbishop replies.

11*

"But you had him assassinated."

The archbishop does not deny it.

What shall the Pope do? Shall the archbishop be hanged, or shall he be imprisoned? Assassination is a terrible crime, especially when committed by one of the highest prelates of the Church. Shall not Cæsar be at once degraded from his archbishopric? No. The Pope pardons him instead, and the assassin goes on absolving people from their sins, and enjoying all the wealth and honor and power of his position.

But Cæsar is tired of being a priest, and the Pope releases him from his vows, for he has other plans in view for him. Now that he can marry, the Pope demands of the King of Naples the hand of his daughter in marriage with Cæsar. The king refuses.

LUCRETIA BORGIA.

The Pope resolves to have his revenge, and he looks around to see how it can be gratified. He remembers that the French king, Louis XII., for a long while has laid claim to the kingdom of Naples, and also to the dukedom of Milan. Louis is married to a woman whom he hates, and from whom he would like to be divorced, so that he can marry Anne of Bretagne. The Pope sends an ambassador to Paris, with a proposition: If Louis will pay him thirty thousand ducats, and endow Cæsar with two provinces in Dauphine which will yield twenty thousand livres a year, and make Cæsar a duke, and marry him to Charlotte d'Albret, the beautiful daughter of a French count, he will issue a bull taking the crown from the King of Naples and giving it to Louis, and will support his claims to Milan.

As the Pope has the right to give away crowns and depose kings, Louis accepts the proposition. The Pope decrees the dissolution of Louis's marriage contract, and issues a bull taking the crown from the King of Naples and giving it to Louis, who at once sets his armies in motion to take possession. It is the beginning of a war in which many hundred thousand men lose their lives, towns and cities are destroyed, and the land made desolate.

Lucretia is tired of her husband, Lord Sforza, and the Pope can see a

THE TIBER, ST. PETER'S, AND CASTLE OF ST. ANGELO.

chance to marry her again, and so divorces her from Sforza, and marries her to Duke Alfonzo of Naples. He soon discovers, however, though he is infallible, and can make no mistake in anything, that Alfonzo is a poor fellow, whom he must get rid of. Lucretia has been divorced so many times that it will hardly do to issue another divorce so soon after her marriage. There are assassins in Rome, and if Lucretia's husband should happen to disappear some night, it would only be such a fate as falls to other men. Singularly enough, one evening, when Alfonzo is walking through St. Peter's, an assassin stabs him. It is not a mortal wound; but on another day some ruffians steal into the chamber of the wounded man, and finish him by strangulation, and the Pope knows who the ruffians are, and it is whispered that he hired them to put Lucretia's husband out of the way.

During these years the Spaniards have discovered a new world in the West, while the Portuguese have sailed down the coast of Africa, discovered the Cape of Good Hope, and opened a new way to the East; and the Pope gives America to Spain, and the eastern lands to Portugal.

Being God's vicar on earth, being above all kings and emperors, able to give away crowns, to alienate subjects from their sovereigns, compelling potentates and all in authority to kiss his feet, owning all the world, he can give away the Western continent to whomsoever he will, as if it were but a bit of land which he had always owned, and no one may question his authority.

The Pope loves wine, and drinks so much that his eyelids grow heavy; he falls asleep in his chair and rolls upon the floor, but the business of the papacy goes on just the same, for Lucretia opens his letters, issues orders to the Holy Office, to the cardinals, and bishops.

The Pope is fond of Lucretia, and wants to see her married once more, and finds a husband in the Duke of Ferrara.

Some of the princes of Italy combine against the Pope, who finds out what is going on. He soothes them with honeyed words, and invites them to a banquet. While they are at supper, a band of assassins breaks into the hall. The Pope and Cæsar slip out of a side door, while the assassins fall upon the princes and put three of them to death. The others make their escape.

The Pope is in need of money; and as the men are dead, he confiscates their estates; and as the others have leagued against them, he throws them into prison and seizes their property.

All the while there is a great show of religion in Rome. The priests go every day in procession to the churches, wearing robes embroidered with crosses; after they have performed mass, they spend the remainder of the time in idleness, or in something worse.

There comes a night in August, 1503. The Pope has invited nine of the cardinals to a banquet. He has a little scheme which he wishes to carry out: he wants to make Cæsar king. To do that he must have more money; and though the people all over the world are paying him Peter's-pence and purchasing indulgences, the gold does not come in as fast as he would like. If he could only create a few cardinals, he would be in

THE PRIESTS' PROCESSION.

funds, for he can sell a cardinal's office for thirty thousand ducats. If the nine cardinals would only die, he could reap a rich harvest—more than two hundred thousand ducats—by selling their offices! With such an amount of money, he could carry on war, conquer cities, and make Cæsar king.

Cæsar prepares the banquet in the garden of the Vatican. It will be delightful for the old cardinals to sit there in an arbor on a summer night and quaff their wine. He will have a particular kind of wine for them— one cup, which none but the nine shall drink. He prepares it himself, and gives it into the hands of a trusty waiter.

" Let no one drink of this except the cardinals : it is for them alone. Be careful now," he says to the servant.

The servant carries the flagon into the arbor.

" Why do you put that goblet by itself ?" asks the vintner who has charge of the wine.

" It is very choice wine.   Only the cardinals are to drink it."

The Pope and Cæsar enter the arbor, and the cardinals will soon be there.   The Pope discovers that he has forgotten to put his charm upon his neck.   It is a precious affair—a gold locket, with a crumb of holy bread in it.   A fortune-teller has assured him that so long as he wears it no harm can come to him.

" Run and get it; you will find it on my table," he says to the servant who has brought in the flagon of choice wine.

· The servant hastens away.

" I am very thirsty.   I will take a glass of wine, if you please," he says to the vintner.

Is there any wine too good for the Pope ?   The vintner thinks not. He will give him some of the choice vintage which is reserved for the favored few, and brings a glass for the Pope, and another for Cæsar.

The cardinals come, and the Pope and Cæsar receive them graciously, and all take their seats at the table.

But suddenly the Pope utters a piercing cry, and rolls upon the ground. He is in terrible agony ; and Cæsar is also seized with excruciating pains.

There is running here and there for doctors, who come in hot haste.

" Poison !"

They have drunk the wine which was prepared for the cardinals. Cæsar recovers, but the Pope is burning up.   There is a fire in his bones. His flesh grows putrid ; his tongue becomes black, and hangs from his mouth ; ulcers break out upon his body, which swells to enormous size. His servants flee.   There is no one to care for him.   Alone in his chamber, he groans till death relieves his sufferings.

CHAPTER X.

THE BOY WHO SUNG FOR HIS BREAKFAST.

ON that day when Christopher Columbus went out from the Alhambra, sad and dejected, there was a little boy in a town in Germany who was experiencing a sorrowful childhood. He was born on St. Martin's Day, 1483, and his parents have christened him Martin. They are very poor. The father is a miner, and works hard in digging copper ore and smelting it. The family have little to eat better than rye bread and herrings.

Martin's father is a passionate man, and his mother is a stern woman. His school-master is hard-hearted and cruel; and between the three the boy gets many whippings. His lessons are dry as dust—the Catechism, Ten Commandments, Apostles' Creed, the Canticles, Psalms, and Latin exercises. One day the brute of a master punishes him not less than fifteen times! There is no joy in life. He hates the Catechism and the Creed, but makes good progress in Latin. The miner has sense enough to see that Martin can learn very little in such a school, and sends him to another, taught by monks, called a *currend* school. The boys attending it sing in the churches on Sunday, and go through the villages early every morning, and sing before the burghers' houses for a bit of bread. They carry little tin boxes with a slit in the cover, and the burghers' now and then drop in money. At times Martin obtains neither money nor bread. On Christmas mornings the boys go out early, Martin singing the solos, and the others joining in the choruses. The solo rises, sweet and clear, upon the wintry air:

> " Praises now from all on earth!
> 'Tis the day of Jesus' birth,
> Of a Virgin born in sooth;
> Angels glory o'er the youth.
> *Kyrie eleeson.*

> " Only child of God's own kind
> In a manger shepherds find;

God-babe sent our sins to free
By suff'ring our humanity.
Kyrie eleeson."

But it is not always Christmas, and there are days when the boys have little to eat. Martin often has only a crust. He grows thin and pale and weak. What shall he do? His father is so poor that he cannot help him; the monks have nothing to give him, and if the burghers do not supply him with food, he must starve.

There comes a cold and bitter morning. Martin goes out to sing through the streets, but the burghers do not like to be awakened so early, and the servants are surly. He sings before a house.

"Go away!"

It is a gruff voice that he hears, and he passes on to another residence; but as soon as he begins to sing, the door opens, and a man's head is thrust out.

"Clear out there! Don't you know better than to disturb the master so early?"

He will get nothing there, and moves on to a third house

THE EARLY MORNING CHANT AT EISENACH.

and sings; but before the carol is finished a servant comes out with a whip.

"Begone, you ragamuffin!"

Charity is frozen on this winter morning. Weak, faint, hungry, disheartened, he turns away. What shall he do? Why should he sing? No one will give him bread.

"I may as well go back to the convent and die," he says to himself.

He is standing before Conrad Cotta's house. The owner is a rich burgher. No one is astir about the premises that he can see. The daylight is streaming up the east, and the burghers of the town will soon be eating their breakfasts; then they will be off to their shops. Oh, if he but once in life could eat all that he wanted!

URSULA COTTA AND MARTIN LUTHER.

Shall he sing?

Herr Cotta is one of the chief men of the town; will he not rush out and whip him? The tears roll down the boy's cheeks as he stands there, irresolute.

Sing, boy! sing! The ages are waiting for you. Sing! sing! All the world will hear you. God knows what will come of it.

Sweet and clear, his voice rises on the morning air. The door opens, and Ursula Cotta stands upon the threshold beckoning to him.

Little does Ursula Cotta know what will come from that lifting of her hand. She has seen the poor boy driven from the neighbors' houses, and the harsh words addressed to him have filled her with pain. She has

seen him on Sunday, and has recognized his voice as being sweeter than
all other voices in the choir. She will give him a good meal. He
goes up the steps. She takes him by the hand, leads him into the house.
He goes to a warm breakfast and a home; henceforth Ursula Cotta will
be a mother to him. Now he can go to school and study all day, sleep
sweetly at night, and have all he can eat at breakfast, dinner, and supper.
The scowl disappears from his face. He is no longer dogged and sullen,

THE STUDENTS' FESTIVAL.

but bubbling over with joy; and in a short time, so diligently does he
apply himself, that he is fitted to enter the university, where he masters
the Latin language, till he can speak it as fluently as his mother-tongue.

One day, while in the university library looking at the books, he comes
upon an old volume into which none of the students or monks ever look.
He brushes the dust from the covers, opens to the title-page, and sees

that it is the Bible. He has heard of the book, but never before has he seen a copy. It is in Latin. He turns the leaves, but his eye falls upon an interesting story about a boy who tended the lamps in the sanctuary on the green hills of Shiloh. Never has he read so interesting a story.

THE AUGUSTINE FRIARS.

Of all books in the library none are so entertaining as this. He reads the volume at every leisure moment. The other students spend much time in celebrating festivals, marching through the streets; but he has no time for play, and even on holidays, when all the inhabitants turn out and decorate the streets, he is busy with his books. He is thirsting for knowledge, and makes such progress in his studies that before he is twenty-seven years old he is made a doctor of philosophy; and his fellow-students, proud of their young doctor, make a grand parade, conduct him to the hall of the university, and install him as their teacher, with appropriate ceremonies, in his professor's chair.

And now, instead of reciting creeds and catechisms, he is giving lectures, and is so earnest and eloquent that students come from far to listen to his teaching. There comes a night when he invites all the students to take supper with him. They drink his health in foaming mugs of beer.

He rises to make a speech. They hurrah and clap their hands. But never have they seen the young doctor so sober. He informs them that it is the last time they will meet together. He has decided to resign his professorship and become a monk. They are astounded.

"Become a monk!"

"Yes."

"Shut yourself up in a convent, shave your head, go barefoot, and wear a hair shirt!"

"Yes."

He bids them good-bye, leaves the room, and at midnight knocks at the gate of the convent of the Augustine monks. The door turns on its hinges, and Doctor Martin Luther passes in, and the door closes upon him. Morning comes. The professor's chair in the university is vacant, while the professor who has occupied it is kneeling on the cold stone floor of his cell, saying his prayers. He is dead to the world, and the world is dead to him : he studies ; he spends his time in praying ; he fasts, eating only a few morsels of bread ; he grows thin and pale, till he is only skin and bones — trying in this way to get rid of his sins. He begs his living. Shouldering a bag, he goes through the villages, asking the people for bread, cheese, geese, chickens—or anything that will support life. Martin before long, however, discovers that the monks, instead of being holier than other men, have like passions, and are ready to help themselves to the best of the things given them by the people. There are frequent disputes which the prior has to settle.

And what do the people receive in return for their gifts ? Nothing.

12

CHAPTER XI.

WHAT THE BOY WHO SUNG FOR HIS BREAKFAST SAW IN ROME.

THERE is a dispute between the Augustine monks of Germany and the vicar who superintends them. The monks object to some of his proceedings. It is a dispute which only the Pope—the man who can do no wrong—can settle. The monks choose Friar Martin to go to Rome and lay the matter before the Pope. Friar Martin is able and eloquent. He has read all the works of the fathers, and he, of all others, will best plead their cause. Although the journey is a long one, Friar Martin is pleased to make it, for Rome is the Eternal City, where dwells the head of the Church—the holy man who is God's representative on earth, who cannot possibly do anything that is not right. To visit Rome will be like going to the very gate of heaven.

The monks give Brother Martin their blessing and benediction, and he starts upon his journey. Although there are thousands of monks tramping through Germany—so many that the people compare them to the grasshoppers that eat up their fields of corn—yet they do not refuse him a bit of bread-and-cheese, and at the convents he finds good cheer among the brothers. He crosses the Rhine ; climbs the Alps, where the shepherds are tending their flocks ; passes along deep gorges, where the water tumbles and foams to the lakes below, and where the rocks rise so high, so sharp and steep, that at noon it is only twilight. He sees the avalanches roll from the mountains with a roar like thunder. Far above him the icy peaks gleam in the sunshine. He climbs above the clouds, crosses fields of snow, goes over the summit, descends the southern slope, and finds himself, as it were, in another world. How pure the air ! How deep and tender the light ! A blue haze rests upon the mountains. Fresh and green the fields ; wide-spreading the chestnut-trees ; fertile the slopes, where the peasants are planting their vineyards. He reaches the plains of Italy, and beholds ruins around him—marble pillars, beautifully sculptured once, but broken now. The Italian brothers of his order welcome him to their monasteries ; but he is surprised to see how luxuriously they live.   They make themselves merry with wine, sing songs, tell unseemly stories, and then rattle off Pater-nosters and masses glibly, to get through with them as soon as possible, that they may take another pull at the wine, or indulge in other pleasures.

Italy is an old land, and Friar Martin is well acquainted with its history—how the Empire of Rome rose and fell.   He gazes upon the sculpt-

OVER THE MOUNTAINS.

ured marbles and broken columns, and recalls the time when Rome was in her glory, with an empire reaching from India to England.   He comes to the Campagna—the wide plain through which winds the River Tiber. He sees the Aqueduct, which the old Romans built to bring water into the city from the Albanian hills.   And there, in the distance, are the gleaming spires of the city—the one spot of all others on earth that he has

longed to see. He falls on his face and gives thanks to God. "Holy
Rome! I salute thee!" he cries, in ecstasy. He passes through the massive gate - way, walks with reverent feet the narrow streets, enters the

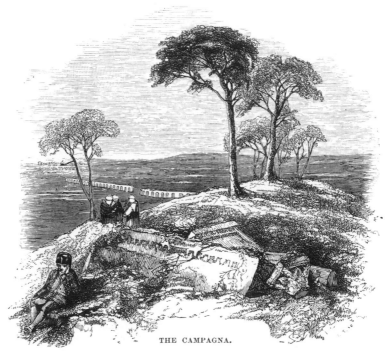

THE CAMPAGNA.

churches, one after another, to say his prayers and thank God anew that
he is in the holy city. He almost wishes that his father and mother were
not alive; for if they were dead and in purgatory, what unspeakable pleasure there would be in obtaining their release by his prayers, which he repeats in every church!

How inspiring to stand in the old Forum where, a century before
Christ was born, Cicero gave utterance to his immortal orations! The
past rises before Friar Martin. He sees, in imagination, the audience of
old Romans listening to Cicero. One of his auditors is Julius Cæsar, six
years younger than the orator: he has led the armies of Rome in triumph
through Gaul, has crossed the sea to the land of the Angles, where men
wear skins of beasts for clothing, and where Druids venerate the stately
oaks, and offer human sacrifices to their deity.

Another of Cicero's auditors is a general who has led the armies to
victory in the East—Pompey—he who profaned the Temple at Jerusalem
by entering into the most holy place.

General Cato is another listener—a man with a soul so calm and serene that nothing disturbs him.

And still another general is there—Mark Antony—a wild, reckless debauchee, who fills Rome with riot and disorder.

Two poets are in the audience listening to Cicero's eloquence—Virgil and Horace, and a historian—Sallust; they are boys. And there is one more—Seneca. Friar Martin has read their works; and there he is upon the spot where the poets, perhaps, have recited their own poems to the people of old Rome.

He walks along a street, past the Temple of Jupiter, and comes to the Temple of Peace, and looks up to its mighty arches, reared by Vespasian, to receive the spoils which he brought from Jerusalem; and the poor Jews whom he brought as prisoners were compelled to work in the clay-pits, making bricks for the construction of the edifice commemorative of their humiliation.

Near by it is the Arch of Titus. What a story in its time-worn stones

THE PLACE WHERE CICERO DELIVERED HIS ORATIONS.

—the history of a perishing, and yet imperishable, people! The Triumphal Arch was erected to glorify the man who thought he had crushed
them out forever. In the sculptured stones Friar Martin sees the procession of Roman soldiers bringing the silver trumpets, the golden candle-
stick, the table of showbread—the sacred furniture of the Jewish Temple,
and escorting the weeping maidens, the stalwart warriors of the conquered
race, prisoners of war, doomed to hopeless captivity.

On the hill overlooking the Forum is the Capitol—the once magnificent marble palace, with its majestic columns, mosaic pavements, courts,
and passage-ways, adorned with statues of nymphs, fauns, and satyrs, and

THE BUILDING WHICH THE JEWS ERECTED.

before which is the statue of the emperor Marcus Aurelius. From this
palace once was issued a decree that all the world should be taxed; and
so it happened that a poor man in Judea started on a long journey with
his wife, to give in his name to the tax-assessor, and could find no room in
the tavern at night, and was forced to lie down in a stable with the cattle,
where, during the night, a babe was born—babe of all others most wonderful! From this palace was issued the order for the beheading of Peter
and Paul; and in yonder prison, in a deep, dark dungeon, Paul was confined.

It is not the palace of the emperors of Rome, but the places where

FROM THIS PALACE WENT FORTH THE DECREE "THAT ALL THE WORLD SHOULD BE TAXED."

Christian martyrs have suffered, that most attract the attention of Friar Martin. It was in the Coliseum that they were torn to pieces by the wild beasts, to gratify the heathen populace of Rome. Jewish captives built it,

THE ARCH OF TITUS.

and the mortar of the masonry was mixed with their tears. In the arena those who would not abjure their faith in Christ were eaten by lions. In the great edifice, rising tier above tier, the people looked down upon the spectacle—emperor, patrician, plebeian—and not one heart in all the vast

THE COLISEUM.

assembly moved to pity at the sight.   What joy to behold the hated
Christians tossed to the beasts — to see fair maidens torn in pieces and
devoured !

The thought does not come to Friar Martin that the men who ask
questions in Spain, at that very moment are roasting men by the thousand ; while there were only a score or two thrown to the lions and tigers
in the Coliseum.

Friar Martin finds that the Pope, Julius II., is an old man, with a
long white beard.   He sits in a golden chair, wearing gorgeous robes em-
blazoned with diamonds and jewels.   Palm-Sunday comes, and there is a
grand procession.   The Pope bears a silver plate on his breast, on which
there is a figure of the Almighty.   It is of pure gold, surrounded by costly pearls.

The cardinals appear in their red hats, red gown, red stockings, and
slippers.   One of them is known as the " Boy-cardinal."   His name is
John de' Medici.   His father lived in Florence, and was very rich.   When
John was only seven years old, his father bought an abbot's office for him.
An abbot had charge of a monastery, and the monks called the boy " their
father."   Quite likely some of them smiled when they thus addressed him.

When he was fourteen, his father bought a cardinal's office for him, and John put on his red hat, slippers, and gown, and became one of the Pope's councillors. He owns a villa, and lives in grand style. He loves music, painting, sculpture, and poetry. He spends all of his income in giving entertainments to his brother-cardinals, and the poets, artists, and musicians. He sets before them the choicest wines, and all the delicious fruits of the season. Sometimes he even pawns his gold and silver dishes to obtain money enough to give a banquet; for he is thinking that the Pope may not live always, and possibly, if he is hospitable to his brother-cardinals and to those who influence public opinion, he may be elected Julius's successor.

In the procession are a great number of bishops—Armenian, Syrian, Greek, and Roman—wearing magnificent dresses, blazing with jewels. The young friar from Germany never dreamed that there was such wealth in the world as he sees around him.

The Pope's chamberlains walk by his side, carrying fans made of peacocks' tails. The cross-bearers go before, bearing huge silver crosses. One official carries the triple crown, set with costly diamonds and jewels.

The Pope sits in his golden chair, on a litter, which is taken up by stout men, and borne upon their shoulders.

FAN-BEARERS.

An officer carries a golden mace — the emblem of authority; and there is a great following of princes, counts, abbots, priests, and monks.

On Corpus Christi Day the Pope is carried around St. Peter's Church, seated in his golden chair, with all the prelates of the Church in his train,

and his body-guard marching by his side with drawn swords — not that anybody will harm him, but to add to the pomp and grandeur of the occasion. The people kneel, and the Pope throws a blessing to them from the ends of his fingers.

Friar Martin sees wonderful things in the churches. In one he beholds the Holy Baby — a rag doll, which performs more cures than all the physicians in Rome. It is taken to the chambers of the sick, and its presence heals disease. The people worship it, offer costly gifts, which go — they know not to whom. The doll performs miracles. Men falling from the tops of houses have called upon the baby to save them, and have not been harmed. Drowning men have called upon it to rescue them, and they have been saved. A lady fell from the roof of a high building, and prayed to the

CARRYING THE POPE'S CROWN.

doll, and the fall was arrested in mid-air. The lady was so grateful for her preservation that she gave an immense sum of money to the doll, and had a picture painted representing the scene.

Every church has its holy relics. In one are the boards of the manger in which Christ was laid at his birth. He sees the Virgin Mary's clothing, one of St. Peter's ribs, a part of John the Baptist's skull, and no end of saintly bones—all very precious and holy.

The people worship the relics, and gaze upon them with reverential awe.   In St. Peter's Church they form in a long line to kiss the foot of St. Peter's statue, which has stood there for many centuries : so many have pressed their lips to the great-toe that it is worn to a stub.   Some sceptical persons maintain that the statue is not Peter's, but an old heathen statue of Jupiter ; that, however, does not diminish the devotion of the multitude.

Julius II., the Pope, is at the head of his army.   Ever since his election, in 1506, he has been at war—fighting the Venetians, the Germans, and the French, at times ; then, making alliance with the Venetians and Germans, he has waged a vigorous war against Louis XII. of France.   He fights not only in the field, but in the cabinet.   He has bribed Henry VIII. of England and Ferdinand of Spain to attack France, and has taken the money which the good people have contributed to support the

THE DOLL THAT WORKS MIRACLES.

Church to pay an army of Swiss, which he has hired to fight against the French.   He has issued a bull releasing the subjects of Louis from their allegiance.

Just before Friar Martin arrives in Rome, the Pope goes out with his troops to attack the town of Mirandola, accompanied by all the cardinals and bishops. His army surrounds the town. The Pope plants the cannon, directs the soldiers where to attack, and issues his orders as commander-in-

KISSING ST. PETER'S TOE.

chief. Day after day the siege goes on. The Pope did not expect such a stubborn resistance, but he is only the more determined to conquer; and when at last the town surrenders, he climbs a scaling-ladder, sword in hand, mounts the wall, followed by his troops, who rush through the streets, enter the houses, plunder the people, and commit terrible outrages upon the men, women, and children.

The Pope sends an army to Ravenna, an allied army, composed of Spanish, Swiss, Germans, and Venetians, all leagued against the French. The armies meet on a plain near the city. The French are commanded by a young general, Gaston de Foix, who, though he is only thirty years old, has won many victories. The commander of the Pope's army is John de' Medici, the Boy-cardinal, who knows nothing about war, but who can give grand entertainments. There are about thirty-five thousand in each army. All day long the battle rages, but when night comes the Pope's army is a routed rabble, and the Boy-cardinal a prisoner. Though the French have won the victory, their brave leader lies beneath a heap of slain. Each army has lost nearly ten thousand men in this conflict, which is only one of many fought on the plains of Italy; and for what? That the Pope may drive the French out of the provinces which Roderick Borgia (Alexander VI.) had given to Louis a few years before.

Friar Martin did not expect to hear the beating of drums, nor the blare of trumpets, neither to behold the Pope marching at the head of his troops through the streets of holy Rome. He had thought of the city as being, as it were, a suburb of heaven; but he finds it a military town. The Pope is such a fighter that the people call him "general." A witty man writes a paper which sets everybody to laughing, representing Julius, after he is dead, as knocking at the gate of heaven for admission.

"Who is there?" Peter asks, looking down from the top of the wall.

"Julius."

"Never heard of you before. What have you done? Give an account of yourself."

"I have been fighting for you. I have marched with my armies, captured cities. I entered one place sword in hand."

"That is not satisfactory. I can't let you in."

"Not let me in, after fighting so bravely?"

"No."

"Why not?"

"My soldiers fight only with the sword of the Spirit."

"If you don't let me in, I'll bring up my cannon, and batter down your walls, as I did the walls of Mirandola."

And so, fearing that Julius will be as good as his word, Peter opens the gate and lets him in. People say that the learned man of Holland, Doctor Erasmus, wrote it; but the doctor will not acknowledge that it came from his pen.

Friar Martin visits one of the churches, that he may say his prayers on the marble steps of the holy stairs up which Christ walked when he was brought before Pilate in Jerusalem. He kneels upon the lower step and says a Pater-noster, for which he will obtain fifty years' release from purgatory. He goes up another step, and repeats the prayer. He has gained one hundred years. He moves another step, and repeats it. One hundred and fifty years has been gained.

"The just shall live by faith."

Who spoke? Was it one of the monks at the foot of the stairs who takes money from those who ascend them? Was it one of the swarm of beggars who hold out their hands at the bottom, and also at the top of the stairs? Was it a fellow-pilgrim? None of these. Who then? Friar Martin certainly heard a voice. He stops in the middle of the Pater-noster,

CLIMBING THE STAIRS.

looks around, springs to his feet, and goes down the steps.

Many times has he read those words, and now, like a flash of lightning from a cloudless sky, they blaze upon his soul. He leaves the church, greatly wondering, and thinking as he never has thought before.

The longer he stays in Rome, the more is he dissatisfied with what he sees. He discovers that the Pope, the cardinals, bishops, and priests are, for the most part, very far from being the pure men he had supposed them to be. The Pope is a military chieftain. The cardinals are living sensual lives. The money which is contributed by the good people of every land for the Church is squandered in riotous living or for the support of armies. It is no longer holy Rome; the city instead is a sink of iniquity. Crime goes unpunished. Men are robbed and murdered at noonday. The offices of the Church are bought and sold, just as men buy and sell houses or cattle. The nunneries and monasteries, instead of being retreats for prayers, meditation, and holy living, are vile places. Cardinals, bishops, priests, monks, and nuns, all live upon the treasure contributed by the people, or taken from them by tithes, or obtained by the sale of indulgences and pardons. He turns his steps homeward, sick at heart with what he has seen.

CHAPTER XII.

THE BOY-CARDINAL.

IT is a great day in Rome, the 11th of April, 1513. One of the grandest processions ever seen in the city is passing through the streets, escorting the newly elected Pope to St. Peter's. Julius is dead, and the cardinals have elected as his successor the man who was defeated at Ravenna by Gaston de Foix, the man who loves pictures, statues, poetry, and music, who gives sumptuous entertainments, and who pawns his silver plate to obtain money for a grand banquet — the Boy-cardinal, John de' Medici. He has had his eye on the Pope's chair for a long while, and all of his grand dinners have been given with the view of making himself so agreeable that when the time should come for electing a new Pope, he would step into Julius's shoes. He is no longer to be known as the Boy-cardinal, but as Leo X. He is amiable and kind-hearted. He never will mount a scaling-ladder, and enter a city sword in hand; he will stay in Rome, and gather painters, sculptors, and poets around him. He loves their society. He loves good dinners and good wine, and drinks so much at times that he becomes limber in the legs. His garments glitter with diamonds and jewels. He rides a superb horse. Triumphal arches have been erected along the streets, marble statues set up, and banners flung to the breeze. Bright-eyed girls strew flowers along the way, and the multitude kneel as he passes by in his gorgeous coach. In the evening Leo gives a magnificent banquet. Since the days of the emperors of old Rome, there has been no such feast. The rarest and richest luxuries are spread upon the tables, and the choicest wine of Italy is drunk from golden goblets.

As soon as the new Pope is seated on his throne he lays his plans for the future. He will have a new church edifice — the grandest in all Christendom. He will have it adorned with the richest marbles. Among the architects whom he employs is Michael Angelo, the greatest of all.

Fortunately, that gray-bearded man, Christopher Columbus, has discovered a new world, rich in silver and gold, and the wealth of those distant lands is beginning to flow to Europe; while England, France, Spain, Germany, and Holland are increasing in riches. There are few heretics now, for the men who ask questions have roasted nearly all of them to death.

THE POPE'S CHAPEL.

The people everywhere love and honor the Pope, and are ready to give liberally to enable him to build his great church. He sends the Gospel to their very doors, so that everywhere the poor, as well as the rich, can purchase salvation not only for themselves, but for their friends in purgatory. The Pope is very kind and accommodating. He bestows his blessings freely—blessing the people, the bells in the churches, even blesses horses!

THE CARDINALS IN PROCESSION.

Anybody can secure salvation or buy a blessing. Priests, monks, and friars travel up and down the country selling indulgences.

One of the Pope's agents for the sale of indulgences is a fat friar, with a thundering voice John Tetzel. He is from Leipsic, in Germany. John does not give himself to fasting, but eats fat meat and drinks good wine. He rides in a carriage drawn by three horses. Once he committed a crime, and was sewed up in a sack, and was about to be thrown into the

THE POPE IN HIS CARRIAGE.

river, but the judge concluded not to put him to death; and now he is carrying the Gospel about the country, with a cavalcade of horsemen to escort him and protect him from robbers.

Just before he enters a town, the sheriff passes through the streets with a trumpeter. The people hear the sounding of the trumpet, and rush out from their houses to see what is going on.

"The grace of God and St. Peter is before your gates," shouts the sheriff.

The good news spreads. The Gospel has come. Now they can purchase salvation, and release their friends from the pains of purgatory.

13*

The people form in procession, the priests leading.   Then come the school-children, the monks, friars, and nuns, and a great number of citizens carrying banners and lighted candles.   They meet Friar Tetzel, and escort him, in his gilded coach, to the church, singing and shouting, for it is a joyful day.   The procession enters the church, the organ peals, a chant is sung, the cross is placed in front of the altar, and the Pope's arms suspended upon it.   Tetzel takes his position in the pulpit.

"Come, friends, and buy my pardons, buy my indulgences.   You can

BLESSING HORSES.

release your friends from purgatory.   Do you not hear them say, 'We are enduring horrible torments?'   A small sum will deliver them."

The people shudder at the words.   Their friends in purgatory!   They will release them at once.

"The very instant the money chinks in the box their souls will fly toward heaven," says Tetzel.

But there are some who do not quite believe all that he says.

"I will excommunicate all who doubt this blessed grace," he cries.

To be excommunicated—cut off from the Church—would be terrible, and they must doubt no longer.

ST. PETER'S AND THE VATICAN.

"Blessed, my friends, are the eyes which see what you see," and Tetzel holds up the cash-box. "Bring your money! Bring your money!" He drops a piece of silver into the box to set an example of benevolence.

A king, queen, and prince must pay fifty dollars for an indulgence; counts and barons, twenty dollars; poor people, five dollars; and if they are very poor, they can get one for a less amount. For particular sins there are specified prices. If a man has committed murder, he must pay a larger sum than he who has committed theft.

The people flock to the church, and all day long the money is dropping into the cash-box. The money not only of Germany, but of all Europe, is flowing toward Rome.

Tetzel travels from town to town, and after a while reaches the city of Leipsic. Little does he know of what is before him. A gentleman comes to buy an indulgence.

"Can you pardon a sin which a man intends to commit?" he asks.

"Certainly; the Pope has given me full power to do so."

"Very well. I should like to punish a man a little. I don't want to hurt him much—just a little. How much do you ask for an indulgence that will hold me harmless, so that I shall not be punished?"

"For such a sin I must have thirty dollars."

"That is too much. I will give ten."

"No, that is too little. I will let you have one for twenty-five."

"I can't pay that. I will give fifteen."

"That is not enough. I will let you have it for twenty."

"Are you sure that it will protect me?"

"Certainly. I should like to know how any harm can come to you. It is the Pope's dispensation; and no one may question my authority."

"Very well; here is the money."

The man takes the indulgence, and goes away; and Tetzel starts for the town of Jüterbogk. He comes to a forest, when suddenly a party of robbers spring from behind the trees. Some of them seize Tetzel and pound him, while others ransack the carriage, find the money-box, and all flee to the woods.

Who are the robbers? The leader of the band is the man who bought the indulgence, and this was the crime that he intended to commit. Tetzel hastens to Duke George, who is Governor of Saxony.

"I have been robbed."

"I will have the robbers hanged," says the governor, and sends the sheriff to arrest them.

The sheriff very soon brings them before the governor.

"You are accused of robbing," he says to the gentleman who bought the indulgence. "What have you to say for yourself?"

"Tetzel has already pardoned me. This is the crime I intended to commit. I paid him twenty dollars for the indulgence. Here it is."

The governor reads the paper.

"I don't see as you have any case, Mr. Tetzel."

The governor cannot send the robber to prison, nor compel him to give up the money. To do so would put an end to Mr. Tetzel's business, for it would show the people that the indulgences are worthless. Ah, Mr. Tetzel, it would have been better for you not to have taken the road to Jüterbogk, and it would be better for you not to go there to set up your fair; but go on, for out of your going will come liberty to the world!

Although so many years have passed since Doctor Wicklif's day, the people all through Europe are still in slavery. They are taxed by emperors and kings, Pope and priest. They are robbed systematically; they are ignorant and degraded. If a man commits a murder, he can flee to the shelter of a church; or if he can once get inside of a convent door, the sheriff cannot arrest him. The civil law, then, is powerless. The bishops and priests are, many of them, ready to burn a heretic to death; while emperors and kings are autocrats. They do as they please. There is no liberty as yet for the people.

John Tetzel sets up his great red cross in the Jüterbogk church, and begins the sale of his pardons. He is very sore over his loss. The people laugh at him, and say it was a good joke that the robber played. Jüterbogk is only four miles from Wittenberg, where the boy who sung for his breakfast is preaching and hearing people confess their sins.

All-saints-day comes. The people from all the country round flock to Wittenberg to see the procession of the holy relics, for, on this 1st of November, the images of the saints and the relics are to be carried in procession through the streets.

The people come to Friar Martin to confess their sins.

"You must leave off sinning," he says to them.

"Leave off sinning?"

"Yes; I cannot grant absolution unless you do."

"But we have liberty to sin."

"Liberty to sin! Who gave you liberty to sin against God?"

"Doctor Tetzel, over in Jüterbogk. Here are the indulgences which we have purchased."

"I care nothing for your indulgences. Unless you repent, you will perish. I will not grant you absolution, unless you promise to leave off sinning."

The people are in despair. They have paid their money for their indulgences, and now their confessor will not absolve them. They hasten to Jüterbogk.

"Our confessor will not absolve us. He says that these indulgences are good for nothing."

"Good for nothing!" Doctor Tetzel will see about that. He goes into the pulpit. He is the Pope's ambassador, and is endowed with authority. He curses the young priest at Wittenberg, who has thus taken it upon himself to say that these indulgences are worth no more than blank paper.

"I have orders from the Pope to burn every heretic who dares to oppose his most holy indulgences," shouts Tetzel; and he orders a fire to be kindled in the market-place, to let the people understand that he means what he says.

Evening comes. In the market-place of Jüterbogk the fire which Doctor Tetzel has kindled is burning. Over in Wittenberg, at the same hour, the people see their young confessor nailing a paper upon the door of the church. They

LUTHER INSPIRED BY SATAN.

crowd around to see what sort of a notice it may be. They read:

"Those who truly repent of their sins have a full remission of guilt and penalty, and do not need an indulgence."

And this:

"He who gives to the poor and lends to the needy does better than he who buys an indulgence."

There are ninety-five paragraphs. The people read in amazement. Here is war against Doctor Tetzel—a war between two doctors.

Doctor Luther goes back to his room in the convent, little knowing what will come of his nailing up that paper—that it is the beginning of a series of events which will go on while time shall last; that out of it will come a great division in the Church; that thrones will be tumbled

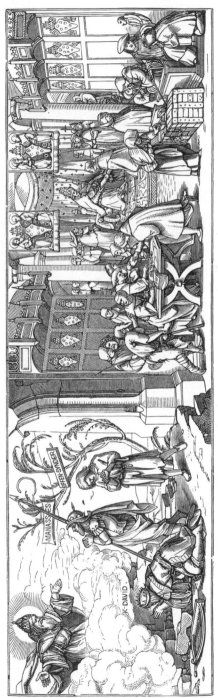

PURCHASING PARDON.

CONFESSION TO GOD.

into the dust; that kings will go down, empires be rent asunder, lands be desolated by war; that there will be massacres and horrible outrages against the lives and liberties of men; that for thirty years continuously war will sweep over Germany. If he could but lift the veil that hides the future, he would see the streets of Paris and the vine-clad valleys of Italy drenched in blood. He would see fires kindled all over England for the burning of men, women, and children. He would see men hurled headlong from precipices, roasted over slow fires, starving in dungeons, subjected to every form of cruelty; but with all this he would see the beginning of the emancipation of men, the advance of justice, truth, and liberty — the beginning of a new era in human affairs. The monk does not know it; but that paper which he has nailed upon the oaken panels of the door is, as it were, the marching orders of the great Army of Freedom.

The people read, and go home to think about it. They see that if what Doctor Luther says is true, then Doctor Tetzel has fooled them. He has sold them worthless slips of paper. Men do not like to be swindled.

Doctor Luther does not rest content with nailing up the paper on the church door. He will call into use the invention made by that man in Haerlem who loved to please his children — Laurence Coster — and which John Guttenberg carried out. He prints the paper, and in a few weeks all Germany is reading it. Tetzel is terribly enraged. At Frankfort he kindles a fire in the market-place, and burns the paper.

"Wait a little, and we will have the heretic roasted," he says.

"Has that monk of Wittenberg an iron head and a brass nose, so that he cannot be crushed?" asks the chief of the Dominican friars.

"Such a heretic ought not to live an hour," cries James Hochstaeter, of Cologne.

Friar Martin is not frightened in the least, but goes on preaching and writing against the sale of indulgences and the practices of the wicked monks.

The priests say that he has sold himself to the devil. They get up a horrible picture, representing Martin as being inspired by Satan. Martin's head is a bagpipe, his nose the flageolet. The devil squeezes the friar's head under his arm, blows the wind into one ear, and plays upon his nose with his claws.

The friends of Friar Martin set themselves to work; and Hans Holbein draws a powerful picture, one part of which represents the Pope and his agents selling pardons; and, in contrast, King David, Manasses, and the humble publican are confessing their sins to

CHRIST, THE TRUE LIGHT.

PAPA, DOCTOR THEOLOGIÆ ET MAGIS-
TER FIDEI.

"A long-eared ass can with the Bagpipes
cope
As well as with Theology the Pope."

God, and receiving his blessing. The people see that they are being swindled. Some
have seen it for a long time, but have made
no open protest; but now they speak plainly. They *take* the liberty of dissenting
from what the Pope has decreed. That
man who was so disgusted with St. Thomas's
shirt, Erasmus, long before Martin nailed
the paper on the door of the church, poked
fun at the friars, and ridiculed the sale of
indulgences in a book which he wrote. In
the old city of Nuremberg there is a man
who mends shoes, and who sings songs ridiculing the monks—his name is Hans Sachs.
The painter Holbein brings out another
picture, which represents Christ as the true
light. The pictures, the songs, the tracts,
the preaching, set men everywhere to thinking. One of the pictures published repre-
sents an ass wearing the Pope's crown, and playing a bagpipe, with a
couplet explaining it. So, from ridiculing the monks and friars, they
began to ridicule the Pope. Lucas Cranach drew a picture which rep-
resented the Pope as being cast into
hell. Up to this time men have regarded the Pope as having all power—as being God's agent on earth;
but now they laugh at the idea, and
consign the Pope to perdition. It is
a sudden breaking of the shackles that
have bound the intellects of men. It
is freedom.

In vain does John Tetzel set up
his cross in the churches; the people
will not buy the Pope's indulgences.
The money which has been flowing
toward Rome ceases to go in that direction. Friar Martin and his followers are drying up the fountains. Leo
is a kind-hearted man. He would
like to have everything peaceful; but

THE POPE CAST INTO HELL.

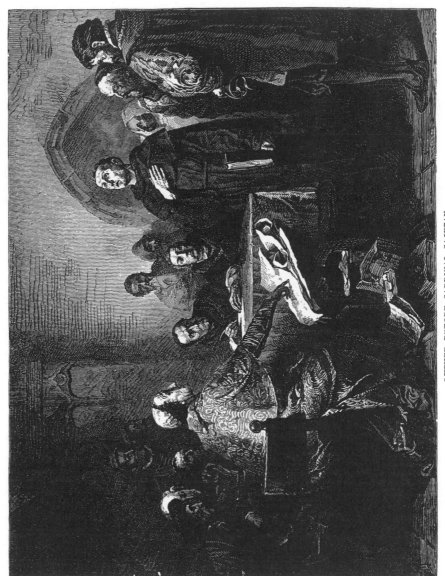

LUTHER BEFORE CARDINAL CAJETAN.

he cannot permit an obscure monk to overthrow his authority. He sends a summons to Martin to appear at Rome and answer for what he has said and written; but Martin will not go. And the Pope summons him to appear before a legate, Cardinal Cajetan, at Augsburg; and Martin obeys.

"Take back what you have said," is the demand of the legate.

"I stand by the truth. I will not take it back."

Doctor Luther knows that his life is in danger; that if Cardinal Cajetan could only get him once inside of a dungeon, he never would regain his liberty. He has appeared and made his answer. He waits four days.

"You are not safe here; you must not remain," say his friends.

He is on foot, but they supply him with a donkey, and an hour before daylight, on an August morning, he mounts the animal, picks his way through the silent streets of the old town. The birds are singing. The sunlight streams up the east. He, too, breaks into singing, for he has stood up for truth and liberty against the mightiest power on earth.

Doctor Luther goes back to Wittenberg to send out more books and pamphlets, in defence of what he believes to be the truth. Peddlers carry them through the country. The people read them, pass them from hand to hand, discuss them by their firesides. It is like the lighting of torches. Men see as they never saw before. Others begin to write and preach against the authority of the Pope. Germany is stirred as never before. The works of the monk of Wittenberg are read by the mountaineers of Switzerland. They are translated into other languages; and so the wave of intellectual life and liberty rolls over the land.

CHAPTER XIII.

THE BOY-EMPEROR.

MAXIMILIAN, Emperor of Germany, is dead, and some one must be chosen in his place. There are three individuals who desire to be elected—Henry of England, Francis of France, and Charles of Spain. Henry is twenty-six years old, Francis twenty-one, and Charles nineteen. It is not long before Henry sees that he has no chance; but Francis and Charles are both confident of success. Francis sends ambassadors to the princes of Germany, who are to elect the emperor, promising to do great things for them; presenting them purses filled with gold. Charles does the same. But the man who patronizes painters and sculptors down in Rome (Pope Leo) has something to say about it. He uses his influence in favor of Charles, who is already King of Spain, Netherlands, and Naples, and who lays claim to a portion of Italy.

The electors meet in the old council-hall in Frankfort, in Germany, and make choice of Charles; and Francis finds that he has spent his money, and been defeated besides. He could put up with the loss of the money; but a wounded spirit, who can bear? It is a bitter disappointment, and Charles knows that Francis will take his revenge.

On a day in May, 1520, the people of Dover, in England, are surprised to see a great fleet of Spanish war-ships sailing into the harbor. What is the meaning of it? There is the flag of the King of Spain, the Boy-emperor of Germany, as they call him, flying at the mast-head of the largest ship. The fleet comes to anchor, and the people soon learn that the young emperor has come to make a visit to his aunt Katherine and uncle Henry. Horsemen ride post-haste to London, and Henry sends his true friend and chief adviser, Cardinal Thomas Wolsey, to Dover to offer his congratulations to his nephew, and to say to Charles that he will hasten down, and that together they will ride to Canterbury, to the tomb of Thomas Becket, and cement their friendship at that shrine.

Cardinal Wolsey is very much pleased to go upon such an errand, for he would like to have a little private conversation with Charles before

Henry arrives; perhaps he may be able to advance his own fortunes. He is getting on well in the world. When he was a boy, he carried joints of mutton and roasts of beef to the people of Ipswich, where his father was a butcher; later, his father sent him to Oxford, where he graduated, and became a preacher; but he led a fast life, and one day the sheriff arrested him, and he was condemned to sit in the stocks for his misdeeds—a strange spectacle to his parishioners!

Thomas could not be content to live in a little country village where a justice of the peace could interfere with his pleasures, and so went to London. The Archbishop of Canterbury was his friend, and introduced him to the king, Henry VII. The king was pleased with him, and, through the archbishop's influence, made him a dean. Being a dean, he was in a position to push his fortunes, and soon became Bishop of York. He was so influential and able, that when Henry VIII. came to the throne, he selected him to be his prime minister. Louis XII. of France wanted to marry Henry's sister Mary; and he seeing that Wolsey had great influence at court, sent him a purse filled with gold. Then the Boy-cardinal, in Rome,

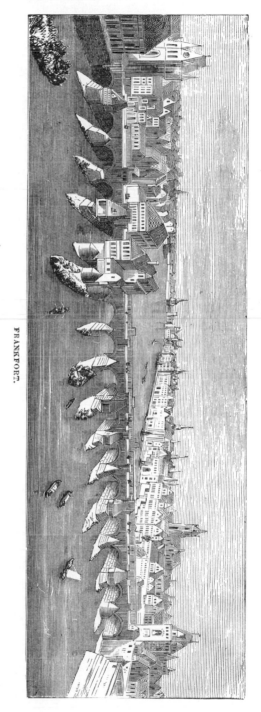

FRANKFORT.

when he became Pope, desiring to secure Henry's friendship, made him a cardinal, and gave him permission to appoint all the bishops, deans, and

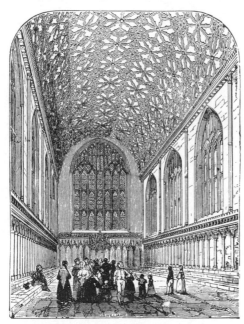

INTERIOR OF CHAPTER-HOUSE, CANTERBURY.

other prelates of the Church in England. It is a power greater than that held by the king. All the Church officials, from the verger who opens the pew-door up to the Archbishop of Canterbury, will take off their hats to him, and all the lords, earls, and barons will wait upon him.

No earl of England lives in greater state. He rides a donkey, to show that he is as humble as his Master, who rode into Jerusalem on an ass; but he spreads a luxurious table, and drinks the best wines. He wears a gorgeous dress, with a massive gold necklace studded with diamonds and pearls. His tippet is of the finest sable, and his robe is trimmed with the whitest ermine. His shoes are of silver and gold, inlaid with diamonds. He has eight hundred men in his train—sons of barons, earls, lords, counts—fifteen knights, and forty squires. His servants are in livery. His cook wears a velvet-satin jacket, and a gold chain upon his neck. A lord rides before the cardinal, carrying the red hat which Leo has given him. Another lord carries a golden mace, while two priests bear massive silver crosses. His saddle-cloth is of crimson velvet, his stirrups of solid silver. Men armed with

THOMAS WOLSEY AND HIS COMPANIONS IN THE STOCKS.

spears and swords, a grand cavalcade of horsemen, with a regiment of servants—more than a thousand in all—make up his retinue.

One of the gentlemen in his train is Thomas Cromwell, who was born in London, 1490. His father was a blacksmith, but this Thomas did not mean to blow the bellows or swing the sledge for a living. He has been a clerk in a store in London and at Antwerp, but has entered Cardinal Wolsey's service, and is on the high-road to fortune. The world will yet hear from this son of a blacksmith. So great a man as Wolsey must have a chaplain, and he has selected Edmund Bonner for that service. This preacher has graduated at Oxford. He is only twenty-five years old, but, now that he is in the cardinal's service, is getting on in the world. We shall see him again.

The cardinal has a great deal of writing to be done, and he has appointed as his chief and confidential secretary Stephen Gardiner. He is an able man, but artful, ambitious, and proud. He was educated at Oxford, and can speak and write several languages. The world will be better or worse for what he will do, as we shall discover farther along.

Cardinal Wolsey rides to Dover to receive the young emperor; but what is he thinking of as he hastens along the dusty road through the hop-fields of Kent? He is thinking of how he shall wind the Boy-emperor round his little finger. He knows what Charles has come for—not merely to make a friendly visit to Katherine and Henry, but to enlist Henry on his side in case Francis begins a war. He has come to persuade Henry to give up

CARDINAL WOLSEY.

a friendly meeting which he is intending to have with Francis, in June, over the Channel near Calais, where carpenters and masons are erecting a grand palace for use during the festivities. Cardinal Wolsey is turning the matter over in his mind. How much can Cardinal Wolsey make out of this visit? In what way can he best wind the boy round his finger, and make him pay for the winding besides? Cardinal Wolsey is taking long looks ahead. He is already master of affairs in England. The Pope will not live forever; and when he dies, who in the world is more worthy to occupy the pontifical chair than he who once carried joints of mutton and beef to the people of Ipswich, but who is now as powerful as

Henry himself? Plainly, it will be for his interest to make Charles under obligations to him; but if he helps the emperor, the emperor in turn must do great things for him: he must have some pay down, and the promise of a great deal more by-and-by.

The cardinal arrives at Dover, and bows with great deference to the pale young man. They talk by themselves. Charles is ready to do anything for his friend the cardinal, and gives him outright a bishopric in Spain. The cardinal need not ever set foot in the country; but he may

THE "GREAT HARRY."

have all the revenue, which shall be collected and sent to him—ten thousand ducats per annum; and when Leo dies, the emperor will use his utmost influence to secure the election of the cardinal as his successor. The cardinal, on his part, will see to it that no harm shall come to Charles from the proposed meeting between Francis and Henry. It is better, the cardinal thinks, that the meeting should take place.

Henry and Katherine and the barons and lords hasten to Dover to pay their respects to Charles, and then they ride up to Canterbury to cement their friendship around the tomb of Thomas Becket. Mass is performed in the cathedral—they have a grand banquet, and then the cavalcade takes the road to Dover once more; for Henry and Katherine, and all the nobles and lords and knights, are on their way to the Field of the Cloth of Gold, which we shall see in the next chapter.

Henry is large-framed and strong. He can pitch a quoit or throw an iron bar with the best men in the kingdom. He has blue eyes and rosy cheeks; while Charles is thin, pale, and spare, and has a heavy underjaw. They ride side by side. Katherine accompanies them, with her little daughter Mary, four years old. So these five persons, who will have much to do with the history of liberty, journey together to Dover—the man who is managing them all riding on a donkey, and his great retinue following.

Henry has a fleet of ships waiting for him and the nobles and knights of England. His largest ship is the *Great Harry*. He bids the emperor good-bye; and the Spanish ships, amidst the thundering of cannon, spread their sails, and shape their course toward Holland; while Henry's steer straight across the Channel to Calais.

CHAPTER XIV.

THE FIELD OF THE CLOTH OF GOLD.

THREE hundred masons, five hundred carpenters, scores of painters, plasterers, decorators, glass-setters—three thousand men in all—have been at work since the 19th of March, and it is now the middle of June, building a royal palace on the Field of the Cloth of Gold. The edifice is in the form of a quadrangle, with audience-rooms, chambers, halls, and courts. Upon the towers of the palace and on the battlements are figures of gods and heroes. The interior is hung with rich tapestries. Adjoining the great audience-room is a chapel, the walls of which blaze with jewels. The altar, the candlesticks, and the crucifix are of silver, and the canopy above the altar is of pure gold.

FRANCIS I.

Near the palace is a grand pavilion, the covering of which is cloth of gold, lined with blue velvet and studded with silver stars. The tent ropes are of pure silk, intertwined with threads of gold. There are many smaller pavilions of the same material, gorgeously decorated.

Henry VIII. of England has erected the palace, and Francis I. of France the pavilion. They have made these preparations for a tournament and fraternal meeting. Francis would like to have Henry his friend while he gratifies his revenge against Charles. Henry is a little jealous of Charles—so much power is too much for a boy of nineteen to wield—and he is quite willing to be on friendly terms with Francis.

Cardinal Wolsey arranges affairs. There will be tilting, mock battles, banquets, dances, promenades; but not much talk about political matters. The King of France shall be well pleased at the hospitality of the King of England; the King of England shall be gratified with the courtesy of the King of France. But the cardinal determines that there shall be no treaties made or promises given that cannot be broken.

TILTING.

What a grand assembly! Two kings, two queens, dukes, earls, lords, barons, nobles, knights, counts, marquises, cardinals, archbishops, gorgeously arrayed in silk, satin, and velvet; in purple, crimson, green, blue, and buff, with gold and silver trimmings, with ostrich plumes and eagles' feathers—their garments glittering with jewels!

Six thousand of the nobility of England are there, with nearly four thousand horses. Thousands of the noblemen of France, and Spain, and Italy, and Germany are assembled; for messengers have been travelling in all those countries, inviting them to attend the grand tournament.

Henry rides a beautiful horse. His coat is cloth of silver, ribbed with gold. His jacket is of rose-colored velvet; his boots of yellow morocco. He wears a black velvet cap, blazing with diamonds, and adorned by a white plume. Around his neck is a heavy gold chain, set with rubies and pearls. On his breast is a jewel that twinkles like a star.

Before the king rides a marquis, carrying the sword of state. Two

CHAMPION OF THE TOURNAMENT.

pages, ready to do his bidding, walk by his side. At his left hand rides Cardinal Wolsey, on his donkey, wearing his scarlet cloak, scarlet slippers, and a scarlet hat. Behind the king is the Duke of Suffolk (Charles Brandon), on a white horse; and following him is the Bishop of Rochester, with a beard so long that it covers all his breast. Sir Henry Guilford leads the king's spare horse. After him comes a grand cavalcade of nobles, magnificently arrayed.

THE TOURNAMENT.

Out from the Golden Pavilion rides the King of France. He is tall, and has a long nose. His face is bronzed. He has long legs and small feet. He wears a coat of satin silver cloth, glittering with precious stones. His cap is of damask and gold, spangled with diamonds. With him are the noblemen of France, in rich attire, riding the most beautiful horses to be found in the kingdom. Some of them have expended so much money in preparing for the tournament that they will be in debt for the remainder of their days.

THE COOKS GETTING DINNER.

A great camp has been established, with magnificent pavilions, where the queens of England and France, with the ladies, may behold the games. The kings have each a private pavilion near by; and there are other tents by the thousand. In one are hundreds of casks filled with the choicest wines. There are dining-halls and lunch-tables, and there is to be no end of feasting. Hundreds of cooks are employed day and night in preparing the feasts.

It is on the 11th of June, 1520, that the tournament begins. The Queen of England (the little girl whom we saw in the Alhambra) wears a rich dress, covered with jewels. Even the cloth upon which she rests her feet is powdered with pearls.

Claude, the Queen of France, is younger than Katherine, and very beautiful. Francis has obtained for her the richest dresses to be had in the realm, and the most costly jewels. She rides in a stately carriage.

THE QUEEN'S CARRIAGE.

Among the ladies in the train of Queen Claude is a girl whom we have seen before, one of the number who went to France with Henry's sister Mary, when she went to be the wife of the king, who was old enough to be her grandfather—Louis XII. Very little happiness did Mary have with Louis, who was afflicted with dropsy, and who died three months after their marriage.

What did Mary do then? Without letting Henry or anybody else know what she intended to do, she married her true-love, Charles Brandon. Henry did not like it at first, but made the best of it, and now the young man is riding by his side as Duke of Suffolk.

The little girl, Anne Boleyn, was only seven years old when she went with Mary to France to be her little waiting-maid; now she is eighteen. Of all the ladies at the tournament, there is none so fair, none more graceful in the dance, none so bright and witty. Henry beholds her in all the freshness and beauty of maidenhood.

The kings put on their armor, the trumpets sound, the heralds make proclamation, and the tournament begins. The kings are victors in the games. It would not do for a subject to disarm the king—he would stand a chance of having his head cut off, or at least of losing the king's favor.

One of the noblemen accompanying Francis is the Duke of Guise, or Duke of Lorraine, as he is sometimes called. He was a poor boy, but he has been making his fortune by fighting for Francis. He was badly wounded three years ago, but has recovered. He is married to Antoinette of Bourbon, and has a little daughter, Mary, who will be Queen of Scotland by-and-by, and the little babe which she will hold in her arms will also bear the name of Mary—Mary Queen of Scots. The duke has a son, Francis Guise, a spirited boy. Little does King Henry imagine that the son by-and-by will wrest the old town of Calais from his daughter Mary—the little girl now four years old—who will be Queen of England, and that the loss of it will break Mary's heart.

Henry and Francis talk of betrothing Mary to Francis's son Henry, who is only two years old; but such a marriage never will be consummated. The son of the French king, whom we shall see by-and-by on the throne as Henry, will find a wife beyond the Alps in the old city of Florence, where she is at this moment sucking her thumbs in her cradle in a palace near the grand old cathedral—the palace in which Pope Leo was born. She is Leo's grandniece, Catherine de' Medici, who, when she is fourteen, will come to France to be married to Henry. Let us keep this Florentine baby in remembrance, because she will play a terrible part in the story of liberty.

The tournament lasts three weeks. When it is ended, Francis returns to Paris, and Henry and Cardinal Wolsey set their faces toward England; but before crossing the Channel they ride out from Calais a little way, and

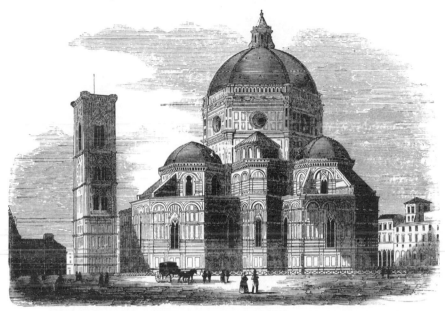

THE CATHEDRAL, FLORENCE.

whom do they meet? Charles, who has been waiting conveniently near for an interview; and Charles is greatly pleased to hear from the cardinal that Henry has entered into no alliance with the King of France. He will do in return all that he can for Cardinal Wolsey.

CHAPTER XV.

THE MEN WHO OBEY ORDERS.

ON that day when the boy who sung for his breakfast was standing before Conrad Cotta's door, there was another boy in Spain who was waiting upon King Ferdinand. His father was a nobleman. The boy never knew what it was to be poor. We may think of him as running here and there carrying letters and despatches. He learns to obey—to do whatever he is commanded to do without asking any questions. It becomes the habit of his life. Obedience is a virtue, and he accomplishes his work with energy and despatch. He is faithful in all his trusts.

Years pass. Ferdinand is dead, and Charles V. is King of Spain. The page is a young man. He has suffered a great disappointment—a lady whom he loves has rejected his suit; and so when Francis I. of France, a few weeks after that meeting with Henry at the Field of the Cloth of Gold, sends an army to drive Charles out of Navarre, and force him to give up the territory which Ferdinand wrested from Catherine de Foix, the cavalier Ignatius Loyola eagerly engages in the war, to forget, in the excitement of the camp, the fair lady who has rejected his suit. He is wounded and taken prisoner. Through the weary days he lies upon his cot. The time is long. His spirits chafe. He offers vows to the Virgin Mary that if she will cure him he will make a pilgrimage to Jerusalem. His wound heals, and he keeps his vow, for he has learned faithfulness in the court of Ferdinand. He has wonderful visions; the Virgin appears to him, surrounded with supernal glory, to reward him for his fidelity.

Loyola returns to Spain, and has so much to say about his vision that the men who ask questions thrust him into prison as a heretic; but he makes his escape, and flees to France. He is deeply religious, fasting and praying all night. He consecrates himself to the service of the Virgin—to go wherever she may send him, to do what he can in converting the world.

In Paris he makes the acquaintance of Peter Faber, Francis Xavier, and four other young men, whom he fires with his own lofty enthusiasm for the conversion of the world. They fast and pray, and form themselves into a society, with Loyola as their general, who shall tell them

IGNATIUS LOYOLA.

what to do, and they will do it; where to go, and they will go, without asking any questions. They take four solemn oaths:

1. To obey their general, no matter what he may command them to do.

2. Never, as individuals, to own any property, but to obtain all they can for the Church.

3. Never to marry.

4. To do whatever the Pope commands.

They are animated by one lofty idea—to put forth all their energies to convert the world. For this they will suffer hardship, hunger, poverty, privation, sickness, and death. Nothing shall deter them, no obstacle turn them back.

In April, 1538, these seven brethren kneel before Pope Alexander Farnese, in Rome, and ask him to accept their services. They will go or come, and will do all that he shall order. The Pope sees that he can use

such men to good advantage. He accepts their services, and recognizes
the Society of Jesus as an agency of the Church. He issues a bull ex-
empting the brothers from all control except his own. They are not answerable to cardinals, archbishops, or anybody else—not even to kings or
emperors, neither to any civil or ecclesiastical law. They never shall be
called upon to pay any tithes or taxes.

Loyola draws up a set of actions for the society—not based on the Ten
Commandments, nor on Christ's Sermon on the Mount, but on the idea
that if an object to be attained is good, they may use any means to obtain
it, even though the means may not be good.

"A good motive makes any action right."

That is what Loyola believes. It is right to tell a lie, to take a false
oath, to defraud, and commit even murder, if the act is done for the good
of the Church. So if the members of the society judge that the Church
will be benefited by having a king or queen, or anybody else, put out of
the way, it will be right for them to take any means to accomplish it.

*"No action wicked in itself is really wicked unless the intention is
evil.*

*"In taking oaths, the members of the society may make mental res-
ervations to break them, if they can benefit the Church by so doing.*

*"If called upon to justify any of their actions, they may give a
false motive instead of the real one.   They may equivocate, may justify fraud and deceit, without any scruples of conscience."*

The Pope promises to grant them absolution for whatever they may
do that in itself would be wrong, but which he will make right, because
it is for the good of the Church.

*"No member of the society shall submit himself to be examined be-
fore any court of justice without the permission of his superior."*

This makes the society superior to the State—to kings and emperors
—superior to all law.

*"If the members are cast into prison for refusing to testify, they
are to account it all honor to suffer for the good of the Church."*

With the Pope's blessing resting upon them, the members of the society go forth, in their enthusiasm, to establish the Church in every land—
threading the jungles of India; traversing the deserts of Africa; sailing
along the rivers of China; making their way amidst the mountains of Ja-
pan; crossing the Atlantic; penetrating the wilds of America; planting
the cross on the plains of Brazil and the peaks of the Andes; establishing
missions amidst the fertile vales of Mexico; making themselves at home
in the wigwams of the Indians of the New World; sailing their canoes

on the great lakes; threading the wilderness beyond the Mississippi; establishing missions everywhere; bringing myriads of the human race un-

THE JESUIT MISSIONARY.

der the dominion of the Church; persuading men where persuasion will accomplish what they desire, and employing force where force is possible, regardless of natural rights and liberties.

We shall see, by-and-by, what will come from such an organization, established on a code of morals which sets up vice for virtue, falsehood for truth, deceit for honesty; which claims to be superior to king, emperor, Parliament, or Congress; which makes itself a despotism over the hearts and consciences of men; which places its spies in every household, taking note of the actions and beliefs of every individual; trampling on all law; setting aside all authority; acknowledging only one whom they are bound to obey—the Pope of Rome!

15

CHAPTER XVI.

PLANS THAT DID NOT COME TO PASS.

HOW easy it is to plan! How nice it would be if we could only carry out our plans! So we think. Why do we not carry them out? Because there are other plans besides our own. Before we get through with this Story of Liberty, perhaps we shall see that, somehow, almost all of the great plans of kings and emperors have been overturned; that things have not come out as they intended. Perhaps we shall see that behind all the plans of men to advance their own interests, there will seem to be another plan—that circumstances and events will take such shape that we shall be able to discover a new arranging of things—a plan superior to all others, as if God had a plan and were behind all the overturnings and defeats of men.

The King of France, who has gone back to Paris from the Field of the Cloth of Gold, is laying his plans. He intended to be emperor, but Charles has won the prize, and now he will have his revenge. He will march his armies across the Alps and pounce upon Milan, and perhaps carry his victorious legions to Naples.

Cardinal Wolsey, who had the private interview with Charles, and promised to manage Henry in Charles's interest, is laying his plan, and every move that he may make in life will have reference to it; he is going to be Pope when Leo dies. Charles has promised to place him in the pontifical chair. Henry has not yet laid his plan; what it will be we shall see by-and-by. He would like to lead his armies to victory; but the people of England have no desire to go philandering over the Continent searching for some one whom they may conquer. Henry is wishing that he had a younger wife—a lady fresh and fair, sparkling and witty. Such a one as Anne Boleyn, for instance, for the wrinkles are coming in Katherine's cheeks, and she will soon be an old woman.

Anne Boleyn has gone to London. She is bright and beautiful. Whatever plans she may be laying, she keeps them to herself; but the king smiles upon her, and she is graciously received at court.

Charles has laid his plan to be emperor, and has carried it out.   Now what shall he do?   Why not aim to be ruler of the world, and be as great as Cæsar or Alexander.   He is master of more than half of Europe—Spain, Netherlands, Germany, Naples, and part of Italy, all the New World—the empire in the West.   Why not go on and crush France?   He will.

Leo is building his great church in Rome.   He is employing sculptors and painters.   He will make his pontifical rule so brilliant that people in all coming time shall praise it.   There is only one thing to mar his plan: that monk in Germany, who, on All-saints-eve, in 1517, nailed a paper upon the door of Wittenberg church, has created such a disturbance that the people have stopped giving money.   He must have money, or he cannot go on with his grand project.   He will have the heretic put out of the way, and the heresy suppressed.

On the very day that Cardinal Wolsey takes Charles one side to have a confidential talk after the Field of the Cloth of Gold, Leo writes an order commanding Friar Martin Luther to stop preaching and writing. He gives him sixty days, in which he must take back all that he has said; if he does not retract it in that time, he will condemn him as a wicked heretic.   All persons having Friar Martin's writings are commanded to throw them into the fire; and all who have supported him must at once abandon him, or they will be excommunicated, and also condemned as heretics.

Leo has been giving so much attention to the building of St. Peter's and the painting of pictures, that he has not kept himself fully informed in regard to what has been going on in Germany the last three years.   He does not know that since All-saints-day, in 1517, only two and a half years ago, half of the people of Germany have become heretics.   Many good men in the Church and out of it are heart and soul with Doctor Luther, who is no longer a friar.   Some of them are writing books.   Doctor Luther's friend, Philip Melancthon, is hard at work with his pen. Some of the bishops are writing in his favor, others against him.   When King Henry gets home to England, from the Field of the Cloth of Gold, he takes his pen and writes against the doctor, which so pleases the Pope that he gives Henry a new title — Defender of the Faith — borne by all the sovereigns of England from that day to the present hour.

The order of the Pope is published, and people wait to see what Doctor Luther will do.   Will he yield?   Not he.

There comes an evening in December.   The snow is on the ground. The air is chill, but, though dreary the night, it does not prevent the students at Wittenberg from assembling in procession.   They march out

through the gate of the town.   Doctor Luther leads them.   They kindle
a fire, and as the flames rise the doctor burns a lot of the Pope's books.
If the Pope can burn Luther's books, Luther will let the world know that
he can burn the Pope's.   The book which he throws into the flames con-

MELANCTHON.

tains the claim of the Pope as being superior in all things—as lord of the
liberties, rights, actions, hearts, and consciences of men.   He also casts the
Pope's bull into the fire.   The students shout and hurrah, and the procession goes back into the town.

Christmas comes.   The Wittenberg students, seeing the boldness of their beloved doctor, lose all fear of Rome. They have a carnival. One of their number dresses himself up to represent the Pope. Some wear red cloaks and hats, to represent the cardinals. The other students seize the mock pope, put a paper cap on his head, carry him on their shoulders through the streets, and tumble him into the river. They strip the red cloaks from the mock cardinals, beat them and hustle them about, amidst the shouts and laughter of the people.

The Pope cannot permit such a heretic as Doctor Luther to go unpunished. He sends word to the emperor, Charles V., that he must be seized and sent to Rome. The emperor is young and ambitious. He has his plans against the King of France : it will not do for him to take action which will offend his subjects in Germany, for he wants their aid ; but here is half of Germany ready to support the heretic.

"I cannot strike such a blow without first consulting my councillors," is the emperor's reply to the Pope.

One of his councillors is Frederick of Saxony.

"What shall we do with Doctor Luther ?" Charles asks of Frederick.

Frederick does not know what reply to make. But that learned man from Holland, just at this time, makes Frederick a visit—Doctor Erasmus, who was so disgusted at the sight of St. Thomas's shirt in England.

"What do you think of Doctor Luther ?" Frederick asks.

"He has committed two great sins : he has attacked the Pope's crown and the monks' bellies," Doctor Erasmus replies.

Frederick laughs.

"Please give me a serious answer."

"Well, then, the cause of all this trouble is the hatred of the monks and friars to knowledge. They see that if the people acquire such knowledge as Luther wishes them to have, there will be an end to their tyranny and power. If the emperor imprison Luther, it will be a bad beginning for him. The world is thirsting for truth. Let the matter be examined by wise men : that will be the best thing for the Pope and for all concerned."

They are wise words, and Frederick repeats them to the emperor. Charles will not seize Doctor Luther.

Doctor Luther makes appeal to the Council of the Empire, or Diet, as the Germans call it, which is composed of the emperor, the electors, princes, counts, barons, representatives of the free cities, and other great men of the realm.

"The Pope is superior to all others," say those opposed to Luther.

"The council is superior to the Pope," Doctor Luther replies.

The Pope does not wish for a council. The very fact of its meeting will be the upsetting of his claim of superiority. It will be a declaration of liberty. What shall Charles do? He would like to please the Pope; he wants him on his side in the fight which he is going to have with Francis: he wants, at the same time, to please his German subjects, for he needs money and troops. If he seizes Doctor Luther, will they not be offended? Upon the whole, it will be better to have the council.

The council meets in the old city of Worms. The emperor sends his marshal, dressed in a gorgeous uniform, bearing a golden eagle, as the emblem of imperial authority, to summon Doctor Luther to attend it.

The Town Council of Wittenberg obtain a carriage for their preacher Three of his friends accompany him—to die with him, if need be, in behalf of liberty. They reach the old town of Weimar. The Pope's agents are there posting up a paper, in which everybody is commanded to abandon the heretic.

" Will you go on ?" asks the herald of the empire.

" Go on! Yes; though I am interdicted in every city. The emperor has given me his safe-conduct—the promise that I shall not be harmed while going or coming," Doctor Luther replies.

" They will burn you as they burned John Huss," say his friends.

" Though they should make a fire extending from Wittenberg to Worms, and flaming to the skies, I will pass through it in behalf of truth and in the name of the Lord," is the reply.

" The emperor will deliver you over to be burned, as Sigismund delivered John Huss. Don't go," is the word which one of Frederick's chief advisers sends him.

" Though there be as many devils in Worms as there are tiles on the roofs, I will go," is the word which Luther sends back.

He arrives in sight of the city where he is to stand up before the great men of the empire in behalf of truth and liberty. Has the boy who sung for his breakfast forgotten how to sing? Not yet. He stands up in his carriage, and his clear voice breaks forth in a hymn :

> " God is a castle and defence,
>   When trouble and distress invade;
>   He'll help and free us from offence,
>   And ever shield us with his aid."

There is great excitement in Worms. Everybody is asking if he will come.

" He is coming !" The shout rings through the streets. A great crowd pours out from the city-gates—a multitude far greater than that

A STREET IN THE OLD TOWN.

which went out to meet Charles V., for he and the princes, barons, knights, archbishops, and bishops are already there. Noblemen escort Doctor Luther into the city.

The Pope's ambassadors are disappointed. They did not want Doctor Luther to come. They hoped he would be frightened, and stay away— not obey the order, and then the emperor would be obliged to seize him. The emperor did not think that he would come.

" Here he is. What shall we do ?" the emperor asks.

" Pay no attention to his safe-conduct ; seize him at once," is the advice of a bishop who hates Doctor Luther.

" I should not like to blush as Sigismund blushed before John Huss," Charles replies. He is young, but he has a mind of his own, and he will not outrage honor and justice by such a perfidious act.

" The council must be held," is the decision of the emperor.

It is the 17th of April. The storks have arrived from the south, and are building their nests on the chimneys. The children are never weary of seeing them, or of listening to the twittering of the swallows, wheeling in the air ; but to-day they have something else to engage their attention. Never has there been such a gathering in the old town ; all the great men of the realm, besides thousands of people from surrounding towns, are gathered to see the great heretic.

" He is a monster," says one.

" They say he has horns."

" And hoofs."

" And a tail."

" He is a devil in disguise."

" He is a bad man," say Luther's detractors.

" He is a good man ; he tells the truth," say his friends.

So the people talk in favor of or against the man who has made such a commotion.

The bell strikes four — the hour when Doctor Luther must appear before the council. The herald of the empire comes for him, but the crowd is so great in the streets that the herald cannot proceed.

" Make way there !"

But the crowd will not make way.

" Give room !"

He may shout till he is hoarse, but the people will not stir. They cannot, for the street is full. Every window of the quaint old houses, whose upper stories jut over those below, is filled with heads, for all want to see the man who, by his writing and preaching, has set the world in an uproar. The people will not, or cannot, move, and the herald has to take Doctor Luther through gardens and by-ways to the council-chamber.

The emperor is seated on a throne. Around him are his brother (the Archduke Ferdinand) and the electors of the empire. There are eighty lukes, thirty archbishops and bishops, the ambassadors of France and England, the Pope's ambassador — more than two hundred great dignitaries in all.

No wonder the Pope did not want the council to meet. Has he not forbidden Doctor Luther's speaking? Yet here he is about to address the greatest assembly ever seen in Germany! Has not the Pope forbidden everybody from listening to him? Yet here is an immense multitude waiting to hear what he will say. Has not the Pope declared that he is an outlaw, with no rights that any one is bound to respect? Yet here he is recognized as having rights which the emperor is bound to acknowledge. Liberty has made some progress since that evening when the young preacher, who sung for his breakfast in boyhood, nailed that paper upon the door of the Wittenberg church.

After much struggling and pushing, the marshal and Doctor Luther reach the council-hall.

"I have two questions to ask you," says the Archbishop of Treves, opening the examination, and pointing to some books on the table.

"Did you write these books?"

"I do not deny having written those books," is the answer, after the titles are read.

"Will you take back what you have written?"

"As to taking back anything in accordance with the Word of God, I must act deliberately. I will give you my answer to-morrow."

The council breaks up for the day. The crowd in the streets admire the courage of a man who dares to stand by his rights and for the truth in such an assembly—who even compels all the archbishops and the emperor to wait upon him.

Again Doctor Luther stands in the council. He is about to speak. The Archbishop of Treves cannot bear to have a man whom the Pope has forbidden to speak stand there and compel everybody to listen to him.

"Will you, or will you not, retract?" shouts the archbishop.

Doctor Luther looks around. He is in the council's hands. What shall he say? Shall he take all back? Liberty has led him; shall he now desert her? God has walked, as it were, by his side; shall he distrust the Being who has protected him hitherto?

DR. LUTHER AT WORMS.

"*I cannot and I will not retract anything. God help me! Amen!*"
Leo has his answer.

"The court will meet again to-morrow to hear the emperor's judg-ment," is the proclamation of the marshal; and the great throng breaks up. Doctor Luther goes back to his hotel. A servant comes in with a silver tankard filled with beer, sent by the old duke, Eric of Brunswick.

"As the duke remembers me to-day, so may the Lord Jesus remember him in his kingdom," is the blessing uttered by the doctor.

Once more the council assembles. The emperor gives his decision.

"A single monk, misled by his own folly, stands up against the faith of Christendom. I will sacrifice my kingdom, my power, my treasure, my body, my blood, my mind, and my life to stop this impiety."

Then the emperor goes on forbidding any one to give Doctor Luther anything to eat or drink, or to aid him in any way. As soon as the safe-conduct expires, all officers are ordered to seize him, and hold him as a prisoner, till the emperor shall decide what shall be done with him.

So the emperor, twenty-one years of age, decides. He has made one mistake. He makes the decision himself, and does not consult the princes, dukes, and electors. It is only a few months since he was elected em-peror, and now he takes all the responsibility of deciding a momentous question, affecting the interests of all his subjects. The dukes and nobles think that they are entitled to have something to say upon public affairs. Why did the emperor call them into council, if they are to have no voice in the matter? Are they dummies only? They do not altogether relish the course pursued by the young man from Spain.

Doctor Luther is on his journey homeward, riding through a dark for-est, along a lonely road. Suddenly a party of horsemen make their ap-pearance. They seize him, throw a cloak over him, compel him to mount a horse. It is the work of a moment, and then they disappear with him through the woods. He is gone almost before the men who are with him know what has happened. Have his enemies spirited him away? His friends wring their hands in despair.

The horsemen ride with him, fast and furious, through the forest, along lonely roads—sometimes turning back and riding over the road a second time—turning east, west, north, and south, so that no one shall be able to follow them. They strike into paths that seem to lead nowhere. Once they stop and rest, and give him a drink of water. No one speaks. Night comes, but on they ride in the dark, beneath the tall trees, over hills, through valleys. At last they climb a steep hill, and come to a great stone castle. The heavy gate swings upon its hinges, and the horsemen pass in.

It closes.   They take him from his horse, lead him to a chamber, and point to a knight's uniform which lies there.

LUTHER AND THE POPE.
(From an Old Print.)

"Take off your clothes and put it on," says one of the men.

The doctor obeys.

"Your name is Knight George.   You are to let your hair and beard grow."

The horsemen go out.   He is in a small room, with one little window. A servant brings some food, but does not talk with him.   He lies down upon his cot, and awakes in the morning.   He can look out through the gratings of the little window and see a great forest — nothing more. Where is he?   He does not know.   He only knows that he is a prisoner; that he has a new name; and that his captors treat him kindly.

What an upsetting of plans there has been since last night!   The emperor had his plans—to have Doctor Luther arrested as soon as his safe-conduct expired.   So would he keep on good terms with the Pope.

Leo had his plans.   He was going to burn the heretic.   But Luther has suddenly disappeared, whither he does not know.   With the arch-heretic burned, the heresy would soon die out, perhaps; but now it will go on.   All of the emperor's plans to please the Pope and secure him as his ally against the King of France have been overturned.   The bulls which Leo has issued are so much waste paper, and the cause of liberty will go on.   It will roll like a wave over Germany.   It will sweep across the sea to England; and as the centuries go by, it will surge across the Atlantic to the New World, which those sea-captains from Bristol discovered; and in time it will sweep around the globe. All this will have a vital connection with the thought which has come to Frederick, Elector of Saxony, that it would be a good thing to seize Doctor Luther secretly, and shut him up where nobody will be able to find him. Whence came the thought? What put it into Frederick's head? Was there not a plan higher than the emperor's and the Pope's?

Months pass. Doctor Luther's friends think of him as having been secretly put to death. His enemies begin to think that the heretic will trouble them no more; and yet all the while he is hard at work doing for Germany just what Doctor Wicklif did for England—translating the Bible, and so helping on the cause of liberty.

In the solitude and quiet of the old castle, shut in from the world and his enemies, he translates the great text-book of human freedom — the Bible.

Three hundred and fifty years have passed since then; and of Luther's translation it is estimated that three hundred and sixty million copies of the Bible have been printed.

VIEW FROM ALBERT DÜRER'S HOUSE.

A large number of the priests join Luther, some preaching against the Pope, others writing pamphlets. Printing-presses have been set up all over Europe; poets write songs, painters produce pictures, and the hawkers peddle them through every hamlet; and people discuss questions which, till now, they never have thought of discussing. By thinking for themselves, men begin to assert their rights and liberties.

Nearly all the great artists and painters in Germany and Holland sympathized with Luther, notwithstanding the Pope was their patron. One of them—Albert Dürer, of Nuremberg—was greatly grieved when he heard that Luther had been seized, and probably killed. Dürer's house looked out upon the old Castle of Nuremberg, which stood on a high hill. In the castle was a torture-chamber, filled with terrible instruments for inflicting pain: pincers, thumb-screws, clubs, knobby tables, and a great iron Virgin, as it was called, which embraced the victim with its iron arms, pierced him with spikes, and then, when life was extinct, the victim's body would drop into a well two hundred feet in depth, and none would know what had happened.

The revolt of the people was not only against the abuses of the monks and the authority of the Pope, but it was the first clear insight which had come to them of their natural and individual rights.

CHAPTER XVII.

THE MAN WHO SPLIT THE CHURCH IN TWAIN.

KATHERINE OF ARAGON is forty-four years old. The freshness has faded from her cheeks. She is a true wife, but Henry is tired of her. He is thirty-eight, in the full vigor of manhood. He is not a true husband, for he finds more pleasure in the society of Anne Boleyn than with Katherine. Anne is a lady of the court. Henry kisses her at a ban-

WOLSEY'S PALACE.

quet which Cardinal Wolsey gives in the magnificent palace that he has erected with the money which he raked in from Charles, from Henry, from the sale of church-livings, from taxation. It is a grand pile of buildings, with spacious grounds around.

The king sits by Anne's side, gazing upon her fair face, charmed by her pleasing ways, and enchanted by her matchless beauty.

Strange that a woman's smile should change a nation's destiny; that a fair face should be the means, as it were, of giving a new direction to the current of human affairs! Wonderful that through the love of a man for a woman should come the rending of the Church of Rome! Marvellous that in the reckless passion of a hard-hearted, cruel despot should lie enfolded, as it were, the rights, the liberties, the advancement, of the human race!

Great changes have taken place in Europe since Henry met Anne,

HENRY AND ANNE.

twelve years ago, at the Field of the Cloth of Gold. It is 1532. Doctor Martin Luther, of Wittenberg, has been preaching and writing. Thanks to Laurence Coster and John Guttenberg, the world may know what is going on, and what people think. Men do not now take all their opinions from the Pope, especially in Germany, in Holland, and France. Martin Luther's doctrines have made little progress in England. Henry and Cardinal Wolsey are fast friends of the Pope. Henry is Defender of the Faith—a strong pillar to the Church.

Leo X. is dead; but his nephew, another of the Medici family, is seated in the pontifical chair. Cardinal Wolsey intended to be Pope, and expected that Charles, for whom he had done so much, and who had made him so many solemn promises, would aid him; but the cardinal has discovered that kings can play false as well as other men.

During these twelve years, Charles and Francis have been at war. In February, 1524, their armies met at Pavia, in Italy, where Francis was defeated, and captured. Charles kept him in prison a year, and subjected him to humiliating terms before releasing him. Charles is a good Catholic, but he has been fighting the Pope, and his troops have sacked the city of Rome.

MAIN ENTRANCE TO WOLSEY'S PALACE.

Cardinal Wolsey rode next the king at the Field of the Cloth of Gold, and he rides next him now. He has had his own way in everything. He lives in great state. Lords and nobles do his bidding. He is proud and arrogant. One day the Duke of Buckingham is holding a gold basin while Henry washes his hands, and Cardinal Wolsey dips his own hands into the dish, whereupon the duke spills the water upon the cardinal's red slippers.

"I will sit on your skirts, sir," says Wolsey.

What he means by that Buckingham soon discovers, for the sheriff comes with an order from Henry for his arrest and commitment to the Tower. He has spoken imprudent words, and Wolsey persuades Henry that the duke is meditating treason. In the "Bloody Tower" Buckingham meets his fate.

"Off with his head! So much for Buckingham."

The King of England can cut off the heads of his greatest nobles as well as of his poorest subjects. He is supreme, and the people are slaves

BUCKINGHAM.

to his will. Will the time ever come when kings will be amenable to law? Yes; and this despot will himself unwittingly strike a great blow for human freedom.

Henry is tired of Katherine; how shall he get rid of her? He has been thinking the matter over. He recalls the question whether or not it was right that he should marry his brother's widow. He protested when the betrothal was proposed; but that was in his boyhood. His father came to the conclusion before his death that the betrothal was illegal, and dissolved the contract; but Henry loved Katherine then, and would not break the engagement. Katherine is the mother of his only child, Mary; but, for all that, Henry begins to doubt if the marriage was legal, notwithstanding the Pope gave his sanction. If it was illegal, then he ought to be divorced; but, if divorced, then Mary would not be heir to the throne. What shall he do? He loves Anne. The passion grows; he must have her for a wife—she is so fresh and fair, so witty and captivating.

Henry places the matter in the hands of Cardinal Wolsey, who sends an ambassador to Rome to lay the matter before the Pope, who promises to set aside the marriage.

Charles finds out what is going on. Katherine is his aunt, and he enters his protest. What shall the Pope do? Charles is powerful; his troops have once plundered Rome, and may do so again. Henry must wait a little. He sends Cardinal Campeggio to England to sit with Wolsey, as legates, with power to decide the question of divorcement. He writes out a bull setting aside the marriage, which the cardinal may show to Henry; but he is not to give it him till he can make things right with Charles.

The cardinals hold a court in Blackfriars Palace, and Henry and Katherine appear before them.

"I am ready to stand by the decision of the Pope's legates," says Henry.

"I am your truly wedded wife," is Katherine's exclamation as she falls at Henry's feet. She will not recognize the cardinals, turns her back upon them, and leaves the room.

Cardinal Campeggio goes back to Rome. Months pass. Henry is impatient and dissatisfied with Wolsey, who has had the management of affairs. But what shall he do?

One day Doctor Thomas Cranmer, of Cambridge, is dining with

BUCKINGHAM ON HIS WAY TO PRISON.

Stephen Gardiner, Cardinal Wolsey's secretary, whom we saw at the Field of the Cloth of Gold.

"Why does not the king lay the matter before the chief ministers and doctors of Europe, and let them examine the lawfulness of the marriage?" Doctor Cranmer asks.

It is a new idea, and Gardiner makes it known to Henry, who invites the doctor to London, and finds that he is able and learned.   He lays the matter before the Oxford doctors, who decide that the marriage was illegal; the Cambridge doctors say the same.   He sends a learned man to

THE COURT AT BLACKFRIARS.

Italy, and some of the doctors there coincide with the opinion.   They discover a lot of old Greek manuscripts, which show that the doctors in old times were of their way of thinking.   Henry consults the Jewish rabbies, who say that in Judea, when a man died leaving no children, a brother might marry the widow to preserve possessions, but they thought it would be illegal out of Judea.

The Paris doctors, after three weeks' study, agree that the marriage was a lawful one; and the doctors at Toulon, Angiers, and Orleans are of the same way of thinking.   John Calvin, a learned doctor in Geneva, says it was illegal.   Philip Melancthon, another learned doctor, Martin Luther's best friend, thinks that it was lawful, but that it may be set aside.

Henry sends Doctor Cranmer, Stephen Gardiner, and Edward Bonner to argue the matter before the Pope.   The Pope listens, but makes no answer.   Henry is impatient; he will wait no longer.   As the Pope has promised to set aside the marriage, and has once written out the bull, as the doctors of Cambridge and Oxford say it was illegal, Henry leaves

Katherine, and is privately married to Anne.   No longer may the true-hearted queen live in one of the king's palaces.   She goes into the country.   She is not even permitted to have Mary with her.   With a breaking heart, she writes to Charles of the indignity heaped upon her; and Charles stirs up the Pope to summon Henry to appear at Rome and give an account of himself.

"Appear at Rome and give an account of myself!   Tell the Pope that I am a sovereign prince, and that he has no authority in England."

Out of this reply shall come the freedom of a nation.   The people, the nobles, are with the king.   Cardinal Wolsey makes all the Church appointments in England; and as he is managing affairs for the king, it will be for the interest of all the prelates to be on the king's side.   Parliament decides that no cause affecting the interests of the kingdom shall be judged outside of the realm: any person executing any censure of the Pope shall be punished.

Never before has the Parliament of England exercised such independence.   New times have come.

Henry appoints Doctor Cranmer Archbishop of Canterbury.   There is no reason why the Pope should not confirm so able and learned a man, and, though Henry and Parliament are taking things out of his hands, he sends a bull for his consecration.   The doctor does not desire the office, and upon taking the oath makes this protestation:

"Not to be bound by anything contrary to what I conceive to be my duty to God and to the king."

It is the right of private judgment.   He will think for himself.   Parliament takes up the marriage of Katherine.   Was the marriage lawful?   Seven lords say it was,

THE OLD GUILDHALL, LONDON.

fourteen say it was not. Of the Commons, two hundred and sixteen say it was not; none say it was. The question goes to the bishops, who hold their court. They summon Henry and Katherine before them; but Katherine will not recognize them as a court. The Pope is the one to whom she appeals. The bishops declare her contumacious of their authority; and they decree that the marriage of Henry and Katherine is null and void.

A few days later there is a grand pageant on the Thames. The Lord Mayor of London comes down from Guildhall, and steps into his gilded barge, to lead a procession of boats. He wears a scarlet cloak trimmed with gold-lace, and is accompanied by all the great men of the realm—filling fifty barges. In one boat sits a dragon with a long tail. From the monster's mouth issues a stream of fire. Another barge carries the representation of a mound supporting a tree covered with red and white roses, for the Wars of the Roses (the houses of York and Lancaster) are over, and the great families are living in peace. Upon the tree sits a white falcon. Beneath its branches sit a group of girls, waving flags and singing songs. There are high-born young ladies, who grace the occasion by their presence. Thousands of boats follow in the wake of the procession.

There is still another barge, more gorgeous than all others, containing another company of high-born ladies, one of whom is seated in a golden chair beneath a golden canopy. We have seen her before. We first saw her here upon the Thames, twenty years ago, when she was but seven years of age—on that stormy day when Mary, King Henry's sister, took her departure for France, to be the wife of old Louis XII. We saw her again at the Field of the Cloth of Gold, twelve years ago—the fairest and wittiest of all the ladies there. Now she is the wife of King Henry, and to-morrow she is to be crowned Queen of England—Anne Boleyn.

As the royal procession passes up the stream, the people look out upon it from the quaint old houses huddled along the shore. The rowers ply their oars; the cannon thunder; bells ring; the people rend the air with shouting. The procession moves from the king's palace in Greenwich to the Tower. King Henry greets Anne at the landing with a kiss, and escorts her into the Tower.

This on Saturday. On Sunday morning all London is astir, for there is to be a grand coronation procession. The houses along the streets through which the procession is to pass are hung with crimson and scarlet. The Lord Mayor, in crimson velvet, leads the procession. After him rides the French ambassador, in a blue-velvet coat, with sleeves of blue and yellow. Then come the judges, in their gowns; then the Knights of the Bath, in velvet gowns and hoods; then the abbots, the bishops, the Archbishop of York; the ambassador from Venice; the Archbishop of Canterbury; the great men—lords, earls, dukes; the Lord High Constable, Duke of Suffolk (Charles Brandon), who married Mary after the death of Louis XII. Anne Boleyn rides in a litter borne by two horses—one before, and the other behind. The litter is covered with cloth of gold. The horses are caparisoned with white damask, and led by footmen in livery.

Anne wears a dress of silver tissue, and a mantle lined with ermine. Her hair hangs in loose tresses upon her shoulders. Upon her brow rests a coronet set with rubies. Four knights bear a canopy, to shelter her from the sun.

Two chariots filled with ladies, and fourteen ladies on horseback, with thirty waiting-maids, follow the queen, accompanied by noblemen, who act as guards. Besides these, there is a great following of merchants and of children.

Fountains of Rhine-wine are erected along the streets, and the people drink all that they wish, at the expense of the king—forgetting that, after all, they will have to foot the bill by increased taxes. School-children

WESTMINSTER, 1532.

sing ballads; poets recite verses. A gentleman presents Anne with a purse filled with gold. There are triumphal arches, festoons, banners; the cannon thunder again, the bells clang once more, and the people shout themselves hoarse, as the procession moves from the Tower to Westminster Abbey. All the great men, all the noble ladies of England, are there. The mayor carries Anne's sceptre; the Earl of Arundel, her ivory rod; the Earl of Oxford, the crown; the Duke of Suffolk, the silver wand;

Lord Howard, the marshal's staff. The Bishops of London and Winchester hold the lappets of Anne's robe; the old Duchess of Norfolk carries her train.

Anne takes a seat in a gilded chair; while the Archbishop of Canter

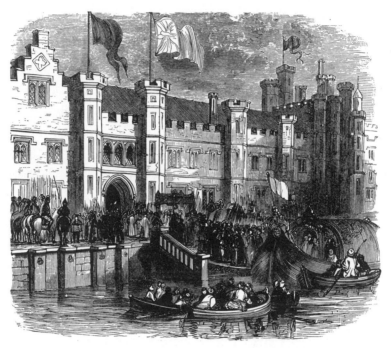

RETURN FROM THE CHRISTENING.

bury reads the Collects, anoints her forehead and breast, places the crown upon her brow, and hands her the sceptre. The choir sing a *Te Deum*, mass is performed, and the procession returns to Westminster Hall, to the banquet.

At the dinner, the Earl of Essex is chief carver; the Earl of Arundel, chief butler; twelve noblemen act as cup-bearers; Lord Burgoyne is chief larder; Viscount Lile, chief pantler—his chief business is to look after the bread; while the Marquis of Oxford keeps the buttery bar. It is Sir Thomas Wyatt's business to pour scented water on Anne's hands. The Countess of Oxford and the Countess of Worcester stand near Anne, with a cloth in their hands, to wipe her nose, in case she needs such service. Two ladies sit at the queen's feet. When all are in their places, the Duke of Suffolk and Lord Howard ride into the hall on horseback, escorting the Knights of the Bath, who bring twenty-seven dishes for the queen. The trumpets sound, and the feasting begins. King Henry takes no part in this demonstration of his subjects, but looks on from a little closet, and enjoys the scene.

Not many weeks after the coronation, Anne gives birth to a babe—a daughter. There is great rejoicing; but there would have been greater joy if it were a son. There is still another grand pageant on the Thames when the babe is taken to Westminster, where it is christened Elizabeth.

Cardinal Wolsey is in his glory—still the most powerful man in the realm. He gives grand banquets and entertainments in the great hall of his palace. But there are often sudden changes in the prospects of great

HALL IN CARDINAL WOLSEY'S PALACE.

men. Henry is angry with him for his mismanagement of the divorce business. Anne has a grudge against him, for she has discovered that the cardinal did not intend that Henry should make her his wife. The nobles hate him, for he was only a butcher's boy, and not high-born. Henry discovers that he has been accumulating great wealth. He will

OLD CHURCH AT AUSTERFIELD.

bear with him no longer. He orders the cardinal to give up the seals of his office to Sir Thomas More. The Duke of Norfolk brings the message that all his property is confiscated to the king. Shakspeare pictures the scene in the hall of Wolsey's palace:

> "*Norfolk.* So, fare you well, my little good lord cardinal.
> *Wolsey.* So farewell to the little good you bear me.
> Farewell, a long farewell, to all my greatness!
> This is the state of man: to-day he puts forth
> The tender leaves of hopes, to-morrow blossoms,
> And bears his blushing honors thick upon him:
> The third day comes a frost, a killing frost,
> And—when he thinks, good easy man, full surely
> His greatness is a-ripening—nips his root,
> And then he falls, as I do."

The cardinal bids farewell to London, and goes up the great road leading to York—the road over which Margaret, Henry's sister, travelled when she went to Scotland. In the old manor-house, at Scrooby, he finds a home for a while. It is lonely there. His greatness has all gone by, but the good people of the little hamlet of Austerfield still do him reverence when he enters the old stone church. They see that his locks are growing white, that he has a sad face, that he walks feebly. He gives money to the poor, and they think that, after all, he has a kind heart. From Scrooby he goes to Esher. A few months pass, and the cardinal is on his death-bed, with this lament upon his lips :

"If I had but served my God as faithfully as I have my king, he would not thus desert me in my old age."

Liberty has not yet dawned upon the people of England. To read the Bible is a great crime. Sir Thomas More is Lord Chancellor. He lives at Greenwich, and is very zealous for the faith as held by the Church. He issues a proclamation against heretics, ordering all laws against them to be put in execution. He burns all the Bibles he can lay his hands upon. Thomas Bayfield, a monk, is discovered to have a New Testament in his possession, and is brought before Bishop Tunstal, of London. In St. Paul's, Tunstal strips off his gown, and while the poor monk is kneeling at the altar the bishop strikes him a blow with his crozier, which knocks him senseless to the floor. Out in Smithfield, where the cattle-dealers market their beeves, he is chained to the stake. The wood is green, and for half an hour he roasts in the flames. The fire curls around his left arm

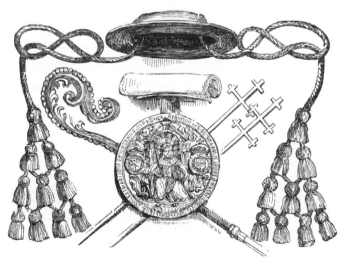

THE CARDINAL'S HAT AND SEAL.

and burns till it drops from the body. All the while the brave-hearted man is praying for Sir Thomas More and Bishop Tunstal, and all his enemies.

Another of Sir Thomas's victims is James Bainham, who is burned on the Smithfield muck-heaps.

"The Lord forgive Sir Thomas," he prays, as he stands there clothed with flames. His face is radiant. "I feel no more pain than when lying on a bed of down; the fire is as a bed of roses," he cries.

Thomas Bilney is a student at Cambridge. One day a Testament

MORE'S HOUSE.

in Latin, translated by Erasmus, falls into his hands; he has seen Latin Testaments before, but none with such smooth-flowing sentences as that. A verse arrests his attention.

"This is a faithful saying, and worthy of all acceptation, that Christ Jesus came into the world to save sinners, of whom I am chief."

If that is true, then fasting, and penance, and masses, and indulgences are of no account. He begins to preach, and brings Hugh Latimer and many others to his way of thinking. He travels through the country doing good, giving alms, sharing his humble fare with the poor, till he is imprisoned. He renounces his doctrines, and is released; but his conscience troubles him, and he begins to preach again. He is as gentle as a lamb. He has nothing to say against the Pope, or the bishops, or the Church; but he preaches the truth as *he* understands it, not as taught by the Pope and bishops. It is private judgment. Sir Thomas More cannot permit that, and sends an order to have him burned. It is at Norwich, just outside the city walls, that the officers chain him to the stake. He smiles upon them. There is no anger in his heart toward any one. The people love him, he is so sweet and tender, and they scowl upon the friars who have maliciously accused him.

It is a strange request which the friars make of him:

"Oh, Master Bilney! the people think that we have caused you to be put to death, and they will no longer give to us, if you do not speak to them in our behalf."

The man, with the light of heaven on his face, turns to the people:

"I pray you, good people, be never the worse to these men for my sake. They are not the authors of my death."

Not they—but the Lord High Chancellor, Sir Thomas More, as zealous for the Church as Paul when he held the clothes of those who hurled stones at Stephen just outside of the gate at Jerusalem. Another day will come to Sir Thomas. Now he is burning the meek-hearted man who stands for the right of private judgment. The time will come when he will assert *his* right of private judgment, and then we shall see what will happen to him.

One hundred years have passed since the monks dug up the bones of Doctor Wicklif. If there was little liberty in the world then, there is very little now, although a century has gone. If the monks and priests

SIR THOMAS MORE.

were corrupt then, it is certain that many of them are leading scandalous lives in these days of Henry VIII. The bishops have their courts, and punish with a light penance a crime in a priest, which is atoned for only by death if committed by common people. Thomas Wyseman, a priest, who has led a scandalous life, is sentenced to do penance by offering a wax-candle at the altar of St. Bartholomew's Church, and say five Pater-

nosters, five Ave - Marias, and as many Credos. Having done this, he pays six shillings and eightpence into the Bishops' Court, and is absolved, and can go on saying mass and absolving the people. But the same crime committed by one of the people is punished with death.

There is a long list of priests who are leading scandalous lives: The vicars of Ledburg, of Brasmyll, of Stow, of Clome, the parson of Wentnor, of Rusburg, of Plowden, the Dean of Pamtsburg, and many more.

THE GUILDHALL, NORWICH.

The people are losing confidence in priests who live in sin, or who can atone for sin by offering a wax-candle. They are losing faith in the Church that makes atonement so easy for a priest, while it metes out death to everybody else. The rhymers write ballads lampooning the priests.

> "I, Collin Clout,
> As I go about,
> And wondering as I walk,
> I hear the people talk;
> Men say for silver and gold
> Mitres are bought and sold.
> A straw for God's curse!
> What are they the worse?

> "What care the clergy though Gill sweat,
> Or Jack of the Noke?
> The poor people they yoke
> With sumners and citations
> And excommunications.
> * * * * * *

" But Doctor Ballatus
Parum litteratus
Dominus Doctoratus,
At the broad-gate house,
Doctor Daupatus
And Bachelor Bacheleratus,
Drunken as a mouse,
At the ale-house,
Taketh his pillian and his cup
At the good ale-tap,
For lack of good wine.

* * * * *

" Such temporal war and hate,
As now is made of late
Against Holy Church estate,
Or to maintain good quarrels:
The laymen call them barrels
Full of gluttony and hypocrisy.
What counterfeits and paints,
As they were very saints!"

It is the year 1547. Fourteen years have passed since Anne Boleyn's coronation. A great man, with a round, bloated face, double chin, coarse features, fat paunch, weak and helpless, with an offensive ulcer on one of his legs, lies in bed. A fair-looking, kind-hearted woman sits by his side, taking care of him. The man is fifty-six years old, and has been a king thirty-six years. His will has been supreme; he has had things his own way, but can have them no longer, for one mightier than he is about to make him a visit—the king of terrors—Death.

We saw him at the Field of the Cloth of Gold; we saw him putting away Katherine of Aragon, and marrying Anne Boleyn. Three years later, he chopped off Anne's head, and married Jane Seymour the next day, who died the next year in giving birth to a son — happily for her. He married Anne of Cleves, and was divorced from her. Then he married Katherine Howard, in July, 1540, and cut her head off, February 12th, 1542; and married Katherine Parr, in July, 1543—the woman who is sitting by his side and soothing his pain.

Important changes have taken place during these years, in which great things have been unwittingly done for liberty by this man, so powerful once, so weak and helpless now. The changes have been brought about through his passion for Anne Boleyn.

The timid Pope—destitute of conscience or moral principle; afraid of Charles; afraid of Henry—promised to grant him a divorce from Kath-

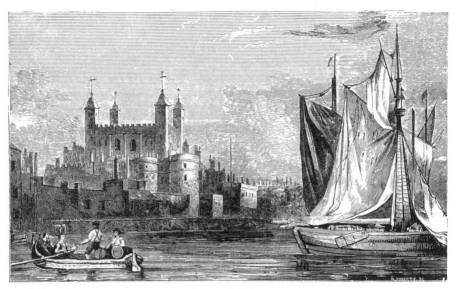

THE TOWER.

erine, and then failed to keep his promise. Archbishop Cranmer, speaking for the bishops of England, pronounces the marriage with Katherine illegal, and sanctions his marriage with Anne. The Pope declares that the bishop cannot make such a decision—all power belongs to him. The Parliament will see about that, and declares that the Pope has no authority in England. The bishops decide, in their sessions, that the Pope has no more authority in England than any other foreign bishop, which is none at all.

The king has always appointed the bishops, and Parliament makes the king the head of the Church—thus setting the Pope aside. Parliament declares that Elizabeth, and not Mary, is the true heir to the crown, because the marriage of Henry and Katherine was illegal; and they require all the nobles and bishops to swear to support the law. If any one refuses, he shall be deemed guilty of high treason. Sir Thomas More, who has resigned his office to Thomas Cromwell, whom we saw with Wolsey at the Field of the Cloth of Gold, is living at Greenwich. His daughter Margaret is married to Mr. Roper, and lives with him. He is called upon to appear at Lambeth Palace and take the oath. He comes up the Thames in a boat, with his daughter's husband, and appears before the commission. He is willing to take part of the oath—to support Elizabeth whenever she may come to the throne; but he will not swear that the marriage of Henry and Katherine was illegal. He sets up his private judgment, just as

Thomas Bilney and Thomas Bayfold set up theirs.   It was for having a
New Testament in his possession, for preaching the truth as he under-
stood it, not as dictated by the Pope, that Sir Thomas sent the good man
to his death; and now he sets up his own judgment against the law of
the realm.   It is treason, to be punished with death; and he goes to the
Bloody Tower, a prisoner, entering by the Traitor's Gate, with Bishop
Fisher, an old man eighty years of age, who also will not take the oath.
In Westminster Hall, where Anne Boleyn sat down to the grand banquet,
Sir Thomas has his trial.   He will not swear, and is found guilty of high
treason.

At the Tower stairs, he bids farewell to his beloved daughter Margaret, who has affectionately waited upon him in prison.

At nine o'clock on the morning of the 6th of July, 1535, Sir Thomas
and the sheriff come out from the Tower.   A great company has assembled to see him executed.   Some of the people do not like him.   They

THE BLOODY TOWER.

remember how he has sent many a poor man to the stake, and there is no
pity in some of the faces around him; but there are others who are sorry
to see him suffer for conscience' sake.   He goes with a brave heart.   His
life has been sweet and pure.   The scaffold stairs are weak.

" See me safe up, Mr. Sheriff. As for the coming down, I can take care of myself," he says, with a smile on his face.

" I ask your prayers, good people. I die in the faith of the Holy Catholic Church. I am a faithful servant to God and to the king."

He kneels, and repeats a Psalm.

The sheriff kneels to him, and asks forgiveness for what he is about to do.

" Pluck up spirit, man, and be not afraid to do thine office. My neck is short. Take heed how you strike."

He himself ties a handkerchief over his eyes, and lays aside his white beard.

" Pity it should be cut; it never has committed treason."

They are his last words. He lays his head upon the block, and all is over.

" What measure ye mete it shall be measured to you again."

SIR THOMAS MORE AND HIS DAUGHTER MARGARET IN THE TOWER.

Many times those lips, motionless now, have sentenced men and women to death for reading the New Testament—for not believing that the bread of the sacrament is Christ's body. They were heretics, and died for conscience' sake. Sir Thomas dies for conscience' sake, not as a heretic, but as a rebel, disobedient to government.

The king goes on burning Catholics who will not recognize him as head of the Church, and heretics who say that there is no purgatory. But amidst all this burning and hanging a great revolution is going on. The people have lost confidence in the Church. There are more than six hundred monasteries and nunneries in England, and the country is overrun by a set of lazy monks and priests and nuns, who own immense estates. The Pope has always had control of the monasteries; but now he has no authority in England. The king is the head of the Church; and commissioners are appointed to visit the monasteries. They report them rich, and that the monks, friars, and abbots lead scandalous lives.   Parliament makes a law suppressing them.   The lands, jewels, and estates are seized; and the men and women, who have been living on the people so long, are turned adrift, to get their living as they can.   The king fills his coffers, the nobles, dukes, earls, and baronets take good care to fill their own pockets, with the spoils.   One woman, Widow Cornwallis, makes a pudding for the king, which is so good, with so many plums in it, that he, in return, makes her a present of all the lands of an abbey.

Workmen tear down the monasteries to get the lead and iron; and the stately stone edifices, which have stood so long, soon are heaps of ruins.

Though Stephen Gardiner and Edmund Bonner, the nobles, the king, are spoiling the abbeys, they are at the same time burning heretics.

SMITHFIELD IN 1546.   THE BURNING OF ANNE ASKEW.

Anne Askew is arrested for not believing that the bread of the sacrament is the flesh of Christ.   She is brought before the Lord Mayor of London.

"You do not believe that the bread becomes Christ's body?"

"No, your honor."

"What if a mouse should eat the bread after it is consecrated?" the mayor asks.

"What say you to it, my lord?" Anne asks, in return.

"I say that the mouse is damned."

"Alas! poor mouse!"

The Lord Mayor sees that he has made a little mistake.

Anne is put upon the rack in the Tower, and two of the questioners throw off their gowns, and work the winches till her limbs are all but torn from her body. They carry her in a chair to the place of burning, at the Muck-heap of Smithfield, and bind her to the stake with a chain. Two others are to suffer with her. The executioner fastens bags of powder to their bodies. The Lord Mayor, the Duke of Norfolk, and the Earl of Bedford sit upon a seat by St. Bartholomew's Church, but, though several rods away, are afraid that the powder will hurt them.

ALL DAY LONG THE PEOPLE READ IT.

Anne Askew has a countenance like that of an angel. She smiles upon the executioners.

"Here is a pardon if you will recant," says the sheriff.

"I came not here to deny my Lord."

With these heroic words upon her lips, she gives her life for liberty.

But notwithstanding all these burnings, liberty is advancing. The king has ordered that the Bible, in English, shall be in every church in England. Desks have been put up, and the books chained to them. All day long the people stand there hearing them read, and as the reading goes on they think for themselves, and heretics are multiplying.

The woman who sits by the bedside of the king—Katherine Parr—secretly befriends those whom Stephen Gardiner and Edmund Bonner have thrust into prison, and they resolve that she too shall suffer; but she finds out what is going on, and cares for Henry very tenderly. Gardiner comes with his accusation.

"Get out, you knave!" is the salutation which he receives when he makes his business known.

Henry knows that he cannot get well. Jane Seymour's son, Edward, is ten years old. Who shall conduct affairs till he is old enough to wear the crown? There are two great parties in England now—the old party and the new. The old party do not wish to have the Bible in the churches, and they believe that the Pope is their head of the Church. The new party accept the king as head of the Church, and the Bible, and not the Pope, as authority in matters of religion. Henry selects men of the new party to direct affairs. Edward is to be king, and after him Mary and Elizabeth are to be heirs to the throne.

On the 28th of January, 1547, the despot who through life has been trampling upon the rights of men, who has cut off the heads of his wives and nobles, who has plundered the people at will through an obsequious and

GOLD MEDAL OF HENRY VIII.

time-serving Parliament, yields his sceptre to one mightier than himself. He has been a wicked man, a tyrant; yet, through his wickedness and tyranny, liberty shall dawn upon the oppressed and suffering people of England, and, through them, upon all the world.

CHAPTER XVIII.

THE QUEEN WHO BURNED HERETICS.

ON the 1st of October, 1553, Mary Tudor, daughter of Henry VIII. and Katherine of Aragon, is crowned Queen of England. There is a grand procession, and Mary rides in a gilded coach drawn by six horses. She is thirty-seven years old, small in stature, thin and pale. Her eyes are bright and sparkling, but she has a voice deep and resonant like a man's. She wears a blue-velvet dress trimmed with ermine, and a richly embroidered mantle ornamented with pearls. A golden fillet encircles her brow, set with diamonds and precious stones, and so heavy that she has to support her head with her hand.

Mary is very religious. She counts her beads, and repeats her Paternosters and Ave-Marias regularly, and never fails to attend mass.

In the procession is her half-sister Elizabeth, Anne Boleyn's daughter. She is twenty years old, the picture of health.

There have been stirring times in England since midsummer. Mary's half-brother Edward, Jane Seymour's son, died on the 6th of July. He had been king six years. He had no children to succeed him. Then came the question as to who was entitled to the crown. Henry made a will, and declared that after Edward, Mary was to have it; and after Mary, Elizabeth; and after Elizabeth, the descendants of his sister Mary —the Mary whom he compelled to marry the old Louis XII. of France, but who, as soon as Louis died, married Charles Brandon.

Mary and Charles have a granddaughter—Jane Grey—a lovely girl, seventeen years old, and just married. Edward wished the crown to go to her, and the day after Edward died, the council proclaimed Jane Grey queen. She was in the country, and when word came to her that Edward was dead, and that she was to be queen, she burst into tears. She did not desire to wear the crown, and to be burdened with all the cares and responsibilities of State.

Not so with Mary. She wished to be queen. She sent word to the council that the crown belonged to her. There was a great party that wished her to be queen, and she was proclaimed in August. Her party has succeeded, and she wears the crown. There is eating and drinking and great rejoicing by all good Catholics, for Mary is a devoted friend of the Church. Some of her councillors are hard-hearted, revengeful men. They suffered under Henry, were obliged to keep quiet while Edward was king, but now they are in power, and will make their power felt.

The news of what is going on in England reaches Charles V., who is in the Netherlands. He has been negotiating a marriage for his son Philip with the daughter of the King of Portugal; but here is a chance to make a better bargain. He will bring about a match between Philip and the woman to whom he himself was once betrothed, and whom he agreed to marry when she was twelve years of age, but saw fit to break the agreement. Mary is thirty-seven, and Philip twenty-seven.

Charles sends Count Egmont to England to make a proposal. Mary accepts the offer, but many of the English people do not like the match. "No foreigner for us!" they shout, and Sir Thomas Wyatt heads a party and raises an insurrection; but Mary's troops soon suppress it, and Wyatt and many of the men who joined him are executed. Jane Grey's husband is one. Jane looks out of her prison in the Tower, and sees his headless body in a cart. The executioner then comes for her. She walks to the scaffold with a firm step, and ascends the stairs as lightly as if going to her chamber to a night's repose. There are no tears on her cheek, nor is there any trembling of her eyelids. She reads a prayer, and then ties a handkerchief over her eyes.

"What shall I do?" she asks of the executioner.

"Kneel by the block."

"Where is it?"

She feels for it, lays her head upon it, to receive the fatal stroke.

"Lord, into thy hands I commit my spirit."

The axe falls, and the head of the brave girl drops from the body. What has she done to merit such a

THE BEHEADING-BLOCK.

fate? Nothing. A great political party has used her to advance its own interests; that is all. Perhaps Mary breathes easier when she hears that her cousin is dead, and perhaps not, for on this same "Black Monday," as people call it, from eighty to one hundred men are hanged—some in St. Paul's church-yard, some on London Bridge, some at Charing Cross, others at Westminster. The next week she hangs forty-eight more; and a few days later, twenty-two common men, besides several officers.

TRAITOR'S GATE.

Now comes the arrest of her sister Elizabeth, who is in the country, sick. She is brought to London, and taken to the Tower in a boat, entering it through the dark and gloomy Traitor's Gate. Mary is determined that Elizabeth's head shall roll upon the pavement in the Tower yard; but Bishop Gardiner and Bishop Bonner, and other men among Mary's councillors, much as they wish it, see that it will not do to cut off the head of one on whom the people have already set their affections, and who has had nothing whatever to do with the insurrection.

On the 20th of July, 1554, a fleet of Spanish ships—one hundred and fifty or more—sails into the harbor of Southampton. Philip of Spain has come to be married, with a great train of Spanish noblemen, and six thousand troops. The English noblemen meet him at Southampton. Philip is accompanied by a gray-bearded man, sixty years of age, who has done a deal of fighting for Charles V.—the Duke of Alva, who has a hard countenance and a harder heart. His eyes have a cruel look. We shall see him again.

Mary is at Winchester impatiently waiting for Philip. He sets out on Monday morning, in a driving rain-storm, on horseback, and splashes through the mud, reaching Winchester at sunset. He goes at once to the cathedral, and listens to a *Te Deum*. In the evening he goes to the bishop's palace, where Mary, with a company of ladies, is waiting. She never has seen her future husband. He enters the hall, and she beholds a small man with spindle-legs, small body, a broad forehead, blue eyes, large mouth, heavy underlip, and protruding jaw. He has a deep sepulchral voice; but Mary could sing the bass quite as well as he, for she has a tremendous voice. He is proud and haughty, and cares nothing for men except to use them; but on this occasion he kisses his wife that is to be, and not only her, but all her ladies. He has already been once married —in 1544, to Maria of Portugal, when he was only sixteen. The next year a son was born to him. One day, soon after the birth of the babe, there was a grand spectacle in front of the royal palace at Valladolid— the burning of a lot of heretics by the men who ask questions—and Maria's nurses left her alone, that they might see the men and women roasted to

PHILIP.

death; and while they were gone Maria helped herself to so much water-melon that she sickened and died the next day.

The marriage between Mary and Philip is consummated, and the wed-ded pair enter London beneath triumphal arches and amidst the blazing of bonfires, the roaring of cannon, and ringing of bells.

Mary is firmly seated on her throne. She is married to the son of the mightiest monarch in the world. She has put out of the way her political enemies; and now she will begin with heretics. Her father Henry, through his guilty passion for Anne Boleyn, severed England from the Church; she will bring it back again. Men shall no longer think for themselves, but shall be in subjection to the Pope. There shall be no

WINCHESTER.

more reading of the Bible. The thousands of married ministers shall be turned out of their pulpits. Heresy shall be crushed out. In 1547, all acts punishing heretics were repealed; but now Parliament restores them.

On St. Andrew's Day, Nov. 30, 1554, a high mass is sung in Westminster Abbey. Philip, the Duke of Alva, and another great don from Spain (Ruy Gomez), with six hundred Spanish grandees, the Knights of the Garter, the English nobles, the archbishop and bishops whom Mary has appointed in place of those appointed by Henry and Edward, whom she has turned out, are there, dressed in gorgeous apparel. After mass, they have dinner; and then there is another gathering in Westminster Hall. On a platform, in three golden chairs, are seated Mary, Philip, and Cardinal

Pole, the Pope's ambassador. Above them is a canopy of gold. The bishop sits near by. The Hall is the place where the Commons meet, and the members are in their places.

Stephen Gardiner, Lord Chancellor, in his big wig, bows to Mary and Philip, kneels, and presents a petition to the Pope's legate, requesting his forgiveness for all that has been done against his authority in the past, and praying that the nation may be taken back again into the bosom of the Church.

Cardinal Pole rises to reply for the Pope. Mary and Philip and all the rest fall on their knees, and receive the absolution which the Pope gives through the cardinal.

"Amen! Amen!"

The voices of the assembled multitude echo amidst the oaken rafters. The organ peals; the choir sing a *Te Deum.* Tears of joy roll down the cheeks of the queen. Her heart's desires are gratified. The nation is once more in the fold of the Church. She has been the one to lead it back. Some persons in the assembly, in their ecstasy and joy, throw themselves into the arms of their friends.

"We are reconciled to God. Blessed day for England," they say.

A GRANDEE.

Cardinal Pole, sitting in his chamber at midnight, writes to the Pope: "What great things may the Church, our mother, the bride of Christ, fancy for herself! O piety! O ancient faith! this is the seed the Lord hath blessed!"

The letter reaches Rome, and the Pope embraces the messenger, falls on his knees, says a Pater-noster, gives orders to ring all the bells in Rome, to fire the cannon of the Castle of St. Angelo, light bonfires, to give indulgences and pardons to all who want them.

The Pope has given his absolution, and the nation is once more back in his fold. But how about those monasteries and abbeys which Henry tore down? How about the lands and estates that were seized and divided between the crown and the great men, and given to women who made good puddings? They must be given up. The Pope demands it.

ST. MARY OVERY, SOUTHWARK.

The Members of Parliament have been willing to fall on their knees and receive absolution, but, having obtained it, conclude to hold on to their spoils. They are willing that heresy shall be rooted out, but they will not let the Pope have authority in England. The queen shall still be head of the Church. They are good Catholics, but they will not change Henry's will, and after Mary the crown shall go to Elizabeth. Philip wants to be crowned. Charles urges it, the Pope desires it; but there are some sturdy Englishmen who say, "No foreigner for us," and Philip is obliged to smother his resentment.

The Commons, the Lords, the great men have submitted to the Pope in behalf of the nation, and now the people themselves must submit.

"If any one before Easter, 1555, does not acknowledge the authority of the Pope, he shall suffer for it," is the edict.

"Come and register your names," is the command given by the priests; and registers are provided in every parish.

There shall be no more reading the Bible, nor Prayer-books; no more liberty of conscience; no more thinking for themselves.

Stephen Gardiner opens his heresy court in St. Mary's Church, Southwark. Goodwin, Bonner, Tunstal, and three other bishops are the judges. The court is the Inquisition under another name. There are several men for whose blood they are thirsting. Mr. John Rogers is one. He is a preacher—a learned man; and when Tyndal and Coverdale were over in Antwerp translating the Bible into English, he went over and aided them, and is therefore an arch-heretic. Besides, he went to Wittenberg, and studied with that monk who, when a boy, sung for his breakfast—Martin Luther. He married a German wife, and has ten children. The Pope does not allow priests to marry. He was preaching at St. Paul's when Mary came to the throne; he could have fled: but he is an Englishman, and has done nothing contrary to his conscience. He will stay, come what will. He has been a prisoner for many months in Newgate, with Mr. Hooper, of Gloucester.

The world does not often see a man like John Hooper. He was educated at Oxford, and was a Bachelor of Arts two years before that meeting on the Field of the Cloth of Gold, and became a monk; but after reading the Bible he left the monastery. When Henry was king, he had an interview with Stephen Gardiner, who was astonished at his learning. He had to flee to France, however; but when Edward came to the throne, he returned, and Edward made him Bishop of Gloucester. When everybody else was getting rich on the spoils of the monasteries, Bishop Hooper was making himself poor by feeding the hungry. He sat down with them at the table to let them know that he loved them. But he is a heretic; besides, he is married. For a long while Gardiner has had him in prison—confined in a room with robbers and murderers, with nothing but straw to lie upon, and an old counterpane for a covering. He and Mr. Rogers are brought before the court, and condemned to be burned.

"Shall I not be allowed to bid farewell to my wife and children?" Rogers asks.

"No," is the savage reply of Gardiner.

It is four o'clock in the morning, February 4th. The frost is on the window-panes. In the cold and gloomy prison Rogers is quietly sleeping. The jailer's wife taps him on the shoulder.

"Bishop Bonner is waiting for you."

He rises and goes out into the hall, where Bonner is waiting to degrade him from his office as a priest. That done, Rogers bids farewell to Hooper, and the sheriff leads him out. It is still dark; but the people have heard that he is to be burned, and a crowd has assembled to see him die.

"He will flinch," say his enemies.

His wife and children are waiting for him, and though Gardiner has said that he shall not see them, he kisses them, and goes on with a firm step to the stake. The executioner binds the chain around him and heaps the fagots. In the dim gray of the winter morning the people see him standing there, looking up into heaven, with a smile upon his face.

"You can have the queen's pardon if you will recant," says Sir Robert Rochester, who has come to report his behavior to Gardiner. But he has nothing to recant.

The fire curls around him. He bathes his hands in the flames as if it

STREET IN LONDON IN THE TIME OF MARY.

were cold water. They who look to see him beg for mercy hear nothing but prayer and praise, while those who expected he would stand firm rend the air with their shouts of joy.

Ah, Mary! out from those applauding cries shall come liberty to the human race! Go on, Gardiner, Bonner, and Tunstal, with your court of heresy; send men and women to the stake—for the brief period of your power; but every fire which you thus kindle shall be a beacon to light the human race in its march to freedom!

BEARING FAGOTS.

"Hooper is an obstinate, false, detestable heretic; let him be burned in the city which he has infected with his pernicious doctrines," is the order for the burning of the aged bishop.

Mr. Gardiner has made a mistake. If he wants to put a stop to heresy, he had better not send Bishop Hooper to the city where everybody loves him as children love a father, where he has fed the hungry and clothed the poor. Surrounded by guards, he rides out of London on horseback. He is old, feeble, and wasted almost to a skeleton with his long imprisonment and with sleeping on his bed of straw. He eats dinner at a tavern where a woman rails at heretics; but he is so tender, so childlike and forgiving that she too becomes a child before him, and with tears begs his forgiveness, and does what she can for him. Love is more potent than fire to subdue the human heart. A great crowd awaits his coming. For a mile outside of Gloucester gates the road is filled with people. It is evening, and the sheriff will give him one more night on earth; and the people go to their homes, wondering if their good old bishop will stand firm at the final hour.

Sir Anthony Kingston, who has often heard the bishop preach, is sent by Gardiner to see him burned. In the morning Sir Anthony enters the prison.

"Do you know me?" Sir Anthony asks.

"Oh yes, Sir Anthony; and I am glad to see you in such good health. I have come here to lay down my life for the truth."

"Would you not like to live?"

"I can live; but I never should enjoy life at the expense of my future welfare. You would not have me blaspheme my Saviour by denying him, would you? I trust that I shall bear with fortitude all the torments which my enemies may be able to inflict."

Sir Anthony is not a hard-hearted man, and the tears stream from his eyes.

"I shall be sorry to see you die."

" It is my duty to stand for the truth."

A little blind boy who has heard the bishop preach comes to bid him farewell, and he falls on his knees at the bishop's feet.

" I am blind, but you have opened the eyes of my soul. May the good Lord be with you, and bring you into heaven !"

The good old man lays his withered hand upon the head of the boy and blesses him. A bigoted man comes in to revile him.

" You are a wicked heretic."

The man who has fed the hungry and clothed the naked makes no reply. The mayor, who has sat under the bishop's preaching, comes with the sheriff to conduct him to the stake. Gladly would the mayor give him his liberty, but then he, quite likely, would be roasted alive, if he were to do so humane an act.

" I could have had my life, but I would not take it here to lose it in the next world. Please, Mr. Sheriff, make the fire a hot one, so that it may be quickly over."

It is nine o'clock in the morning. The winter air is chill, but all of Gloucester, and the people from the surrounding country, have gathered to see their dear old friend lay down his life. He is weak and feeble from long imprisonment. He has ridden all the way from London on horseback, and he walks with a feeble step, supporting himself with a cane ; but how brave of heart ! He looks round upon the multitude with a smile on his face. He would like to speak to his old friends, but the sheriff will not let him. Stephen Gardiner and Bishop Bonner will have no farewell address to stir the hearts of heretics ; but those lips, so eloquent once, were never so eloquent as by their silence now.

The bishop, when he arrives at the stake, throws his arms around it as if it were a friend. He kneels and prays.

The sheriff holds a paper in his hand.

" Here is a pardon, if you will recant."

" A pardon if I will recant ! Take it away !"

The sheriff strips him of his garments, ties bags of powder under his arms, fastens a chain around his neck, another around his waist, a third around his legs, piles the fagots, and applies the torch.

At the windows, on the house-tops, in trees, are the people. In a room over the college gates are some priests looking down to see the heretic burned. It is a damp and windy morning. The fagots are wet. The smoke smothers the martyr — the fire scorches and blisters his legs, but does not touch his body, for the wind blows the flame aside.

" More fire !"

The people hear the bishop calling from the pillar of smoke. The sheriff heaps on more fagots, and the withered hands, reaching out from the fire, draws them closer. A handful of flame leaps up and scorches his face. The hands wave to and fro.

"For God's love, good people, give me more fire!"

The minutes go by. His legs are burned to a cinder.

"More fire!" he cries.

Once more the fagots are piled, the flames leap up, and the powder explodes.

"Lord Jesus, receive my spirit!"

Those who stand nearest hear the words — the last that fall upon their ears; yet still his lips

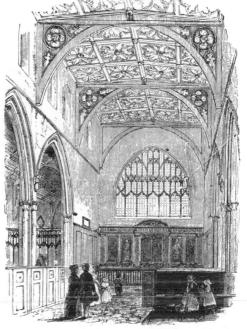

HADLEIGH CHURCH.

are moving. Three-quarters of an hour have passed since the fagots were lighted, and still the scorched hands are beating on his breast.

It is over. He who spread the table for the poor, whose every act was for the good of man, whose life was pure and holy, who was the impersonation of good-will to men, is nothing but a cinder now. He will preach no more heresy. So, perhaps, Stephen Gardiner and Mary and the priests, with hate in their hearts, may think; but when the sun goes down at night there are more heretics in Gloucester than in the morning.

At this same day and hour there is a similar scene in the town of Hadleigh, not far from London.

ST. BOTOLPH'S CHURCH, ALDGATE.

Rev. Rowland Taylor, the minister who has preached there, has been in prison a year. It is two o'clock in the morning when he is brought out from his cell. The good man's family are on the watch, by St. Botolph's Church. All through the weary winter night they have stood there. They hear the tramp of feet — discern a body of men.

BRIDGE AT HADLEIGH.

"Oh, mother, there they are; there is father!" cries the daughter Elizabeth.

"Rowland, are you there?" the wife asks.

"I am here."

The sheriff is not altogether a brutal man.

"Stop a moment, and let him speak to his wife!" is his command to his men.

The minister takes his little Mary in his arms, presses her to his bosom, feels once more her hands upon his neck. He puts her down, and kneels with his family, and all repeat the Lord's Prayer. Then he kisses them.

"Farewell, dear wife; be of good comfort. God will be a father to my children."

"God bless thee, Mary dear, and make thee his servant."

"God bless thee, Elizabeth; stand strong in Christ."

Once more he presses them to his heart, feels the scalding tears drop upon his cheek in the darkness.

The streets of the old town of Hadleigh are crowded with people, who have come to see their old pastor die. They cannot see his face, for the sheriff has covered it with a hood, with two holes in it, so that he can see without his face being seen. At a foot-bridge a poor man, with his five children, kneels before him.

"God help thee, Doctor Taylor, and succor thee, as thou hast many a time helped me."

He passes the almshouse. Many times has he been into it to give things to the poor. The people are looking out of the window to see their old friend.

"Is the blind man yet alive?" Mr. Taylor asks.

ALMSHOUSES AT HADLEIGH.

" Yes."

" And the poor old blind woman ?"

" Yes."

" Here is some money for them ;" and he throws a glove, in which are a few coins, into the window.

He reaches the stake. No longer will he wear the hood, but tears it from his face, and the people see once more the smiling and genial face of their dear old pastor. His beard is white, and he is pale from long imprisonment. He would speak to the people, but one of the sheriff's men rudely thrusts a staff into his mouth.

They pile the wood around him, and a brutal fellow hurls a stick into his face. The blood trickles down his cheeks.

" Oh, friend, what need of that ?" Mr. Taylor mildly asks.

He is placed in a barrel smeared with pitch. The flames whirl above his head, and then a soldier knocks out his brains.

No more heresy, no more private opinions in Hadleigh.

William Hunter, nineteen years old, is learning to weave silk with Thomas Taylor in London. He does not go to mass, as Mary has commanded everybody to do on Easter-morning, and the priest threatens to have him up before the bishop.

THE MARTYRS' STONE.

" You had better go home for a little season," says his master, hoping that if William is out of the way for a little while the priest will forget all about it; and the boy goes home to Brentwood. He strolls into the church, and sees the Bible chained to the desk. Since Mary has come to the throne, only the priests are allowed to read it; but William dares to open it.

" Reading the Bible ! What right have you to read it ?"

It is the shout of the beadle, who opens and shuts the doors.

" I read it because I like to."

The beadle runs for the priest, who comes in hot haste.

" Sirrah ! who gave you leave to read the Bible ?"

" I found it here, and I have read it because I wish to."

" You have no business with it."

" I intend to read it as long as I live."

" You are a heretic."

"No, I am not."

The priest cannot permit any reading of the Book in his parish, and hastens to Esquire Brown, who sends for William's father.

OLD CHAPEL AT BRENTWOOD.

"Your son is a heretic, I hear. Bring him to me at once, or I will put you into jail."

"Would you have me seek my son to have him burned?"

"Go and bring him."

The constable soon has hold of William, who, to give him a taste of what is before him, puts him in the stocks, where he remains twenty-four hours, and then brings him to Esquire Brown.

"Is the bread turned to flesh when the priest blesses it?" asks the squire.

"I do not think it is."

"You are a heretic. Recant, and I will let you go."

"If you will let me go, and leave me to my own conscience, I will keep my opinions to myself."

"Will you go to confession?"

"No, sir."

"Put him in the stocks, and feed him on bread and water."

For two days and two nights he sits there, with a crust of bread and cup of water by his side; but the brave boy will not touch them. The bishop comes to make him say that he will go to confession and mass; but William refuses to accept liberty on those terms.

"If you will recant, I will help you on in life."

"Thank you, bishop; but I cannot, in my conscience, turn from what I believe to be truth."

"You must go to prison and be burned, if you do not recant."

"I cannot help it."

On the 27th of March, 1555, the boy goes to his death. His brother Robert walks by his side to comfort him.

"God be with thee, my son!" says his father, bidding him farewell.

"We shall meet again, father." He kneels upon the fagots and prays.

"Here is the queen's pardon if you will recant," says the sheriff.

"I cannot accept life on those terms."

"Put the chains around him."

"As you are about to burn here, so shalt thou burn in hell," says a bigoted priest. The fagots kindle.

"Good-bye, William; be of good cheer."

"Good-bye, Robert. I fear neither torture nor death. Lord Jesus, receive my spirit." So he lays down his life for liberty.

THE OLD BOCARDO PRISON, OXFORD.

Bishops Latimer and Ridley are very obnoxious to Mary. On the 16th of October, 1555, they are burned at Oxford.

Archbishop Cranmer loves life. In a moment of weakness he signs a paper condemning the Reformation; but he repents of the act, and is burned, March 21st, 1556. When the fire rises around him, he holds his right hand in the flames till it is burned to a crisp.

"This unworthy hand!" he exclaims, and then commits his soul to Jesus.

The Sheriff of Oxford makes out his bill to the queen:

TO BURN LATIMER AND RIDLEY.	£	s.	d.
For 3 loads of wood fagots	0	12	0
1 load of furze fagots	0	3	5
For the carriage of these 4 loads	0	2	6
A post	0	1	4
2 chains	0	3	4
2 staples	0	0	6
4 laborers	0	2	8
	£1	5	9

TO BURN CRANMER.	£	s.	d.
For 100 wood fagots for the fire	0	6	0
For 100 and ½ of furze	0	3	4
For the carriage of them	0	0	8
For 2 laborers	0	2	8
	£0	12	8

Latimer, and Ridley, and Cranmer were heretics. But Mary had another reason for burning them : they had given an opinion in the question

OLD MARSHALSEA.

of her mother's divorce. Henry demanded their opinion, and for giving it they must be put to death.

For three years the fires blaze. It is not that Mary has any personal hatred toward the men and women whom she causes to be executed. But they will not acknowledge that the Pope is the head of the Church ; they do not believe that the bread is changed into the body of Christ when the priest blesses it. They think for themselves ; and that is not to be tolerated. It is heresy, to be exterminated. Mary thinks of herself as being responsible for the eternal welfare of the people. The Church of Rome demands the rooting-out of the heretics, and she must obey, or lose her own soul. Thousands are cast into prison; and the poor men and women suffer terrible hardships, lying on the cold stones of the Old Marshalsea

BURNING THE HAND.

Prison, in London, or in the Bocardo, at Oxford. Families are broken up. Orphans beg their bread from door to door, or else starve in the streets. By way of warning, some heretics are burned on the hand and liberated. Women are compelled to do penance in public, standing all day with a lighted torch in their hands, exposed to the insults of a motley rabble. No one may succor them—no one take pity. They suffer for

OLD PAUL'S CROSS—RIOTS IN 1556.

conscience' sake. It is the protest of heroic souls in behalf of liberty. They will suffer every indignity, and give their bodies to be burned, rather than yield their convictions of right and duty. Through such sacrifice freedom comes to the human race.

Does such harshness exterminate heresy? On the contrary, the harsher the treatment of heretics, the more they multiply. Those who witness

THE MARTYR'S MEMORIAL, OXFORD.

their heroism in death begin to think that there must be something in their cause which should command respect. The people are weary with the burnings. They begin to murmur. When the priests ascend the pulpit at St. Paul's Cross to preach, the mob hoots them down.

Philip is tired of England. He intended to be king; but Parliament will not let him be crowned. He is only a figure-head—a man of straw, with no voice in public affairs. He is tired of Mary; she is almost old enough to be his mother—pale, weak, sickly, querulous—always repeating her prayers. He is gross in all his tastes. He loves bacon-fat, and can eat a dish of it at a meal. He cannot gratify all his tastes in England; he will cross the Channel to Brussels, and visit his father. He bids Mary farewell, promising with his lips soon to return, but intending never to set foot in England again unless he can be king. We shall see him at Brussels.

CHAPTER XIX.

HOW LIBERTY BEGAN IN FRANCE.

THIRTY years have passed since Doctor Luther nailed his paper upon the door of the Wittenberg church. During this time men have been thinking for themselves in France as well as in Germany. In the old town of Meanx men first began to be independent in thought. It was a wicked place, and the priests were no better than the people—drinking wine and leading dissolute lives.

One day a man came to Meaux bringing a Bible which a priest—James Lefevre—had translated into the French language. He told the people that they must repent of their wrong-doing and live righteously, and preached so faithfully that in a short time the place became one of the most orderly in all France. Instead of swearing, the peasants sung psalms. Instead of carousing after the work of the day was over, they held prayer-meetings. Some of the peasants be-

BERNARD PALISSY.

came preachers, and went into other towns, and so the new religion began to spread. One of those who accepted the new faith was Bernard Palissy, a poor potter. He could set glass, draw portraits, and used to paint images of the Virgin. He travelled from village to village, getting

HEATING THE FURNACE.

a scanty living. He went down into the south-west corner of France, to
Saintes. One day he saw an enamelled teacup, of Italian manufacture.
Nobody in France could make such a cup. How was the glazing put on?
It must be by heat. What was it composed of? He would find out. He
built a furnace, made experiments, but the glazing would not melt. He

sat six nights in succession watching the furnace, but the enamel would not fuse. He was in despair. The fuel was giving out. He must have more heat. What should he do? He had no time to go after more wood; besides, he had no money to pay for it. He seized the chairs, broke them up, and hurled them into the furnace. Still the glazing did not melt. Then he split up the table. His wife and children looked on in amazement. Was he crazy? "More wood! More wood!" That is his only answer. Victory! He has discovered the secret. The glazing melts, and from this time on there will be a new era in the manufacture of earthen-ware.

The potter turns preacher. Others imitate him. Churches are gathered. It is a crime to read the Bible. But the printing-presses are at work; and peddlers are carrying the book in their packs, selling copies here and there, which the people read secretly; and so the new religion gets a foothold all over the kingdom.

Those who accept the new faith no longer spend their time in carousing, but sing psalms instead. Those who laugh at them for being so religious call them *Huguons*—people who sing in the streets. They soon are known as *Huguenots*.

The priests cannot tolerate the heretics. One day a company of soldiers, led by priests, enter the town where the potter is at work. The soldiers are blood-thirsty wretches.

WINE AND GARLIC WILL MAKE HIM STRONG.

"Where are the heretics? Let us cut their throats!" they shout.

They seize the unresisting inhabitants, cut out their tongues, gash their faces, or cleave their heads open. Some are thrust into prison, fourteen burned to death, others maimed for life.

JEANNE D'ALBRET.

From Meaux the soldiers and priests go on to the town of Merindol. The soldiers are let loose upon it. They plunge their spears into the breasts of the defenceless, unresisting people; hurl men and women from the walls upon the rocks below; seize all the goods; tear down the houses, and leave it a scene of indescribable desolation. Have the people revolted? No. Have they committed any crime? No. Are they not law-abiding and peaceful? Yes. They have only stayed away from mass, have been reading the Bible, and worshipping God in their own way. That is all

"All printing must be stopped!"

And now to go back a little. We have previously seen that, after Ferdinand of Spain had driven the Moors out of that country, he made war upon the Queen of Navarre, and seized the southern half of her kingdom, because she was weak, he powerful, and because he wanted it. In his estimation, might made it right.

The Queen of Navarre had a son, Henry, who was only seven years old at the time, and who all through life tried to recover what Ferdinand and Isabella had stolen from him, but failed. His life was one long disappointment. He had a beautiful daughter, Jeanne d'Albret, who was married to Anthony of Bourbon, brother of Antoinette, who married the Duke of Guise, whom we saw at the Field of the Cloth of Gold with Francis I., King of France. There came a day when the gray-haired man, whose life had been so bitter, held a babe in his arms—a grandson.

"Ah! this is the boy who will redress my wrongs! To make him strong, I will give him a little good old wine and garlic," says the delighted grandfather; and he pours wine into the babe's mouth, and rubs its lips with garlic.

Eight years pass, and Jeanne d'Albret and her boy Henry go to Paris to attend a wedding. The grandson of Francis I. is to be married—a boy sixteen years old, named for his grandfather, Francis. His mother is the baby who was born in Florence about the time the kings and nobles met at the Field of the Cloth of Gold. She is the niece of Leo X., and her name is Catherine de' Medici. She is Queen of France. Her confessor in childhood was one of the men who obey orders — a Jesuit priest; and she believes, with them, that if a thing is good in itself, it is right to use any means to attain it. Catherine has four children—Francis (the oldest), Charles, Henry, and Marguerite, a wilful girl, seven years old. Who is the bride? A beautiful girl from Scotland, Mary by name. Her mother is sister of the Duke of Guise, whom we saw at the Field of the Cloth of Gold; and her grandmother was Margaret, sister of Henry VIII., who spent a night in the old manor-house at Scrooby, when she was on her wedding-journey. She has been several years in France. She can write Latin, French, and

CATHERINE DE' MEDICI IN COURT DRESS.

English, and speak the languages fluently. She can sing, is quite a poet, and is very beautiful. Among the guests from Scotland is a learned man, George Buchanan, who composes a nuptial poem:

"To the brave youth a royal kindred lent,
True to thy tender cause, a glad consent,
That dearly made a sister queen a wife,
The gentle partner of thy throne and life;
While beauty, birth, and virtue, nobly fair,
And plighted faith and mutual love, were there."

The King of France, Henry, is greatly pleased with the strong, brave boy from the Pyrenees.

"Will you be my son ?" the king asks.

"No, sir. There is my father, Anthony of Bourbon," the boy replies.

"Ha! ha! you are a brave boy! Will you be my son-in-law, then ?"

"Oh yes, sir."

Perhaps the boy has already taken a fancy to little Marguerite; but, be that as it may, the answer so pleases the king that Henry of Navarre and Marguerite are betrothed on the spot.

The wedding takes place, and there is great rejoicing. The King of

HENRY AND MONTGOMERY AT THE TOURNAMENT.

France holds a tournament, and himself enters the lists against the Duke of Montgomery, from Scotland; but the Scotchman's lance breaks, a splinter pierces the king's eye, who reels from his horse and tumbles to the ground. Nevermore will Henry II., King of France, lead his soldiers to battle. Death comes; and Francis II. and Mary of Scotland are king and queen.

Francis is a spendthrift. He borrows money, lays it out in rich dresses for himself and Mary, and lavishes it upon his favorites. The people come for their pay, and the king laughs in their face. They grow importunate.

"Pay us!" they say.

CHÂTEAU OF AMBOISE.

" Help yourself, if you can."

" You have our money. Pay us !"

" Take yourself off, or the king will have you hanged," says the Cardinal of Lorraine, who sets the carpenters to work building a gibbet in front of the Palace of Fontainebleau.

The cheated creditors hear the sound of the axe and hammer, and turn sadly away. Liberty for the king, but none for the people. In their anger, some who were Catholics turn Huguenots; and so the Huguenots become a political party.

FONTAINEBLEAU.

The priests erect statues of the Virgin Mary along the streets, and watch to see who bows down and worships, and who passes by. The passers-by have a black mark set against their names. War breaks out. The Duke of Guise, who commands Francis's troops, is hard-hearted. He strings Huguenot captives on pales, and throws them into the river Seine. Some die firmly, without a quivering of the lip or trembling of the eyelids.

" How brazen-faced and mad these wretches are ! Death does not abate their pride," says the Cardinal of Lorraine.

The Huguenot leaders are exasperated.   They resolve to rid the country of the Guises, and seize the king, who is in the castle at Blois.   But a traitor reveals the plot, and the Guises remove Francis to the Château of Amboise, on the banks of the Loire, and seize the Huguenots.   What a spectacle is that which Catherine de' Medici, Francis, and Mary, and Catherine's two younger sons, Henry and Charles, witness as they stand on the balcony of Amboise !   In the yard before them are gibbets, with corpses dangling beneath them ; stakes are driven into the ground, and Huguenots are roasting in the flames ; soldiers are hacking unarmed men to pieces, and pitching the dead bodies into the river, till it is choked with corpses. Twelve thousand Huguenots are put to death.

Francis has been king fifteen months.   There comes a day when there is a commotion in the royal palace.   Francis has an abscess above his ear, and he has fainted.   The doctors come, but their skill is of no avail. By the bedside of the dead king stands Mary of Scotland.   The brief days of happiness are ended ; henceforth her life will be full of trouble and sorrow.

Charles IX. is king—a boy ten years old.   Mary must return to Scotland.   With tearful eyes she bids farewell to France — to its joys and pleasures, its sunny skies and blooming fields.   She has been tenderly cared for—servants in livery to wait upon her, to carry her sedan.   She sails to Scotland from Calais.   She sits upon the deck of the vessel, gazing sadly, till the land is lost to view, and then writes an

"ADIEU TO FRANCE.

" Farewell to thee, thou pleasant shore !
     The loved, the cherished home to me,
   Of infant joy—a dream that's o'er ;
      Farewell ! dear France, farewell to thee !

" The sail that wafts me bears away
      From thee but half my soul alone ;
   Its fellow-half will fondly stay,
      And back to thee has faithful flown.

" I trust it to thy gentle care ;
      For all that here remains to me
   Lives but to think of all that's there,
      To love and to remember thee !"

While Mary is thus sailing to her distant home, where we shall see her by-and-by, the boy who was fed on wine and garlic is quietly pursuing his studies in Paris, preparing himself for the duties of life, little knowing the part which he is to play in the great drama of history.

CHAPTER XX.

THE MAN WHO FILLED THE WORLD WITH WOE.

NEVER before was there an assembly in Brussels like that which gathers in the great audience-chamber of the king's palace on October 25th, 1555. Princes, nobles, dukes, lords, ladies, archbishops, and a crowd of church prelates are there. The clock strikes three, and those

CHARLES V.

for whom they are waiting enter the hall. Who are they? There comes a broad-shouldered man, with an ugly face, shaggy beard, white hair, crooked nose, and large underlip. He has lost all his teeth, except a few stubs. Once he was straight as an arrow; but now he walks with a crutch, and has to lean upon another's arm. He looks to be seventy, yet is only fifty-five. It is Charles, Emperor of Germany, King of Spain, Naples, and the Netherlands—the man before whom Doctor Luther made his plea for liberty at Worms. For more than a third of a century Charles has been at war—his armies marching through Spain, Germany, France, and Italy. He has an empire in the New World larger than all his domains in Europe, for, since he came to the throne, Hernando Cortez has overturned the throne of Montezuma. They have discovered the Pacific Ocean, have found mountains of silver and gold in Peru. They have been in the Floridas, and marched under De Soto to the Mississippi. His empire is greater than that ruled by Cæsar. Although he is so great a potentate, the gout has got hold of him. He is an enormous eater. At five o'clock in the morning he eats a chicken fricasseed in sweetened milk; then he has a long nap. At twelve o'clock he has a superb dinner of twenty dishes, and drinks a bottle of wine. At four o'clock he eats his first supper, a heartier meal than his dinner, with pastry and sweetmeats, and drinks goblets of beer. At midnight he eats his second supper, and drinks more beer. He is always hungry, yet everything tastes alike; for, abusing his stomach, he has lost the sense of taste.

The man upon whose arm he leans is only twenty-two, tall, handsome, with dark-brown hair, broad forehead, and clearly cut features. He has brown eyes, and wears a mustache and beard. Although he is so young, he has been appointed commander-in-chief of the army which has been fighting against Admiral Coligny, general of the French armies. People call him William the Silent and Prince of Orange. He is the son of William called the "Rich." He came to Brussels, when he was only eleven years old, to be educated. Charles V. was here, and took a liking to the boy, making him a page at court. He was so fond of William that he wanted him always by his side. He revealed to him all the secrets of State. There are but few men in the throng that know more of state-craft than this young man. He is quick to hear; he understands the intrigues that are all the time going on among kings and princes, to build up and to tear down; but he has the faculty of keeping his thoughts to himself, or of letting them be known at the right time. Let us keep him in remembrance, for, of all the men that walk the earth, few will do more for liberty than he.

Behind the emperor comes Philip, with spindle-legs, a face like his father's (large mouth, heavy underjaw), twenty-eight years old, proud, gross, eater of bacon-fat. Little regard has he for justice. What cares he for the rights and liberties of men? Nothing.

One of the bishops is Anthony Perrenot, of Arras, who can speak seven languages. He has been Charles's chief adviser. He detests the people, and hates heretics. The year after Charles was elected emperor he persuaded him to issue an edict against heretics. These were some of the provisions :

"No one shall print, write, copy, keep, conceal, sell, buy, or give in the churches, streets, or other places, any book written by Martin Luther or any other heretic.

"Any person who teaches or reads the Bible, any person who says anything against the Church or its teachings, shall be executed.

"Any person who gives food or shelter to a heretic shall be burned to death. Any person who is *suspected*, although it may not appear that he has violated the command, after being once admonished, shall be put to death.

" If any one has knowledge of a heretic, and does not make it known to the court, he shall be put to death.

"An informer against a heretic shall recover one-half of the estates of the accused. If any one be present at a meeting of heretics, and shall inform against them, he shall have full pardon."

The Jesuits establish their torture-chamber. Thousands are put to death. The prisons are filled with accused heretics. Other thousands flee the country, seeking a refuge where no priest shall find them, or where they may be free from persecution. Their estates are confiscated, the property being divided between the men who ask questions, the king, and those who inform against the heretics.

Charles has wrenched money from the people of Holland to enable him to carry on his wars in Germany and Italy. He has trampled on their ancient rights and privileges, making himself a despot. But he is weary of life, and is about to resign his crown to Philip. This is the day selected for his abdication. Since he came to the throne he has burned, or hanged, or otherwise put to death, more than one hundred thousand men and women for reading the Bible. He began to burn them in 1523. The first victims were two monks, who were burned in Brussels. The priests incited the people to hunt the heretics out of the land. Not a week passed, scarcely a day, that there was not a burning of heretics ; but though so many were disposed of, they seemed to multiply faster than ever. In 1535, Charles issued another edict. Thus it ran :

"All heretics shall be put to death.

"If a man who has been a heretic recants, he may be killed by the sword, instead of being burned to death.

" If a woman who has been a heretic repents, she may be buried alive, instead of being burned."

For twenty years this has been the law of the land, and the smoke of the burning has been going up to heaven all the time.

Through all these years the emperor has been plundering the Netherlanders, wrenching from them more than two million dollars per annum. Through all these years he has been crushing out the liberties of the State and trampling upon the rights of the people. While heretics are burning,

BURNING THE MONKS.

he gives thanks to God for permitting him to carry out such a glorious work. He is very religious—will not eat meat on Friday, goes regularly to mass, counts his beads, says his prayers, and yet looks on with glee while men and women are smouldering in the flames.

The scene is over. Philip wears the crown, and Charles sails to Spain. He goes to Valladolid; and the bishops and priests of the Inquisition get up a jubilee in his honor—the burning of forty men, women, and children, who have dared to think for themselves. So this man—whom we first saw counselling with Henry VIII. and Wolsey, just before the Field of the Cloth of Gold, and just after it; before whom Martin Luther stood at Worms; whose army has sacked the city of Rome; who took Francis prisoner, and treated him inhumanly; who has filled the world with woe —retires to spend the remainder of his life in seclusion, not fasting and praying, but eating like a glutton, reading despatches, counselling Philip —requiring him to hang and burn till there shall not be a heretic remaining in all his dominions. Even in his retirement he fills the world with woe.

CHAPTER XXI.

PROGRESS OF LIBERTY IN ENGLAND.

THE Duke of Guise has captured Calais, which England has held for a long time, and the loss is a terrible blow to Mary Tudor. " When I die, Calais will be found written on my heart," is her lament over its loss. Her life has been filled with disappointment. It is just forty years since she went, with her mother Katherine, to the Field of the Cloth of Gold. She has seen her mother's divorce and humiliation. All her dreams of happiness which she had fondly indulged in regard to Philip have faded; he has deserted her, and is over in Holland, leading a disreputable life. She hoped to re-establish the authority of the Pope in England; but though she has burned so many men, though the prisons are filled with heretics, though she has compelled thousands to flee the country, the Pope's authority is not re-established. She knows that she is hated, that her subjects will rejoice at the news of her death. She is weak, sickly, querulous, prematurely old. Possibly a sweet, sad face, smeared with blood—the countenance of a lovely, innocent girl—may haunt her at times, when she thinks of the beheading of Jane Grey. In her dreams maybe she sees the good Bishop of Gloucester, or Latimer and Ridley, or the boy of Brentwood, with steadfast faith looking into heaven amidst the flames which she has kindled. Unloved and unlovable, her life is going out in darkness. On November 17th, 1558, she ceases to breathe. This is the epitaph that may be sculptured upon her tomb: "*Died of disappointment.*"

" God save Queen Elizabeth ! Long and happily may she reign !"

The Bishop of Ely (lord chancellor) proclaims it in Parliament. Bells ring, cannon thunder, bonfires blaze, tables are spread in the streets. *Te Deums* are sung. No more burning of heretics ; no more Spanish grandees stalking through the streets insulting the people ; no more spying and plotting by Jesuits to send men to the stake—but liberty, such as never before has been enjoyed !

Elizabeth is at Hatfield; but she comes to London, attended by a thousand nobles, knights, and gentlemen and ladies, accompanied by bands of music. Companies of singers greet her with songs; the people fall on their knees, pouring forth their prayers and praises. So the daughter of Anne Boleyn rides to the Tower, entering it, not now by the Traitor's Gate, but in regal pomp, sovereign of the realm.

On the 12th of January, 1559, she is crowned in Westminster Abbey. Never before has there been so gorgeous a pageant in London. The river swarms with boats and barges, the rowers in livery, the canopies of cloth of silver and gold. The nobles and their ladies appear in their richest robes—coats and gowns of velvet or satin, trimmed with gold and

THE RIVER AVON.

silver lace. Cannon thunder once more, the church-bells ring. All London is astir. Triumphal arches are erected, with allegorical characters. One represents the queen trampling Ignorance and Superstition beneath her feet. Another represents Time leading his daughter Truth by the hand, carrying a Bible, which she presents to the queen. Elizabeth receives it graciously, kissing it, and pressing it to her heart.

"I thank the City for the gift; I prize it above all things," is the queen's reply.

Elizabeth is twenty-five. She has her mother's fair complexion, her father's proud and independent spirit. Now that she is queen, there are plenty of men who would like to marry her. The first to offer himself is the man who eats bacon-fat, Philip, who hurries on his suit almost before

Mary is in her grave.   He sends an ambassador to the Pope to obtain permission to marry, without waiting to see if Elizabeth will say yes or no to

ROOM IN WHICH SHAKSPEARE WAS BORN.

his proposal.   She does not consult the Pope, but sends her answer—No!
The King of Sweden makes proposal; so does the Archduke Charles of
Austria: but Elizabeth will not resign her independence to them.   The
Earl of Leicester is one of her favorites, and the court gossips are sure
that he is to be the favored one.   The Earl of Essex is another favorite.
But Elizabeth will not be beholden to any man; she will rule in her own
royal right.

The people love her, for any one—the poor as well as the rich, the low
as well as the high—may approach her with their petitions.   If she makes
a promise, she never fails of keeping it.   She has a wise man to advise
her, Sir William Cecil, who conducts the affairs of State with great ability.

The bishops will not accept Elizabeth's authority as head of the
Church, and she puts them in prison, and appoints others in their place.
There are no more burnings; but has liberty come to the people?   Not
yet.   The queen, by the uttering of a word, the lifting of a finger, can
imprison men and women, confiscate their estates, or send them into exile,
for no crime but that of incurring her displeasure.

Mary Grey, Jane's sister, marries Martin Keys, who is a judge, and
a good man; but Elizabeth does not like the marriage, and both are put
into prison, where Mary languishes for more than three years.

Notwithstanding the queen exercises such arbitrary power, liberty advances. Men can think and speak more freely than ever before. Those who believe in the Pope, and those who do not believe in him as the head of the Church, if they are not violent in their language, may speak their minds.

A golden age for literature has come. A boy who was born on the banks of the Avon, down which the dust of Wicklif floated to the sea, the boy who went to school in the old town of Stratford, and sat at an oaken desk — William Shakspeare — is reading his plays to Elizabeth, and they are being acted in the theatre of London. A people far enough advanced to read such poetry cannot long be slaves.

As Geoffrey Chaucer gave a great uplift to freedom by his "Canterbury Tales," so does William Shakspeare by his dramas. Men behold the spectacles upon the stage, and see the weaknesses, the follies, the tyrannies

SHAKSPEARE READING ONE OF HIS PLAYS TO ELIZABETH.

of kings, as never before. They begin to understand that monarchs are but men, that the Pope is but a chief priest in the Church, that all men have certain rights, and are entitled to liberties which they never yet have enjoyed. We shall see ere long what will come from their thinking.

CHAPTER XXII.

HOW THE POPE PUT DOWN THE HERETICS.

DUKE HENRY OF GUISE is Prime Minister of France, and his brother, the cardinal, is his chief adviser. They are proud and arrogant, and hate the Huguenots. They believe in the Pope, and are ready to do his bidding. The Huguenots and heretics in France are to be put down.

One Sunday the duke, with his followers, is in the country. He hears the sweet tones of a bell in the village of Vassy.

"What is that bell tolling for?" he asks.

"It is the bell of the Huguenots."

"Are there many heretics here?"

"Yes, and they are rapidly increasing."

The duke, when disturbed in spirit, has a habit of biting his beard; and now he champs it between his teeth as a horse his bit.

"Forward!" It is a word of command to his followers, who draw their swords and ride into town, trampling upon the people. A man hurls a stone, which strikes the duke in the face. The butchery begins, and when it is over there are forty-two corpses and two hundred wounded men, women, and children, weltering in their blood! What have the people of Vassy done? What crime have they committed? Only this —peaceably met to worship God in their own way.

The duke returns to Paris, but the fame of his exploit has preceded him; and the archbishop, carrying the host—the bishops, the priests—all come out in grand procession, meeting him at the city gates, and escorting him through the streets as one who has done a glorious deed. What rights have the Huguenots? None. France is in uproar, for one-fourth of the people are Huguenots. Their leader is the Prince of Condé. His soul is on fire. He thirsts for revenge. He has a talk with his friend, Theodore de Beza, an old minister.

"I can raise fifty thousand men to avenge this insult," he says.

"That may be; but the true Church of God should endure blows, and not give them."

" But only think of the slaughter !"

" God will avenge. Remember that his anvil has used up many hammers. Wait !" So the old minister seeks to restrain the vengeance of the prince.

The Cardinal of Lorraine issues a command for the extermination of the Huguenots. In a little town the Catholics and Huguenots have lived side by side in peace; but, at the command of the cardinal, the Catholics surround the Huguenot church one Sunday, seize all within, take them to a high rock, and pitch them from its top into the river. The Huguenots in Nîmes, maddened by the outrages, retaliate by killing one hundred and ninety-two of their neighbors. It is the beginning once more of civil war. Great battles are fought, towns destroyed, and the country is in terrible turmoil. No one's life is safe. Henry of Navarre is in Paris, attending to his studies. His mother is a Huguenot; but she is in her own dominion, in the Pyrenees. His father —Anthony Bourbon—is a Catholic, and is killed in battle. The Huguenots look to Henry's mother as

THE CARDINAL OF LORRAINE.

their protector. Everybody sees that possibly her son Henry may by-and-by be King of France. Will he be Huguenot or Catholic ? Catherine de' Medici means that he shall be a Catholic; while his mother hopes that he will be a Huguenot. She comes to Paris. Catherine receives her with great demonstrations of affection ; but in a very short time Jeanne d'Albret discovers that, wherever she goes, officers and nobles in Catherine's interest follow her. If she rides in the park of Fontainebleau, or strolls along the walks, there are men always following her—she is a prisoner. She resolves to make her escape. One day there is a grand chase, and her nobles go out with her. They chase a deer through the woods. Suddenly

Jeanne and Henry turn their horses, and a few noblemen who are in her secret turn with her. They ride away, mount fresh horses, ride all day and all night, and so escape from Paris.

The war goes on. France is a battle-field, and so is Europe. There is fighting in Holland, in Germany, and in Italy. Henry is in the great battle of Jarnac, fighting for the Huguenots. He sees his leader, the Prince of Condé, fall, and the Huguenot army defeated. He is only fourteen years of age; but the Huguenot nobles choose him for their leader, and he takes this oath: "I swear to defend religion, and to persevere in the common cause, till death or victory has secured for all the liberty we desire."

CATHERINE DE' MEDICI.

Amidst the Alps there is a beautiful valley, where for many years have lived the Vaudois. It is a small territory — only sixteen square miles. The Vaudois are brave mountaineers. They have always loved freedom. They are peaceable, gentle. They have always thought for themselves, and never have acknowledged the authority of the Pope. They have been many times persecuted; now they shall be exterminated. No longer shall they be permitted to read the Bible, to sing their songs in peace, or pray to God, and not to the priest.

The Pope, Philip, and Catherine de' Medici join to destroy the heretics. An army enters the valley. Jesuit priests accompany it, urging the soldiers to exterminate the Vaudois—men, women, and children; all are to be put to death. The people flee; the soldiers pursue them. The old are slaughtered first. Men who cannot move are stabbed in their beds; women afflicted with palsy, and unable to lift a finger, are killed in cold blood. The soldiers seize whatever pleases them in the houses, and then apply the torch. Men and women and children who lag behind in the

THE VALLEYS OF THE VAUDOIS.

TOWNS: 1. Lucernette; 2. Lucerna; 3. La Tour; 4. St. John.—VALLEYS: 5. Valley of Salabial, or Lucernette; 6. Valley of Lucernette; 7. Valley of Lucerna, or Pelis; 8. Valley of Angrogna (the lower part opening into the Valley of Lucerna); 9. Basin of St. John.—MOUNTAINS: 10. Mt. Friouland; 11. Mt. Brouard; 12. Mt. Palavas; 13. Le Cournaout; 14. Mt. Vaudalin; 15. Peak of Cella Veilla; 16. Cote Roussine; 17. Mountains of La Vachere; 18. Les Sonnaillettes; 19. Costiere of St. John.

flight are cut down without mercy. In vain their cries. The Jesuits
have aroused a spirit of hate in the soldiers, and their cries are unheed-
ed. Weary with wielding the sword, the soldiers take their unresisting
prisoners to the tops of high cliffs, and pitch them upon the rocks below.
To vary the work of destruction, they dig graves, and bury the women
alive. When weary with that, they fill the mouths of the captives with
gunpowder, and blow their heads from their bodies. They crop off their
ears and nose, cut off hands and feet, and leave the poor creatures to die
by slow degrees.

Day after day the massacre goes on. Day after day a great pillar
of smoke ascends from the burning of the homes of the Vaudois. The

JEANNE AND HENRY ESCAPING FROM PARIS.

ground is drenched with blood. Corpses lie in the fields, by the road-
side, at the foot of rocky cliffs, devoured by wolves, eaten by the eagles.

Some of the Vaudois have escaped to the higher Alps, and the soldiers
follow; but suddenly they are confronted by the brave mountaineers, who
fire upon them from the heights above, who hurl rocks upon them, grinding them to the earth. Other soldiers rush up, but are driven back, with
great slaughter. Once more they advance. The Vaudois, concealed behind the rocks, take deadly aim; every bullet tells. A pitiless storm of
leaden rain beats in their faces. Twelve hundred fall. The Vaudois, in-

BURYING THE HERETICS ALIVE.

stead of surrendering, leap, like the chamois, from rock to rock, secrete themselves in caves, and, when the soldiers least expect it, assail them once more. Winter comes, and they are not subdued. Count Trinity, who commands the army, withdraws his troops. In the spring he will finish his work.

In caves or in rude huts, living on the chamois which the hunters kill, eating the bark of trees, the Vaudois, with their wives and children, pass the terrible winter.

In the spring Count Trinity returns, with ten thousand men, to complete the extermination. The Vaudois have selected a spot in the Valley of Pra del Tor, where they have erected a barricade. There they will lay down their lives, if need be, for liberty. In the fastness are their wives and children; for them, for the right to think and act for themselves, they will make a last stand. The drums beat, the trumpets sound. With banners and crosses, the army of Count Trinity moves up the secluded valley. The Italian troops are in advance; behind them are the Spaniards. They are clad in armor—brave men; no troops may stand against them in the open field. But now they are amidst the mountains, hunting a starving people, destitute of everything, ready to die rather than yield; for to yield is to die at the stake. There are ten thousand against a few hundred. Quickly will the veterans of Spain and Italy sweep the all but famished rabble away. Up over the rocks march the infantry of Savoy.

Crack! A soldier rolls down the mountain-side, shot by an unseen foe. Above them hangs a handful of smoke; but no foe is in sight.

Crack! crack! Other soldiers go down, and others still. The battalions fire, but their bullets flatten against the rocks. Faster fall the sol-

THE VALLEY OF PRA DEL TOR.

diers. Only now and then can they see a Vaudois. It is but a glimpse; for they are behind the crags, loading, and firing with deliberate aim. Wherever the soldiers attempt to advance, they are met by a storm of bullets. The ground is strewed with dying and dead. The soldiers hear a chorus of voices ringing out above them. It is the Vaudois chanting a psalm. God is their helper, and to him give they thanks.

For four days the Pope's troops keep up the assault. While the men defend the barricade, their wives supply them with food. Count Trinity is enraged. He will charge with his whole army, and trample the Vaudois beneath his feet. Thus far the Italians have been in the forefront of the attack; but now he orders up the Spaniards. The Jesuit priests bestow their blessings, and stand with uplifted crosses, to urge the soldiers on.

A mass of men ascend the rocky path. Those in front go down; but the men behind sweep over the fallen, up to the barricade. Though they have reached it, they cannot mount it. Muskets flame in their faces. The barricade suddenly swarms with men, who beat them back, tumbling them one upon another—the dead upon the living, and the living upon the dead. In consternation they flee down the mountain-side, leaving all behind them. Soldiers and officers alike are panic-stricken. The Vaudois, leaping from the barricade, chase them down the valley, flinging them from the precipices into the depths below. The entire army is put to flight; and the Vaudois gather up the rich booty left behind. But who can bring back the slaughtered dead—the children hacked asunder, those buried alive, those blown up with powder? No one. Priestly intolerance has ground them into the dust; and it is yet a long, long while before men can be allowed to think for themselves. Will liberty never dawn?

CHAPTER XXIII.

THE QUEEN OF THE SCOTS.

THE girl who bade adieu to France with many tears is in Holyrood Palace, Edinburgh. It was a stormy voyage which Mary had from Calais to Leith, on the Firth of Forth. In France she had been accustomed to grand pageants; but although the nobles of Scotland come with their best outfits to welcome her, though the people receive her with joy, they can make but a sorry display. As she enters Edinburgh, the only music that greets her ears is the singing of a psalm, and the scraping of three-stringed fiddles, and the playing of bagpipes. She is beautiful and refined; but the people whom she has come to rule are uncouth. She is a Papist; they, for the most part, Presbyterians, and intolerant of Papists. Before Mary lies a sea of troubles.

Elizabeth never has forgotten that Mary claims to be the rightful heir to the throne of England; nor will Mary renounce her claim.

MARY, QUEEN OF SCOTS.

Elizabeth wishes her to marry a man of her choosing, Robert Dudley; but Mary will bestow her hand upon whom she pleases, and declines the marriage. She loves literature, and, besides attending to the cares of State, finds time to study Latin, and selects for her instructor George Buchanan, who wrote her nuptial ode when she married Francis. The tutor is fifty years old, and his has been a varied life. He was a poor boy, but an uncle sent him to Paris, where he was educated. He wrote a poem exposing the wickedness of the monks. Cardinal Beaton thrust him into prison for the offence, but Buchanan made his escape. In Portugal, the Jesuits arrested him again, but he escaped a second time. He has been professor in several universities, and is a great scholar. We shall see farther along what he will do for liberty.

LORD DARNLEY.

Mary's cousin comes to see her — Henry Stuart — a tall, beardless young man, who can play the guitar, and sing a song. He can dance gracefully. He is Margaret's grandson—the Margaret who spent a night in the old house at Scrooby. Henry Stuart's father is the Earl of Lennox, who has planned a marriage between his son and Mary. The son is Lord Darnley. They are privately married at Holyrood.

"*Te Deum laudamus!*" It is done, and cannot be undone.

A little, swarthy Italian, David Rizzio, Mary's secretary, who, it is said, is a Jesuit priest, shouts it. Why is he so jubilant? Because it will greatly strengthen, he thinks, the Pope's party in Scotland. Mary does not know what a sad mistake she has made—that her husband is a weak-brained, worthless fellow. He claims the right to rule. He is angered with Rizzio, who has great influence with Mary. He concerts with a ruffian—Lord Ruthven—to put Rizzio out of the way; and one evening when Rizzio is in Mary's apartments, Ruthven and his fellow-conspirators creep softly up a winding stairway, and murder Rizzio in her presence. Darnley tries to persuade Mary that he had nothing to do with the murder. She partly believes him.

On June 19th, 1566, Mary becomes a mother. There is great rejoicing, not only in Scotland, but in England, over the event, for the boy will be heir to both thrones. He is christened with much pomp and ceremony. His mother calls him James, and appoints six women to rock his cradle.

Lord Darnley is so debased that he does not attend the christening, but is having a carouse with some drunken ruffians. Mary has lost all respect for him. The nobles of Scotland are rough, unscrupulous men. The Earl of Bothwell, to whom Mary has given Dunbar Castle, plans a wicked scheme to obtain a divorce from his young and beautiful wife, kill Darnley, marry Mary, and so make himself ruler of Scotland. Mary has shown him many favors, and her letters are full of tender regards. She is still kind to Lord Darnley. He has forsaken her, but, when sick with the small-pox, she does not hesitate to visit him. She remains with

HOLYROOD PALACE.

him one night till eleven o'clock. On her way back to Holyrood she meets a man carrying a bag of gunpowder.

"What are you going to do with it?" she asks.

The man makes no reply, but runs away. At midnight there is an explosion which shakes all Edinburgh. The house in which Darnley was sick is a heap of ruins, and he is a mangled corpse beneath the rubbish. It is soon discovered that Bothwell caused the powder to be placed in the cellar, and hired a man to fire it. He is arrested and tried, but, being rich and powerful, manages to escape conviction.

A few weeks pass. Mary has been out to Stirling Castle to see her baby, and is quietly returning, when suddenly she meets Bothwell and a party of horsemen, who compel her to go with them to Dunbar Castle. She is a prisoner. The earl asks her to marry him. She yields to his solicitations, and they are privately married. Scotland is in an uproar. The nobles will not permit Bothwell to be at the head of Government. They rise against him, and he is driven from the country, to end his days as a pirate. The nobles imprison Mary in a stone castle on a little island in Loch Leven, consigning her to the care of Lord and Lady Douglas. And who are they? Everybody in Scotland knows that Lady Douglas, before marrying Lord Douglas, kept company with Mary's father, and that she is the mother of Mary's half-brother, the Earl of Murray. Lady Douglas claims that she was married to Mary's father, and that the Earl of Murray, and not Mary, is rightful heir to the throne; but very few persons believe that she was ever married to the king.

Mary's best friends desert her. They fear that she knew that Bothwell intended to murder Darnley, and connived at the crime. Her instructor, George Buchanan, writes a pamphlet, in which he sets forth her guilt. He also writes a pamphlet entitled "De Jure Regni"—the Right to Rule. He begins by asking this question, "What is the source of power?" This is his answer:

"The will of the people is the only legitimate source of power."

It is a discovery for which the world has been waiting. Possibly some other man may have thought the same; but George Buchanan puts his thought into print. There is not a king, queen, pope, or priest who will agree with him.

"It originates from a natural, instinctive perception of the principle that men, to have government, must have a governor; and the same principle gives them the right to say who shall govern them."

Kings say that they are appointed by God to rule — their right is divine.

"The people have a right to choose their rulers, and, if they prove to be bad, they have the right to depose them."

The world never heard such a doctrine before. People in England read Buchanan's pamphlet, and begin to take new views of their relations to their rulers. The nobles of Scotland, to carry out the teachings of Buchanan, resolve to compel Mary to resign the crown in favor of her babe, who is not a year old. Two of them visit Mary at Loch Leven, and inform her that she must lay down the sceptre. Of all the sad days of her life, this is one of the saddest. She protests—she pleads with them, with tears; but they are inexorable. We are not to think of the nobles as acting in behalf of the people. Many years must pass before the people will have a voice in government. But if she resigns, the baby will be crowned king, and the nobles, for a long period of years, will be in power, in the baby's name. She is a prisoner, and, against her will, resigns.

On the 25th of July, 1567, Mary's baby is crowned King James VI. The ceremony is performed at Stirling Castle, in the room where, a quarter of a century before, Mary herself had been crowned. And now, through the aid of Lady Douglas's sons, Mary escapes from the Castle of Loch Leven. The nobles who believe in the Pope spring to arms, and war begins. On a hill near Dumbarton the two armies meet, and a fierce battle is fought. The ground is covered with killed and wounded; and when it is ended, Mary sees her followers scattered to the winds. She flees southward. Gladly would she find refuge in France, but there is no ship to bear her to those friendly shores. She reaches England, surrendering herself into the hands of Elizabeth, trusting that she will treat her kindly.

CHAPTER XXIV.

ST. BARTHOLOMEW.

CHARLES IX. of France is a weak-headed boy, and his mother, Catherine de' Medici, keeps him under her thumb. She is a wily woman. She hates the Huguenots, and would like to see the last one in France executed or driven from the kingdom. She has a plan for their extermination; yet it is not wholly hers. The Duke of Guise and the Cardinal of Lorraine are knowing to it, and so is the Pope; and all do what they can to put it in execution. They see that the Huguenots are too powerful to be crushed out in battle. They will bring about a truce, lull the Huguenots into security by fair speeches, and then crush them by stratagem. Catherine remembers that Henry of Navarre— the boy who drank wine and garlic —and her daughter Marguerite are betrothed. They are not lovers. Very few princes and princesses marry for love. Henry is willing to accept Marguerite, because it will heal, he hopes, the nation's troubles; but Marguerite is a proud-spirited girl, and means to have something to say about her own marriage.

MARGUERITE OF LORRAINE.

Charles informs Marguerite that she shall marry Henry whether she does or does not like him. Jeanne and Henry come to the Palace of Blois, and Charles and his mother go out to meet them.

"I give Marguerite not only to Henry, but to the Huguenot party," says Charles.

Little do Jeanne and Henry know what is behind these words.

"I love you, my dear aunt," he says to Henry's mother.

Charles and Catherine take their leave.

"Do I play my part well?" Charles asks of his mother.

"Yes; but it will be of no use to begin, if you do not go on," Catherine replies.

What sort of going-on will it be? Such as the world never saw before, nor since.

Catherine cannot do enough for Jeanne and Henry. She bestows rich and costly presents upon them. One of her gifts to the mother is a pair of perfumed gloves. Jeanne wears them, but in a short time is taken sick. The physicians are baffled by her disease; their medicines do no good. She grows rapidly worse, till death ends her sufferings. The physicians, when asked the cause of her death, shake their heads, or whisper the word "Poison."

CHARLES IX.

The mourning for Jeanne is over, and the marriage of Henry and Marguerite is to be celebrated. All of the great men of the realm come to Paris to attend the festivities — all the Huguenot nobles, wearing their rich dresses. Admiral Coligny, an old man, who has led the Huguenot armies to battle, comes to aid in cementing the peace.

"Don't go; you will be assassinated," say his friends.

"I confide in the word of the king."

He believes that Charles will not see him harmed. The Duke of Guise and all the Catholic chiefs are in Paris. There is a whispering between Catherine and the Catholic leaders.   What is the meaning of it ?

"We will not ask the Huguenots to go into the Church of Notre

ADMIRAL COLIGNY.

Dame to attend the marriage ; we will have it in the street, before the door," says Charles ; and the Huguenots are greatly pleased at his efforts for conciliation.

A canopy and a platform are erected in front of the church.   All Paris is there, every house-top is covered with people, every window occupied.   The ladies of the court are richly robed.   Drums beat ; trumpets sound ; the bells fill the air with their clanging ; cannon thunder, and the royal procession passes through the streets to Notre Dame. The bride and bridegroom stand before the archbishop.

"Will you take Henry to be your husband ?"

Marguerite makes no reply.

"Will you take Henry to be your husband ?"

She does not answer, but pouts her lips and tosses her head.

"Will you take Henry to be your husband ?"

Never by look, or word, or gesture will she accept him.   But she shall, though !   That is what her brother Charles determines.   He knows that she has a proud spirit ; but is the marriage to stop on that account ?   Not if he can make it go on.   He clasps Marguerite's head in his hands, and compels her to nod assent.   The archbishop smiles, and the ceremony proceeds, and Margaret is married in spite of herself.   Then come feastings, and tournaments, and great rejoicings ; for will not this marriage, this union of the Huguenot and Catholic, heal all the divisions, and give peace to France ?   The Huguenots hope so.   But a messenger came from the Pope a few days ago, and he has an interview with the king.

"What is the meaning of all this friendship for the heretics?" the Pope asks.

"I cannot tell you; but the Pope will soon have reason to praise my zeal," is the reply of Charles.

The wedding festivities are over. The Huguenot leader, Coligny, makes ready to leave. He calls and pays his respects to the king, leaves the palace, and walks to his quarters. He is reading a letter as he passes along the street. Crack! The blood spurts from his arm and stains the paper. Some one has fired a pistol at him, and the ball has passed through his arm. He looks calmly around, and sees the smoke curling out of a window. People rush in, but no one is there; the assassin has fled. What is the meaning of it? Is there a trap behind all the feasting and rejoicing? The king hastens to console the brave old man.

"The assassin shall be summarily dealt with," says Charles.

The wedding was on Sunday, and it is now Friday. There are mysterious movements among the Catholics. The Huguenots begin to be alarmed. What is the meaning of the whispering?

Saturday afternoon comes. The Duke of Guise, Duke de Retz, and

NOTRE DAME.

others, are in the king's palace in the Louvre conferring together. Catherine comes into the chamber where they are assembled.

"It must be done to-night. The king must be brought up to issue the order. The Huguenots are leaving."

That is the conclusion of the council. Catherine goes into the king's apartment. She is his mother, has taught him to obey her. He is twenty-one years old—weak, irresolute.

"The Huguenots are going to rise against you. They have sent to Germany for ten thousand men, and to Switzerland for ten thousand," she says.

THE MARRIAGE.

It is a lie; but she can tell a lie quite as easily as she can the truth, when it will serve her purpose.

"You must nip the insurrection in the bud. Coligny is at the bottom of it; you must put him out of the way. If you do not, there will be another civil war."

"I will not have Coligny harmed," Charles replies.

Evening comes. The wax-candles are lighted in the chambers of the palace. Again Catherine enters the king's chamber.

"War is inevitable unless you put Coligny out of the way. Let him be killed, and the rest of the Huguenots will submit."

Charles paces his chamber. He likes the brave old admiral. He has just bidden him a courteous farewell. Shall he turn round and strike him now? In an anteroom is the collector of taxes, Charron, and some of the chief men of Paris, and Count De Tavannes is talking with them in secret.

"You are to put the Huguenot leader, Coligny, out of the way," says De Tavannes.

"We cannot do such a deed."

"Not do it! Then you are not the king's friend. If you do not take hold of it, your own necks will be stretched."

That is not a pleasant thought. The king must be in earnest, and they too will be in earnest.

"Ho! ho! That is the way you take it! We swear that we will play our hands so well that St. Bartholomew shall from this moment be remembered," they reply.

The collector of taxes and those with him take their departure. It is past midnight. Paris is in slumber. Not all are asleep, however. The Duke of Guise, the Duke of Anjou, Catherine de' Medici, and ruffians, with drawn swords, are awake on this Sunday morning—this Day of St. Bartholomew. At daybreak a bell will toll, and the crushing-out of the Huguenots will begin. The Duke of Guise is nervous, and so is Catherine. So many know of what is about to happen, that they fear the Huguenots will hear of it.

Catherine hastens to Charles's chamber once more. He is sitting in a chair, moody, angry, silent. He has acquiesced in the plan till now; but as the hour for its consummation approaches, is irresolute. It will be so mean to have the old admiral, and others who have confided in his word, assassinated. Poor weakling that he is, there is still left a little of

THE LOUVRE.

his better nature. The education that he has received from his mother— that the end always justifies the means—the school of falsehood in which

ASSASSINATION OF COLIGNY.

he has been taught, has not quite obliterated all sense of what is right and honorable.

"Since you will not have the leader of the Huguenots harmed, since you are bent on having war once more, permit me to retire with your brother to a place of safety."

He has always obeyed her. He is a boy, with no mind of his own. He springs to his feet.

"Do it! do it! Kill him! Kill all the Huguenots in Paris, that none may be left to reproach me! Give the orders at once!" He rushes out of the room, and into his own chamber.

"Strike the bell!"

A moment later, and the bell on the church of St. Germain l'Auxerrois begins tolling at half-past one in the morning. The brave old admiral is asleep in his chamber, with his bandaged arm lying upon the counterpane. A Huguenot minister is sitting by his side, and Doctor Ambrose Parr is in a chamber near by.

Boom! boom! boom! The admiral hears the tolling. There is a tramping of feet in the street; men are rushing up the stairway of the hotel. The admiral understands it. His hour has come. He springs from the bed and puts on a dressing-gown.

"Say a prayer for me, my friend. I commit my soul to my Saviour." The doctor comes in.

"What is the meaning of this commotion?" asks the doctor.

"God is calling us. I am ready. Please leave me, and save yourselves."

The minister and the doctor seek safety in flight—up-stairs, out upon the roof, reaching another house. The door of the admiral's room bursts open, and ruffians, with spears and swords, rush in.

"Are you the admiral?"

"Young man, I am. You come against a wounded old man. You cannot much shorten my life."

The spear goes into his bosom.

"Oh, if it were only a man! but it is only a horse-boy."

The ruffian beats him over the head. Others enter and plunge their swords into the prostrate form.

"Have you done it?" It is the Duke of Guise calling from the street. "Yes."

"Throw him down."

The ruffians drag the lifeless body to the window, raise the sash, and throw it out. It falls with a thud upon the ground. The Duke of Guise looks at it. The face is smeared with blood. He wipes it away with a corner of the dressing-gown. "'Tis he, sure enough;" and stamps his heel into the face.

Ah! Duke of Guise, gloating over the form of the noble foe who was ever your equal in the field or in the cabinet, there will come another day. God never forgets!

A soldier severs the head from the body, and takes it to Catherine de'

JUST BEFORE DAYBREAK, SUNDAY MORNING—ST. BARTHOLOMEW.

Medici. So the head of John the Baptist was brought to Herod's wife. To whom does Catherine send it? Who of all on earth will be most pleased to receive such a present? Who but the Pope—her uncle! A messenger carries it to Rome, that the Pope may see with his own eyes that the great Huguenot leader is dead.

Bells are tolling in every steeple. Torches glare in the streets. Armed men are rushing frantically from house to house, breaking in doors, rushing into chambers, murdering men and women in their beds, or plunging their swords into their bosoms as they attempt to flee. Muskets are flashing. Charles himself fires upon the panic-stricken fugitives. All through the hours of the summer night the scene of death goes on. Henry Condé and Henry of Navarre are seized and brought before Charles. Catherine does not want them killed. She has other plans.

"I mean to have but one religion in my kingdom. There shall be mass or death. Make your choice." It is Charles who utters it.

"You have promised liberty of conscience to the Huguenots. I will take time to consider it," is the reply of Henry of Navarre.

"As for me, I shall remain firm in my religion though I give my life for it," Henry Condé replies.

"You rebel—you son of a rebel, if you do not change your language before three days, I will have you strangled!"

Of the throng of Huguenot nobles who come to Paris to attend the wedding, all are seized. The Swiss Guards of the king are let loose upon them, and all are massacred. There they lie in a heap in the court-yard of the Louvre—two hundred of the noblest men of the kingdom. Charles, Catherine, the ladies of the court, go out and behold them—the men with whom they danced three days ago! They gaze upon their ghastly countenances besmeared with blood, and indulge in ribald laughter. So, it is said, the hyenas laugh when they have dug up the bones of the dead, and crunch them beneath their teeth.

PARTING TO MEET NO MORE.

Never before was there such a festival of St. Bartholomew. Families are broken up. There are sudden partings, husbands from wives, parents from children, young men from the maidens whom they love, to meet no more, maybe, this side the grave. In the river are thousands of floating corpses — men, women, children. No age or sex is spared.

"Kill the heretics!" It is the cry of the priests and the soldiers. What though fair maidens plead for mercy? What though mothers pray that the lives of their infants may be spared? There is no pity, and the massacre goes on; and not only in Paris, but in the country—in Lyons, Bordeaux, Orleans. Seventy thousand men, women, and children are slaughtered.

The bells of Rome are ringing, and the guns of St. Angelo thundering; bonfires blaze; and Gregory XIII., attended by cardinals, archbishops, bishops, and a great throng of prelates, march in procession. A *Te Deum* is chanted, and the Pope commissions the painter Vasari to paint the scene of the massacre, and employs an artist to engrave a medal commemorative of the event. The preachers in Rome deliver eloquent orations, and a messenger carries a golden rose to Charles as a present from the Pope.

Fifteen months pass. Charles has acted strangely. The Venetian

THE PICTURE WHICH THE POPE ORDERED TO BE PAINTED.

ambassador, Cavilli, makes the king a visit, and writes of his appearance: "He is melancholy and sombre. He dares not look any one in the face. He drops his head, and closes his eyes. It is feared that the demon of vengeance has taken possession of him. He is becoming cruel."

He grows weak and feeble, and will have no one near him except his nurse. His conscience is awake, and his mind racked with remorse. The screeches of the victims of St. Bartholomew are ringing in his ears.

He sees men, women, and children flying through the streets crying for mercy, pursued by blood-thirsty wretches. The air is filled with ghosts; the ground strewed with ghastly corpses.

"Ah, nurse! what blood! what murder! Oh, what evil counsel have I followed!" Then he prays. "O God, forgive me! Have mercy on me!" Despair sets in. "I'm lost! I'm lost!" On July 30th, 1574, he ceases to breathe, and Henry, Duke of Anjou, Catherine's younger son, becomes Henry III., King of France.

CHAPTER XXV.

HOW THE "BEGGARS" FOUGHT FOR THEIR RIGHTS.

OF all people in Europe, none are more peacefully inclined than the inhabitants of Holland. They are great workers, and have no desire to engage in quarrels with anybody. There was a time when a portion of their land was under the sea. The water was not deep, and the people built dikes—laying down bundles of brush, trunks of trees, heaping mud upon them, so fencing out the ocean. Then they erected windmills, and pumped out the water. They laid off the land into fields and gardens, built their houses, made the canals their highways, and so, as the years rolled on, there grew up a country, as it were, from beneath the sea.

A DOG TEAM.

The Dutch have little time to spend in pleasure. In winter, when the canals are frozen, they get up skating parties; but in summer the butter and cheese must be made, and the cabbages cultivated. Everybody must work. Even the dogs are put into harness. By hard, patient labor they have become a thrifty people. Once they all accepted the Pope as the head of the Church; but they have begun to think for themselves, and are fast becoming heretics. Charles, before he resigned his crown to Philip, began to burn and hang them. He taxed them unjustly, confiscated their property, cast them into prison. The men who ask questions have been sending thousands of men and women to jail. Fires blaze, and men are burned, not because they have committed crime, but because they read the Bible. Since Charles laid aside the crown, Philip has been crushing out the heretics with all his might. More than one hundred thou-

WILLIAM THE SILENT.

sand have been put to death, thrust into jail, or driven from the country. The people have risen in revolt. One of Philip's officers called them a nation of beggars; they have accepted the term, and have elected as their leader the Silent Man, William, on whose shoulder Charles leaned when he resigned his crown. The Silent Man is giving his money, his time, his energies, to the cause. He was a Catholic; but he sees that men have a right to think for themselves, and is ready to lay down his life, if need be, for liberty. He has been defeated in battle again and again, has been so straitened in circumstances that he had not money enough to buy a breakfast; but he has gathered another army, and is determined to drive the Spaniards out of Holland.

In 1574, the Spaniards are besieging Leyden. Philip offers the citizens of the town a pardon if they will surrender. But what have they done that they should accept a pardon? Nothing. They have been thinking for themselves, and reading the Bible, which the Pope has forbidden; but have they not a right to read it? If so, they will not ask pardon of any one.

THE GREAT CANAL.

Philip is in Spain, eating bacon-fat and witnessing the burning of heretics. This is the answer which the people of Leyden send to him:

"As long as there is a man left, we will fight for our liberty and our religion."

General Valdez, one of Philip's officers, is sent by the Duke of Alva to level the city to the ground. After taking Leyden, he will sail up the Great Canal to Amsterdam. Five miles from Leyden is a great dike—the Land-scheiding. Three-quarters of a mile nearer is another, called the Greenway. There is another still, called the Kirkway. Inside of these are the forts and redoubts—sixty-two in all, which are in the possession of the Spaniards. Half a pound of meat and half a pound of bread is all they have to eat a day, the aldermen weighing it out to each person in the city. On every side the Spaniards pitch their tents. The people of Leyden are shut in. Only by pigeons can they send word to the Prince of Orange. They have no soldiers; but every citizen is a soldier, and so is every woman. May and June pass; there are frequent skirmishes.

"We will pay a bounty for the head of every Spaniard," say the burgomasters of Leyden, and now and then a man steals out, kills a

Spaniard, cuts off his head, brings it in, and sticks it upon a pole on the walls, that the Spaniards may see it.

The Spanish general expects to starve the "beggars" into submission. The days go by. The Prince of Orange cannot raise an army large enough to fight Valdez; but there is one thing that can be done—he can let in the sea upon the land, and drown out the hateful myrmidons of the Pope and of Philip. The people hail the proposition with joy. "Better a drowned land than a lost land. We can pump it dry again, if we drown it; but if we yield to the Spaniards, our liberties are gone forever," they say.

"Cut the sluices!" It is the order issued by the Silent Man, and men go to work with their spades digging away the dikes. But what will the people in the country do? They must leave their homes. There is a scene of confusion. They take their pigs, cattle, goats, their goods and chattels, on board their boats, and hasten to Amsterdam. It is hard to see the property disappearing beneath the waves, to behold their houses floating away; but better this than to give up their rights.

A pigeon flies into Leyden with a letter fastened to its neck. The burgomaster reads the letter to the people:

"The dikes are cut. There are two hundred vessels ready to sail to your relief loaded with provisions."

The cannon thunder, the bells ring, the people sing a psalm of thanksgiving over the joyful news, for starvation is staring them in the face.

THE FORTIFICATIONS.

The Spaniards wonder what is going on in the city. It is not long, however, before they know that something is going on outside which they never dreamed of. The water begins to rise around them. What is the meaning of it? It rises slowly. Light dawns upon them. The dikes are broken, and an enemy which they will be powerless to resist is stealing upon them. It rises ten inches, and comes to a stand-still. They are safe. It will not rise any higher. They laugh at the "beggars."

"Go up the steeples, you 'beggars,' and see if the ocean is coming to your relief."

The people go up and look toward the north. They can see water covering the fields, but then it is only a few inches deep, and the Spaniards' camp is still on dry land. They gaze in sorrow, for the bread and meat are nearly gone. People are already starving.

There are sea "beggars" as well as land "beggars," and the "beggars" of the sea are getting ready to come to the aid of their beleaguered brethren.

Admiral Poisot commands them. They are hardy sailors — twenty-five hundred in number. The man on the tower in Leyden discovers the "beggars" of the sea. There they are, only five miles away, two hundred armed vessels loaded with provisions. The vessels have sailed in over the submerged land fifteen miles, passing over fields and gardens. The fleet reaches the great dike—the Land-scheiding, which is guarded by the Spaniards; but the "beggars" of the sea open fire upon them. Some of them leap out of the ships, wade to the dike, and quickly overpower the Spaniards. None are spared, but all are put to death.

Now the "beggars" are at work with their spades breaking down the dikes, the water rushes through, and the vessels float on.

The admiral seizes the second main dike, the Greenway, and breaks it down. He floats his ships to a stone bridge, a fortress in itself, swarming with Spaniards. The admiral cannot take it. His vessels ground. The wind is off the shore, and the water, instead of rising, is falling away. For a week the vessels lie there imbedded in the mud.

The wind suddenly whirls north-west, and the waves roll in once more. The vessels float. They are only half a mile from Leyden, but between the fleet and the city is the Kirkway, and the forts, swarming with Spaniards and bristling with guns. Oh, how dismal the days in the besieged town! Thousands have died of starvation. Bread—there is none. All the malt-cake has been eaten. The people are eating dogs, cats, and rats. A few cows only are left. When one is killed, every scrap is eaten. They boil the hide, make it into soup. They eat the intestines, boil the horns to get the last particle of marrow. The famishing creatures strip

LEYDEN.

the leaves from the trees, dig up the roots of grass growing in the streets, and devour them.

Infants starve in the arms of their mothers, and mothers drop dead in the streets, or creep away to die in some lonely place. The watchmen, as they go their rounds, find corpses everywhere. Eight thousand have died of starvation. The air is reeking with malaria, but still the people of Leyden hold out.

Pieter Van der Werff is burgomaster. He stands in the market-place tall, haggard with hunger, worn out with watching.

There are a few faint-hearted ones. "Give up the city," they cry.

"Would you have me surrender? I have taken my oath to hold the city. May God give me strength to keep it! Here, take my sword; plunge it into my body; divide my flesh to appease your hunger, if you will; but, God helping me, I never will surrender."

Brave Van der Werff! For this heroic firmness your name shall go down the centuries.

"Ha! ha! How do you rat-eaters get on? The sea hasn't come to Leyden yet." It is the taunt which the Spaniards shout, secure in the fortifications.

"You call us rat-eaters. We are; but so long as you can hear a dog bark inside of the walls, you may know that the city holds out. We will eat our left arms, and fight with our right. When we can stand no longer, we will set fire to the city, and perish in the flames, rather than give up our liberties," is the answer hurled into the teeth of the Spaniards.

The night of October 1st comes. The city is at its last gasp. Day after day the wind has been off the shore, and the fleet has lain motionless in the mud. The wind whirls south-west and blows a hurricane. The sea is rolling in. The water rises. The vessels float. "Hurrah!" The cry goes up from the "beggars" of the sea. The morning comes, the fleet is close upon two of the forts. The Spaniards are seized with a panic. They leave the fortifications, and rush along the dike. The "beggars" of the sea chase them, throwing harpoons, and striking them down just as they have harpooned the walruses of the north seas. Only one fort blocks the path of the "beggars" now. Let them but take that, and the city will be saved. Night comes on. In the morning the "beggars" will open upon the fortress with all their cannon. The waves are rolling in, dashing over the dikes. Dark and gloomy the hours. In the city everybody is astir; for when morning comes the citizens will make a sortie, and fight their way to the fleet.

Crash! There is a sound of a falling wall. The citizens stand aghast, for the waves have undermined the wall of the city, and there is a wide gap through which the Spaniards can enter the town.   There is a hubbub in the Spanish camp.   All is lost!   No, not all.   Day dawns.   The forts are silent.   No Spaniards are in sight, not even a sentinel pacing his beat.

Just outside of the fort is the fleet.   The cannon are loaded, and the men stand with lighted matches.   The "beggars" of the sea are determined to sweep all before them.

The admiral sees a man wading through the water toward the fleet, while the people in the city see a boy waving his cap from one of the forts.   What is the meaning of it?

"They are gone!" he cries.

There is not a Spaniard left.   At midnight they fled.   The falling of the wall filled them with consternation.   They think the citizens are making a sortie, and flee along the dike, and now they are miles away.   They might have stayed secure.   The fleet might have been beaten back.   Had they waited till daybreak, they might have marched into the city over the fallen wall.

Up to the town sail the ships; out from their houses creep the starving citizens.   The sailors are tossing meat and loaves of bread on shore.   The starving creatures eat as wolves eat; and then they enter the great church, fall on their knees, and, with tears upon their cheeks, give thanks to God.

THE OLD CHURCH.

Never again shall the Spaniard beleaguer Leyden; never again shall Philip encamp his armies in their fields, over which the sea is rolling. They have drowned their land, but have saved that which is worth more than houses, lands, or life—their liberty.   From this time on they will wage war against the Spaniards till they drive them from the country. There is great rejoicing in Amsterdam.   The people send more supplies to their friends in Leyden. Other cities contribute.   Elizabeth of England befriends them.   She is greatly moved when she hears of their sufferings, and of their bravery

and endurance.   She sends Sir William Davison with money to aid them.
Sir William has a young man for his secretary, William Brewster, who
performs his duties so faithfully that the burgomaster presents him with

AMSTERDAM.

a gold chain.   Let us take a good look at this young man, for we shall
see him by-and-by in the old manor-house at Scrooby, and on the shores
of New England, laying the foundations of liberty in the New World.
Sir William Davison is his friend; and Elizabeth's great minister, Sir
Thomas Cecil, has appointed him to this position.   He is in high favor.
He loves liberty, and his soul is greatly stirred at the outrages committed
by the Spaniards.   He is learning early in life that liberty is worth more
than all things else.

CHAPTER XXVI.

EIGHTEEN years have passed since Mary of Scotland fled from the kingdom. She has been a prisoner the while. Going back to that day when she came, weary and worn, to Carlisle, we see her sending a letter to Elizabeth asking for an interview, which the Queen of England will not grant, but who sends Sir Francis Knollys to give a reason for the refusal. While Sir Francis is on his way, a letter comes from Catherine de' Medici. Thus it reads: " Princes should assist each other to chastise and punish subjects who rise against them, and are rebels against their sovereigns."

Catherine wants Elizabeth to march an army into Scotland to put down Mary's half-brother, the Earl of Murray, who, though ruling in the name of Mary's son, is in reality king.

Sir Francis has an interview with Mary.

" Some suspicions are abroad in regard to the complicity of your grace in the murder of Lord Darnley, and the queen will appoint a commission to investigate the matter," says Sir Francis.

" I am not answerable to the Queen of England. Sovereigns are amenable to no one," is Mary's reply.

" Princes may be deposed by their subjects in some cases—if insane, for instance, or if they have committed murder," Sir Francis replies.

The tears steal down Mary's cheeks. This is the new doctrine. Kings and queens answerable to their subjects? Never. To admit it will be admitting that they can do wrong. It is the doctrine which George Buchanan inculcated in that little pamphlet which he published, written in Latin, and entitled " De Jure Regni." To admit such a doctrine will be admitting that subjects can cut off the heads of sovereigns; whereas from time immemorial only sovereigns have had the right to decapitate subjects.

George Buchanan is superintending the education of Mary's boy, King James. The boy is proud and wilful, and thinks that, as he is king, he may do as he pleases.   One of his playmates is the young Earl of Mar, who has a tame sparrow, which James would like to own.

"Give it to me," is his demand.

"I won't," the Mar boy replies, not wishing to part with his pet.

"It is mine.   I am king," James retorts, and seizes it.

"Take that!" and Mar gives him a blow in the face with his fist.

QUEEN ELIZABETH.

"What is all this fuss about?" George Buchanan asks, as he enters the room.

"He has seized my sparrow," says Mar.

"It was mine.   I am king," James answers.

"King, are you?   I'll teach you not to take things by force;" and the boy-king has his ears boxed.

One day George Buchanan is reading, and James and Mar disturb him.

"Be quiet!" says Buchanan.

"I shall make as much noise as I please. I have the right; I am king."

George Buchanan lays down his book, takes the King of Scotland over his knee, and gives him a spanking. The Countess of Mar rushes in, with her hands uplifted in horror.

"How dare you lift your hand against the Lord's anointed?" she cries.

It is not a very polite reply which gruff George Buchanan makes; but he informs her that the boy, although he is king, must behave himself, and have respect to the rights of others.

Mary's friends—the Cardinal of Lorraine in France, the Duke of Norfolk in England—are intriguing with some of the nobles of Scotland to create disaffection in England against Elizabeth. The Duke of Norfolk will rally his followers; the Cardinal of Lorraine and the Duke of Guise will raise an army in France; the Scots will take the field, bring about a revolution in England, dethrone Elizabeth, liberate Mary, and make her queen not only of Scotland, but of England. The Duke of Norfolk proposes to marry her. He is rich and powerful, and under his lead England and Scotland shall once more be brought under the authority of the Pope.

The Pope knows what is going on. He has a plan for the extermination of all who will not submit to his authority. They shall be crushed out in England and France alike.

"Take no prisoners, but kill all who fall into your hands," is his message to the Duke of Guise.* He sends a present to the Duke of Alva, Philip's blood-thirsty general, who is trying to crush out the liberties of the people of Holland. Fugitives from France and the Netherlands flee to England to find protection, and are protected.

Shall Elizabeth release Mary from prison? It is the one great question. It was a breach of hospitality to put her in prison. Mary came into England a fugitive. For eighteen years she has been a prisoner. Why? Because she is the central figure around whom all the conspirators rally. The Jesuits are travelling through the country denouncing Elizabeth. Philip of Spain is sending his spies throughout the land to stir up the people to rebel. The Duke of Guise will help. The disaffected Scots will rally to overthrow the Earl of Murray.

On February 25th, 1570, the Pope publishes a bull absolving all Eng-

---

* "History of the Popes," Ranke, vol. i., p. 383.

lishmen from allegiance to Elizabeth, and enjoining them not to obey her commands. The Earls of Northumberland and Westmoreland begin the rebellion. Shall Elizabeth remain quiet, and see the affections of her subjects alienated?

Now comes the news that the streets of Paris are running with the blood of murdered Huguenots. If heretics are murdered in France, why may they not be in England?

On September 5th, 1570, the Bishop of London writes a letter to Sir William Cecil, Elizabeth's prime minister: "Men's hearts ache for fear that this barbarous treachery will not stop in France, but will reach us."

Bishop Sandys, who owns the old manor-house at Scrooby, writes to Sir William Cecil: "Cut off the Scottish queen's head forthwith."

Why does Bishop Sandys desire that Mary shall lose her head? Because that she is the one individual around whom all the powers of Spain, France, Scotland, and Rome rally, for the overthrow of the government in Church and State, established by Henry VIII., overthrown by Mary, and re-established by Elizabeth.

Parliament passes a law making it treason for any one to publish the Pope's bull in England, or to deny that Elizabeth is rightful queen; but, notwithstanding the law, the Jesuits are determined to drive Elizabeth from the throne. What care they for law? To the Pope alone are they amenable.

A great number of Jesuit priests—Englishmen, who have been studying at Douay, in France—come one by one.

"Elizabeth is a usurper. She is no longer queen. The Pope has deposed her. Mary is the true queen." They whisper it to the people, to incite them to rebellion. It is not long before the priests are arrested.

"We are not traitors. You persecute us because we are Catholics," say the prisoners.

"For fourteen years none have been persecuted on account of their religion here in England. Do you not support the Pope's bull?" the judges ask.

"The Pope in his bull says it is not binding on us to resist the queen, unless the bull can be executed," the Jesuits respond. That is what Loyola taught.

"That means that when you are strong enough you will drive the queen from the throne. If England is attacked, will you support the queen?"

The Jesuits make no reply. They are condemned as traitors, as inciters of rebellion, and are executed.

Now comes the news, in 1584, of the assassination of William, the Silent Man. Papists did it. All England becomes hot against the Jesuits. They are arrested by scores, and put to death. The Jesuits are suspected and closely watched. Those who have been to confession, or attended mass in secret places, are thrown into prison. The country is in no mood to tolerate liberty of conscience.

Over in Paris is Francis Walsingham, who is beating the Jesuits at their own game. He has his spies everywhere. Servants who wait on tables, hair-dressers, chamber-maids, valets, coachmen—men in all stations —have their eyes and ears open day and night to see and hear what is going on, and Sir Francis pays them. He discovers that there is a plot to assassinate Elizabeth and place Mary on the throne. The conspirators in France and Spain are in correspondence with others in England. Mary knows what is going on. The conspirators in England are arrested and executed. What shall be done with Mary? The ministers appoint a court to try her.

"I am not a subject, to be tried; I am a queen," is Mary's protest.

"You cannot try one who reigns by the command of God," say her friends.

"She has resigned her crown, and is no longer queen," the judges reply.

"She resigned because she was compelled to, and therefore it is not binding," her friends respond.

"*The safety of the people is the highest law*," say the judges, overthrowing at once the doctrine that kings and queens have rights so sacred that they cannot be dealt with. The judges have read George Buchanan's little pamphlet, and the world is beginning to understand that kings and queens are amenable to law as well as common people.

The court declares Mary guilty, and Parliament presents an address to Elizabeth asking her to sign a warrant for her execution, for no one can be executed unless the queen signs the warrant. Elizabeth hesitates. Mary is her cousin. Shall she put her to death? Parliament has declared her to be an enemy to the public peace — a conspirator. If Elizabeth were to die, Mary would claim the throne, and there would be no end of trouble. Henry III. of France sends a letter threatening Elizabeth with vengeance if Mary be put to death. Mary's son James sends commissioners to intercede for her; while Philip II. of Spain prepares to make war on England.

Elizabeth is moody and silent. Those who wait upon her hear her talking to herself.

" Strike, or be struck !"

A letter comes from Spain : " Philip is fitting out a great fleet and army to invade England."

Elizabeth appoints Earl Howard, a Catholic, as lord high admiral, to command her fleets, which gives great offence to some of her friends ; but the earl is an Englishman, and his allegiance to his sovereign is his first duty. Elizabeth will trust him. She talks over Mary's case with him ; what they say no one knows : but when the earl leaves her, he calls in Sir William Davison.

" The queen desires you to prepare a warrant for the execution of the Queen of Scots," he says.

Sir William writes it in secret, though quite likely his secretary, William Brewster, knows what he is doing, for Sir William places implicit confidence in him. When it is ready, Sir William enters the queen's apartment, and Elizabeth signs her name in a bold hand, as she is wont to do. A messenger hastens away with the document ; and in the Castle of Fotheringay the Scottish queen, whose life has been one of so many vicissitudes, who has seen little happiness, but much sorrow, meets her sad and mournful fate. She has committed no crime ; but while she lives, the liberties of England are in danger of being overthrown, and the people breathe more freely when they hear that she is dead.

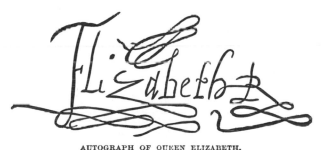

AUTOGRAPH OF QUEEN ELIZABETH.

CHAPTER XXVII.

THE RETRIBUTION THAT FOLLOWED CRIME.

THE Huguenots of France are not exterminated by the terrible mas
sacre of St. Bartholomew; there are still one hundred thousand in
the kingdom.   Catherine de' Medici and the Duke of Guise are determined to root them out, and the young king, Henry III., is a pliant tool
in their hands.

"I will have but one religion in the State," is the edict of the weak
boy-king.   The Huguenots must give up their religion, or fight for life,
liberty, and property.   Give up they will not.   A terrible war begins.
Henry of Navarre is the leader of the Huguenots.   The whole country is
disturbed.   Amidst all the commotion, what is the young King of France
doing?   He is down in the city of Lyons, buying all the little dogs, parrots, and monkeys he can find—paying more than one hundred thousand
crowns for them.   With him are two hundred women, and as many men
—ladies and gentlemen of the court, who have nothing to do but to eat
and drink, dance and sing, and dawdle their time away; while the people, with no security of life or property, with no freedom of thought or
action, are plundered by the tax-collectors of their hard earnings, to maintain the worthless, dissolute creatures in all their mock gentility.

We come to 1588.   The Duke of Guise has been laying a plot to get
rid of Henry III., and also Henry of Navarre, the leader of the Huguenots, who is heir to the throne.   The duke is not content with being a
duke; he must be king.   But how shall he do it?   He will summon the
Jesuits.   He will manage to have his own immediate friends appointed
chief inquisitors.   He consults with the Holy League.   But the king is
aware of what is going on.   He sees through the plan of the wily man,
who is on his way from Nancy, a town in Northern France, to Paris.

"You must not enter Paris without my consent," is the order which
the king sends to him.   What does the Duke of Guise care for that?
Nothing.

"If you will break with the king, I will send you three hundred thousand crowns, and seven thousand soldiers," is the word which comes to the duke from Philip II.

The Leaguers are in Paris, secretly stirring up the people, distributing money to the rabble.

"What a noble, generous man the Duke of Guise must be! He does not spend his money buying poodles and monkeys!" So say the people, as the coins drop into their hands. They are ready to take up arms for such a man against the weak-minded Henry.

At noon, May 12th, a man in a white doublet, black cloak, tall, dignified, with a scar on his face, enters the Gate of St. Martin. All Paris is out to welcome him. "Hurrah for the Duke of Guise!" The shout runs along the streets. The people come out with their arms, and the king flies in terror to a place of safety. Then there are negotiations, and the weak, vacillating king comes to terms, accedes to all the duke's demands, publishes an edict against the Huguenots, and another declaring that Henry of Navarre has no right to the throne. The king appoints to office all whom the duke says must be appointed

HENRY III.

—the duke himself being made lieutenant-general, commanding the army.

Christmas comes. The duke is master. The king feels his degradation.

"What shall I do?" He puts the question to one of his trusty friends.

"Arrest the duke, and have him tried."

"Strike him at once. He is planning your destruction. You never can try him for treason. Strike, and get rid of him," is the advice of another.

Walls have ears; and a servant, a spy of the duke's, hears it. The duke is sitting at dinner, when a servant hands him a note. Thus it reads: "The king intends to kill you."

The duke takes a pen and writes, "He does not dare to." The duke does not know, nor does he care, who sent the note, for he is conscious of his power. To-morrow morning he is to meet the king in council, and he will make new demands more humiliating to the king. Morning comes, and the duke enters the council-chamber. It is cold and chilly.

"Will you kindle a fire?"

A servant lights the wood upon the hearth, and the duke warms himself, eating, while doing it, some plums, which another servant brings him.

"WITH WHAT MEASURE YE METE, IT SHALL BE MEASURED TO YOU AGAIN."

"The king would like to see you in his chamber." The Secretary of State brings the message. Now he will make his demands. Every Huguenot shall be exterminated. He pulls up his cloak, and takes his hat. Some of the councillors have come in. He bows to them with kingly grace, and passes through a door. Whip! whip! whip! whip! whip! Five strokes from as many poniards. Nine men have been standing concealed in the passage-way, and five of them have plunged their weapons into his body.

"God have mercy!" It is his only cry. There he lies, close by the king's bed, his blood flowing from five ghastly wounds.

The king comes from an inner chamber. " Is it done ?"

" Yes."

The king bends over the body and kicks it. Who was he that stamped the heel of his boot into the face of the dead Coligny, sixteen years ago, on the night of St. Bartholomew ? The Duke of Guise, now weltering in his gore, did not stop on that eventful night to ponder the words of Christ concerning retribution, " With what measure ye mete, it shall be measured to you again." But the retributive hour has come, and the words spoken by that Carpenter of Galilee are not fiction, but stern and irreversible fact. The time has been long, but the measure has come at last.

" I am king." Henry speaks the words, and goes to see his mother, Catherine, old and feeble now.

" How are you this morning ?"

" Better," Catherine replies.

" So am I."

" You have had the duke put out of the way, I hear. I hope the cutting is all right ; but now for the sewing." So the mother addresses the son. Thirteen days later, the grandniece of Leo X.— the woman who poisoned Jeanne d'Albret, who planned the massacre of St. Bartholomew, who poisoned her own son Charles, who has been accessory to many other crimes—lies upon her bed, weak, helpless, with death staring her in the face. " Blood ! blood ! There is a river of blood !" she cries. " See ! see ! The devils are after me ! they are dragging me down to hell."

She is a maniac. Death steals on apace. The withered hands move convulsively ; the once fair face is haggard now ; the lips quiver, and the breathing ceases. Death has come, and that is the end ! Is it ? If the good which men do lives after them, does the evil die when the pulse ceases its beatings ? No. A legacy of blood and hate, of war and crime, is what Catherine de' Medici bequeaths to France.

Six months pass. The King of France and Henry of Navarre are at St. Cloud, with their armies. The land is convulsed with civil war. Paris is in the hands of the Holy Leaguers, who fain would exterminate every Huguenot.

It is Tuesday, August 1st, that a monk appears at St. Cloud ; he has come from Paris, with a message for the king.

" You can't go in," says the guard.

" Let him come in," shouts the king from his tent. The monk passes in, bows low before the king to present a paper. A poniard flashes in the air, and the monk drives it to the hilt into the king's abdomen.

"He has killed me!" The shout is heard by the guards, who rush in in season to see the king falling to the floor. Jacques Clement stands

JACQUES CLEMENT KILLING THE KING.

there, with his arms outstretched, as if to make a crucifix of himself in his fanatical hatred of the king. In a moment he is hacked to pieces.

Henry of Navarre and the Duke of Sully are with the army. A horseman rides up at a swift pace, bows to Henry, and whispers in his ear, and the three gallop to St. Cloud. The king is dying, but conscious.

"Navarre is your king; recognize him as the rightful King of France," are the words that fall from the lips of the wounded sovereign.

"We will."

"Swear it."

The noblemen who have gathered round fall upon their knees, and lift their hands to heaven in confirmation of their promise. The dead king is borne to his tomb; and the boy born and nurtured among the defiles of the Pyrenees, whose infant lips were wet with wine and chafed with garlic by a doting old grandfather, is King of France — Henry IV., the first of the house of Bourbon.

Though Henry IV. has come to the throne, the war is not yet ended. The Leaguers are in possession of Paris, and the Duke of Mayenne, youngest brother of the Duke of Guise, their leader. The war widens.

Queen Elizabeth of England sends over six thousand men to aid Henry. On March 14th the two armies meet on the plain of Ivry, Henry with ten thousand, and the Duke of Mayenne with thirteen thousand men.

"My children," says the king, just as the battle is beginning, "if you lose sight of your colors, rally to my white plume: you will always find it in the path to honor and glory. The historian Macaulay tells us about the battle:

> "The king is come to marshal us, in all his armor drest,
> And he has bound a snow-white plume upon his gallant crest.
> He looked upon his people, and a tear was in his eye;
> He looked upon the traitors, and his glance was stern and high.
> Right graciously he smiled on us, as rolled from wing to wing,
> Down all our line, a deafening shout, 'God save our lord the king!'
> 'And if my standard-bearer fall, as fall full well he may,
> For never saw I promise yet of such a bloody fray,
> Press where ye see my white plume shine, amidst the ranks of war,
> And be your oriflamme to-day the helmet of Navarre.'"

The Leaguers are utterly routed. Their commander is a fat man; he seeks safety in flight, but is overtaken and captured. Henry treats him kindly.

"Spare the French," are his orders to his troops. He will not have a Frenchman put to death.

FOR THE SAKE OF PEACE, HE WILL ACKNOWLEDGE THE POPE.

But how shall Henry govern ?   He is a Huguenot, while three-fourths of the people of France are Catholics.   He cares very little for the forms of religion ; but he believes that every man should be allowed to think for himself in religious matters.   He sees that the country is torn by factions. He would have the people united ; and, to bring about a union, decides to give in his adhesion to the Roman Church.   Some of the bigoted Catholics say that he is a hypocrite, while many of the Huguenots accuse him of being a traitor.   For the sake of peace, he acknowledges the Pope as the head of the Church.   He marks out his course of action.   There shall be freedom of conscience to every man, and there shall be no more burning or hanging of heretics.

The country has been drenched in blood since Bernard Palissy, the potter, and his friends began to think for themselves ; but at last, after the weary years, the people may think for themselves, without fear of priest or Pope.

Henry publicly abjures the Huguenot faith, and ranks himself a Catholic ; but on April 13th, 1598, in the old town of Nantes, he publishes an edict guaranteeing protection and toleration to all.   So liberty, like a ship at sea, after breasting the storm and tempest, sails in calmer waters.

CHAPTER XXVIII.

WILLIAM BREWSTER AND HIS FRIENDS.

ALTHOUGH sixty years have rolled away since Cardinal Wolsey made the old manor-house at Scrooby his home, some of the old people living there can remember how he distributed alms to the poor on Sunday, how he fed the lame and the blind from his kitchen-table. It is the year 1590, and the occupant of the old house is the young man, William Brewster—Sir William Davison's secretary. He has seen the hollowness of court life, and is dissatisfied with it. He learns that men who will be great have no end of trouble. Elizabeth has made him one of her postmasters, and there he is, living a quiet and peaceful life, looking after the mail, and the post-riders, and the travellers who go by post from London up the great road to York.

Great changes are taking place in England. Men are beginning to be independent in thought and action. Robert Brown, a zealous minister, has been preaching to congregations in London. Richard Clifton — a man with a long white beard — is also preaching independently of any authority from the bishop. William Brewster believes that every man has the right to think for himself; that neither bishop, pope, king, nor queen should control men in religious matters. Many of his neighbors at Scrooby, Austerfield, Bawtry, Gainsborough, and other little hamlets, are of the same way of thinking. They believe in having a pure worship, and object to the wearing of gold-embroidered vestments by the bishops, to bowing before the altar during service, and making the sign of the cross when their children are baptized. They hate mummery, and so stay away from church, although it has been decreed that everybody in England must attend church, of which Elizabeth is the head. If they do not, the bishops will know why. They have a complicated machinery of courts to compel everybody to believe as they shall direct. Every man and woman in England must believe in the Thirty-nine Articles, which have been decreed by Parliament and the queen. Commissioners have been appointed to inquire about "heretical opinions," "seditious books," and to punish all who shall stay away from church on Sunday. They arrest and imprison all who disobey their commands. The bishops hang John Copping and Elias Thacker, and arrest Henry Barrow and John Greenwood. For what? For not believing as they believe. Although

DANCING ON THE GREEN.

Archbishop Whitgift is himself a heretic, he will not tolerate a man who does not believe as he believes. If the Pope will not tolerate Archbishop Whitgift, he, in turn, will not tolerate John Copping and the rest.

In the great struggle for liberty brave men lay down their lives—not on the battle-field, charging up to the cannon's mouth, but on the scaffold, or else wasting away in loathsome prisons. John Copping and Elias Thacker believe that men should lead pure lives.

The English people, for the most part, are a roistering set. They love out-door sports, hunting and fishing, and games—pitching quoits, wrestling, and dancing. They go into the green-woods on bright summer days, and have a dance—men, women, and children joining in the sport. In the winter the villagers gather in a peasant's cabin, and hold their rustic balls. They are rude in their manners, and spend much of their time in play and idleness.

John Copping, and others like him, think that so much dancing, feast-

"PEASANTS' BALL."

ing, and idleness are a waste of time; that they are not promotive of good morals. Sunday afternoons are given to games and dances. The good ministers believe that Sunday should not be used as a holiday, and they preach boldly for a purer way of living. The peasants are not the only ones who need reforming, for the carpenters, joiners, the tradesmen, and the well-to-do people spend a great deal of time in the ale-houses over their foaming mugs of beer. Archbishop Whitgift does not trouble himself about such things: he has little to say against dancing on Sunday, or against their sports and drinking, or the drunkenness, and idleness, and immorality; but he cannot tolerate a man who will not think as he thinks. He looks sharply after those who dissent from his way of thinking. For six years he keeps Henry Barrow in prison. He does not quite dare to burn him, for the people of England do not intend to have any more roasting of human beings; but one morning, before London is astir, he has the poor man taken out to Tyburn, and speedily put to death by hanging. The same day he arrests John Penry, a Welshman, who

ALE-DRINKERS.

has written a pamphlet in which he maintains that every man has a right to act according to the dictates of his conscience in matters pertaining to religion. Archbishop Whitgift cannot permit any such heresy. On June 7th, 1593, John Penry is taken out and hanged.

Notwithstanding the bishops are hunting down those whom they de-risively call Puritans, it does not deter the postmaster at Scrooby and his friends from thinking for themselves. More than that, Brewster invites his neighbors to come to the old manor-house on Sunday, to hear a man with a long white beard — Richard Clifton — preach: sometimes, when Clifton is not there, John Robinson preaches. After the service Brewster

JAMES I.

gives them bread and beer. He and his friends believe that any body of Christian believers may be a church, and that the minister is their bishop. They believe that the churches organized by Peter, Paul, and the other apostles were just such churches.

Among those who come to hear Richard Clifton is a boy from Austerfield, William Brad-ford. The register in the Aus-terfield church contains the record of William's baptism:

"William son of Willm Bradfourth baptized the XIXth day of March Anno dm 1589."

The next day, after the hanging of Penry, Parliament passes a law imprisoning for three months all who do not conform to the Queen's Church, with the confiscation of all their property, and perpetual banishment from Eng-land.

A non-conforming church has been gathered in London; but upon the passage of this law it is broken up, many of its members being banished, or else seeking safety in Holland. The postmaster of Scrooby and his friends, being so far away, are not molested; and Sunday after Sunday they meet in the old manor-house for worship.

On March 24th, 1603, Elizabeth, who for forty-five years has been Queen of England, draws her last breath, and James of Scotland (who was spanked by George Buchanan), through his descent from Margaret, who in her bridal journey to Scotland stopped at the old manor-house, becomes King of England. He is thirty-six years old. It is to be feared that the spanking did him little good, for he is vain, self-willed, hypocrit-ical, selfish, and superstitious. He believes that wrinkled old women sell themselves to the devil to bewitch the people; and he has been harrying witches at a fearful rate—hanging, drowning, and burning them. He is not the only one who believes in witches. For that matter, everybody believes that they ride about on broomsticks at night, creeping through key-holes, and entering houses to torment the people. Everybody believes that witches should be put to death. It is the spirit of the age.

There are several hundred ministers in England who desire purer ways in the Church, and they present a petition to James, asking that there may be a new order of things. He grants them an audience at Hampton Court —it is not a hearing, for when they begin to present their plea, he inter-rupts them:

"I will have one doctrine, one discipline, one religion. I alone will decide. I will make you conform, or I will harry you out of the land or else do worse—hang you." The bishops are delighted.

The king is greatly pleased with himself. "I peppered them sound-ly," he says, in glee, to the bishops. He issues a proclamation requiring everybody to conform to the Church of which he is the head. What shall the men and women who meet in the old manor house at Scrooby do? They value life; but principle is worth more than property or life. They love their country; but liberty is worth more than country. They will sell their lands, bid good-bye to old England, and find a refuge in Hol-land, where, since the Spaniards have been driven out, men may think for themselves. Not as individuals, but as a church—a body of Chris-tian believers—will they go.

Why not go to the New World, beyond the Atlantic? There is much talk about Virginia just now—its delightful climate, its fertile soil, its fruits and flowers, and inexhaustible riches. The merchants of London are fitting out a colony to settle there; but the power of the bishops will be felt there. Nor will the king let them go. "No Englishman shall transport himself to Virginia without a license;" that is the king's proc-lamation. He will not even permit them to find a home amidst the wolves, and bears, and Indians. Nor will he let them go to Holland. He has the power to banish them; but he will not let them go of their own accord into exile.

William Brewster and his friends resolve to leave the country secret-ly. It is fifty miles to the sea-coast; but they will make their way to the old town of Boston, and take a vessel to Amsterdam. Brewster has been there, and so makes all arrangements. A ship-master promises to take them. They sell their lands, pack their goods, and make their way over the meadows and marshes to Boston. The land is so level that long before they reach the town they can see the tall towers of St. Botolph's Church rising above the horizon. They pass through the narrow streets, and go on board the ship, congratulating themselves that soon they will be beyond the jurisdiction of the bishops. But they are doomed to disappointment. The captain of the vessel is a knave; he has informed the

HOLLAND FARM-HOUSE.

constable, who comes with a lot of policemen, and marches them to the office of the magistrate, who thrusts them into prison, where they are kept many weeks, till he can hear from London; but after much suffering they are allowed to go at large.

Six months pass. Brewster resolves to make another attempt to reach Holland, and this time makes a bargain with a Dutch skipper to take himself and friends on board at a lonely place on the coast. One by one the people leave their homes. The women and children go in a boat. The winds are high, and they are tossed about by the waves, suffering from sea-sickness. The men, carrying heavy packs, make their way through the marshes. They reach the appointed place, but no ship is in sight. The boat runs into a creek for shelter, for those on board are in a miserable plight—sick, weary, disappointed, disheartened, with no home behind them, none before them, so far as they can see. All day, all night, they lie there. The morning dawns, and their hearts are joyful, for there is the ship riding at anchor off the shore a little distance.

The women and children have spent the night on the land. The ship's small boats come in and carry their goods on board. Some of the men are on the ship, some on the land, when a troop of men come rushing over the sand-hills, armed with spears and guns. The bishops' officers are upon them. Those on shore are seized — the women rudely assaulted. The Dutchman, seeing the commotion, and afraid that his ship will be seized and himself thrown into prison, hoists the anchor, spreads the sails, and steers away. It is a sad hour. Husbands and wives are separated, families broken up. There is loud lamentation, for who knows whether they ever will meet again. William Bradford is on board the ship. He is only nineteen years old; he gives this account of the scene: "Pitiful it was to see the heavy care of these poor women—what weeping and crying on every side; some for their husbands carried away in the ship, others not knowing what should become of them and their little ones; others melted in tears, seeing their poor little ones hanging about them, crying for fear and quaking with cold."

The ship, instead of reaching Holland in a few hours, is caught in a tempest, and driven nearly to Norway. For seven days and nights those on board see neither sun, moon, nor stars. Many times they fear that their last hour has come; but after being tossed about for fourteen days, they are safely landed at Amsterdam.

What shall the officers do with the women and children? To imprison them because they were going with their husbands and fathers cannot be thought of; the people will not permit it. No use to send them back to Scrooby and Austerfield, for they have no homes; they can only set them at liberty. King James will gain nothing by keeping them in England; and so, after many delays, they are permitted to make their way to Holland, to join their husbands and fathers.

CHAPTER XXIX.

THE STAR OF EMPIRE.

A CENTURY nearly has passed since Christopher Columbus under-took to reach the east by sailing west. During this period, the Spaniards have seized the West India Islands, conquered Mexico and Peru. They have a settlement in Florida, at St. Augustine. Every ship sailing to Spain from the new Western world carries silver and gold; and the country of Ferdinand and Isabella is reaping a rich harvest. Trade and commerce feel the quickening influence of the precious metals.

Through all these years neither the French or English have made a permanent settlement in North America. Some Huguenots who settled at Port Royal, in South Carolina, have been massacred by the Spaniards; and from St. Augustine northward there is no human habitation, save the wigwams of the Indians. It is the year 1583, when Sir Humphrey Gilbert, of England, with authority from Queen Elizabeth, sets sail, with two ships and three barks, on a voyage of discovery. He drops anchor on the 3d of August, in the harbor of St. Johns, Newfoundland, and is surprised to find thirty-six French vessels at anchor there. The crews are catching fish, and drying them on the rocks. Sir Humphrey informs the fishermen that he takes possession of the island for Queen Elizabeth, and that they must obey the laws of England; and if any one says anything against Elizabeth, he shall have his ears cropped, and lose all his goods: more, they must all worship in the way prescribed by the Church of England. Sir Humphrey grants the fishermen leave to dry their fish—a privilege which they always have exercised; but now they must pay for the privilege. Having established English authority, Sir Humphrey sets sail for England; but never again is he to see his native land: his ship goes down in a storm with all on board; but the vessel commanded by his half-brother, Sir Walter Raleigh, arrives safely in port.

The disaster does not deter Sir Walter from making another voyage. A few months later he is abroad once more, sailing south-west till he reaches the coast of North Carolina, where he drops anchor, and makes the acquaintance of the Indians, who are kind and hospitable. He makes a present of a tin pan to a chief, who bores a hole in the rim, attaches a string, and wears it on his breast as an ornament and shield, and in return gives Sir Walter twenty skins of wild animals, worth a crown apiece; so that the Englishman gives away the tin pan at good profit. The climate is delightful, the air fragrant with flowers; and Sir Walter, who has a great admiration for Queen Elizabeth—so great that he once placed his scarlet-velvet cloak upon the mud for her to walk on when landing at the Tower—names the country Virginia, in her honor.

Sir Walter returns to England, carrying with him some of the tobacco of Virginia. Smoking is unknown in England; and one day when Sir Walter is puffing his Indian pipe, a servant coming in, thinking he is on fire, dashes a pailful of water upon him, wetting him from head to foot.

SIR WALTER ENJOYING HIS PIPE.
(From an Old Print.)

The next year Sir Walter sails once more, with one hundred and fifty men, and makes a settlement at Roanoke, leaving John White to govern the colony. Mrs. Dare, wife of one of the colonists, gives birth to a daughter, whom she names Virginia—the first child of English parents born in America.

Sir Walter returns to England, but sails again to Virginia the succeeding year, to find the houses deserted and weeds growing around them. The colonists have disappeared, no one knows whither. Never are they heard from.

On December 19th, 1606, three small vessels glide down the river Thames, spreading their sails for a voyage across the Atlantic. The largest is of one hundred tons, the next largest forty, and the smallest twenty tons. There are one hundred and five persons on board the vessels. They are leaving England to found a state in a wilderness thousands of miles away. They will find no homes awaiting them, no fields cleared, but a land inhabited by savages. Of the party, four are carpenters, twelve laborers, forty-eight gentlemen, who look upon labor as a degrading occupation. They have an indefinite idea of what is before them, and vague conceptions of what they will do in the land whither they are going; but somehow they all expect to make their fortunes, or else meet with exciting adventures, which will pay for all the hardship they may be called upon to endure.

Captain Newport, who commands the expedition, has been in the New World. He carried two crocodiles and a wild-boar to England, and presented them to the king, and the king has lent his influence to help on their enterprise; merchants have aided it. One of the poets of England has addressed an ode to the gentlemen:

> " You brave, heroic minds,
>   Worthy your country's name,
>   What honor still pursue;
>   While loitering hinds
>   Lurk here at home with shame,
>   Go and subdue.

> "And in the regions far
>   Such heroes bring ye forth
>   As those from whom we came,
>   And plant our name
>   Under the star
>   Not known unto the North."

One of the gentlemen is Captain John Smith, who is only thirty years of age, but who has had an adventurous life. He was born only a short distance from where Doctor Wicklif lived, in 1579. When he was a school-boy, he had such a longing to be a sailor that he sold his books and satchel to get money enough to go to sea; but just then his father died, and left him a good deal of money, and he concluded to remain in England and be a merchant. He was a headstrong boy, and so wild and reckless that his friends were glad when he entered the service of Lord Willoughby, who sent him to France with his son Peregrin. He did not get on very well with his patron, who soon dismissed him, giving him money enough to get back to England; but John, instead of going home, enlisted with the Dutch to fight the Spaniards, and aided the "beggars" in their efforts to drive Philip out of the country. When at last he set sail for England, he was shipwrecked. Instead of going home to his friends, he went to Scotland, made the acquaintance of Mr. David Hume, who introduced him to King James—who was spanked by George Buchanan. The king had nothing for him to do, and he made his way back to England, went into the woods and built a hut, and began to study military science, resolving to be a general. His friends came to see him in his forest home; but he could not stay there. He must be doing something. So he sails for Germany, to enlist in the service of the emperor, who is fighting the Turks. He is robbed of all his money, and suffers for want of food; and one day he lies down, not caring what becomes of him; but a kind-hearted man gives him food,

JOHN SMITH RESOLVES TO BE A GENERAL.

and supplies him with money. This is in France. He discovers the rascal who robbed him.

"You are the villain who stole my purse."

Both draw their swords. Click! click! click! they go, till John has the thief at his mercy.

" Pay me my money, you scamp."

" I have spent it."

The fellow begs for pardon, and John, as kind as he is brave, allows him to go.

At Marseilles he takes a ship for Italy, which is crowded with pilgrims on their way to Rome. A storm comes on. The pilgrims count their beads, and say their prayers, while John calmly looks out upon the waves which every minute threaten them with destruction.

" He is a heretic—a wicked fellow." So the pilgrims whisper to each other.

" He is a Jonah."

" Let us throw him overboard."

They gather around him in anger, and seize him. He makes a brave fight, but it is one against one hundred. Overboard they throw him into the yeasty waves. But he is a good swimmer, and the ship is not far from the shore. The waves toss him to and fro; they roll over him, all but strangle him; but, weak and exhausted, he reaches the shore. The next day a ship comes along, the captain takes him aboard, and in a few days he finds himself at Alexandria, in Egypt. A Venetian vessel sails into port, and a battle ensues between the two ships, in which John makes a brave fight for his friends, who capture their enemy's vessels, and find it laden with silks, spices, diamonds, and jewelry. John's share of the plunder amounts to eleven hundred dollars in money, besides a box of jewels worth a much larger sum.

From Egypt he makes his way into Hungary, joins the Austrian army, and is made a captain of cavalry. His troop is known as the "Fiery Legion." The Austrian general, Count Meldritch, is besieging the fortress of Regal. One of the Turkish generals, Turbashaw, sends a challenge into the Austrian camp: "I challenge any captain of the besieging army to combat."

Many brave men are ready to accept it, but the lot falls on the young captain of the Fiery Legion. The fight is to be in the presence of all the high-born ladies. The combatants meet in the open field, the Turk in a suit of mail wrought with gold, the boy-captain in plain armor. The Turk has eagle's wings attached to his shoulder. Three janizaries attend him: one to carry his lance, the others to walk by his side, and do his bidding.

The ladies on the castle walls wave their mantles as the Turk rides proudly forward to meet his antagonist, and poises his lance and rides at him full tilt; but the next moment the Turk is rolling upon the ground, with his opponent's lance piercing his brain. A loud wail goes up from the multitude gathered on the castle walls, while shouts of victory rend the air from the Austrian hosts.

Another Turkish general will avenge the death of his friend. That

JOHN SMITH'S FIGHT WITH THE TURK.

young Englishman's head shall roll in the dust. He sends a challenge. They meet; each shivers his lance; they fire their pistols, but miss; then whip out their swords. A stroke brings the Turk to the ground; another severs his head from his body; and then Captain John challenges any officer in the Turkish army to fight him. General Mulgro accepts the challenge. The Turk comes out with a sword, battle-axe, and pistols.

THE THREE TURKS' HEADS.

He swings his axe, to annihilate the captain at a stroke; but in an instant John runs him through with his sword, and finishes him. The whole army escorts him into camp, amidst shouts of joy, the three Turks' heads being borne by three horses. Count Meldritch makes him a present of a splendid horse, a belt adorned with jewels, and a costly cimeter, and promotes him to be a major, and the emperor makes him a nobleman. His coat of arms is three Turks' heads, and the motto " *Vincere est vivere.*"

A few days later there is a battle, and the captain of the Fiery Legion goes down amidst a heap of dead, with his blood oozing from a ghastly wound. The Austrians are driven, and he falls into the hands of the Turks, who, thinking that he is a rich nobleman, kindly care for him, expecting that his friends will pay a large sum for his ransom. The pasha sends his prisoner to Constantinople, as a present to his sister. The girl sees how fair he is, and falls in love with him. To save him from being sold, she sends him to another brother, a pasha who lives in the Crimea, on the shores of the Black Sea, asking him to take good care of the fair-faced young man; but the brother shaves the captain's head, dresses him in sheepskins, rivets an iron collar on his neck, and sets him to threshing wheat.

One day the pasha rides out to see how his captive is getting on. He gives the captain a cut with his whip, but in an instant the flail in Smith's hands comes round with a whack upon the Turk's head. Another blow, and he is finished. Smith strips off the clothes of the pasha, secretes the body in a stack of wheat, fills a bag with grain, lays aside his sheepskin clothes, puts on the pasha's, mounts the horse, and flies like the wind across the fields and pasture-lands, reaching the wilderness. The iron collar is still upon his neck, but he muffles it and rides on, day after day, night after night, reaching, after fourteen days ride, the Russian frontier. The military officers are amazed at his story, but help him on, and in a few weeks he surprises Count Meldritch by appearing once more in camp.

When the war is over, he travels through Germany and France to the Mediterranean, embarking on a French ship for Morocco; but, meeting

SMITH'S ESCAPE FROM SLAVERY.

a Spanish ship, a battle ensues. The young captain fights like a tiger, and the Spaniards are conquered. Instead of going on to Morocco, the ship puts back to port, and, tired of adventure, Smith makes his way to England; but he cannot rest, and now is on his way to the New World.

King James has granted the colonists the exclusive right to occupy a strip of country two hundred and forty miles wide, extending from the southern boundary of the present State of Maryland to Cape Fear. The Government is to be a council and a governor appointed by the king. There can be no religion in the colony except that of the Church of England. There is not a single element of popular liberty in the charter. The colonists have no votes—no voice in anything. Besides being subject in all things, in civil and religious matters, to the king, they are, at the same time, under a company of merchants who have contributed to the outfit. Liberty is not a part of the cargo.

The winds are contrary, and the ships steer southward to the Canary Islands, then west to the West Indies, then north-west to the coast of Virginia. On April 26th, 1607, the vessels enter Chesapeake Bay, and drop anchor under the shelter of a point of land where the water is so smooth, the shores so peaceful and pleasant, that the colonists call it Point Comfort; and Captain Newport names the locality Cape Charles, and the headland on the opposite side of the bay Cape Henry, for the king's two sons.

The Indians who inhabit the country gaze upon the vessels with wonder. Captain Newport quiets their fears, and makes them presents, whereupon they invite him to visit their village, where they give him a feast of such luscious oysters as never were seen in England. Captain Smith is sent by Captain Newport to open friendly intercourse with the great chief of the Indians. The man who has had so many adventures in the East finds the chief wearing a crown of deer horns, colored red, with two eagles' feathers in his hair, and a piece of copper dangling on one side of his head. His body is painted crimson, his face blue. The chief receives him courteously, smoking a pipe, and then handing it to Captain Smith.

The ships sail up a noble river, which Captain Newport names James, in honor of the king. He comes to a beautiful island, where he selects a place for a town, erects houses and a fort, and names it Jamestown—the first permanent English settlement in the new home of liberty. The colonists go on shore, the stores are discharged, and the vessels sail away, leaving the four carpenters, twelve laborers, and forty-eight gentlemen to lay the foundations of a new order of things in the Western world. The gentlemen are unaccustomed to hardship; they are unused to labor; nor have they come to work. Labor is degrading. They are soldiers—adventurers. The summer sun blazes in the heavens like a fiery furnace, and they wilt beneath its fervent heat. Their provisions are damaged; the water is unwholesome. Fever sets in, and in a few days nearly every

MEETING THE INDIANS.

man, excepting the laborers, is down with fever. The gentlemen lose heart. Death makes its appearance; four die in a single night.

The governor, Edward Wingfield, is a merchant — avaricious, selfish, grasping. He has come to the New World to amass wealth. He reserves all the choice things for himself—the best tidbits and liquors. Captain John Smith, Captain John Ratcliffe, and Captain John Martin — three Captain Johns—are members of the council appointed by the king, and are so incensed at Wingfield's course that they resolve to depose him.

"You refused me a bit of chicken when I was sick, nor would you let me have a drop of beer; and you gave me mouldy corn," is Ratcliffe's accusation.

"You accused me of being lazy," says Martin.

"You called me a liar," shouts Smith.

They seize the governor, carry him on board a small vessel, and keep him as a prisoner. Ratcliffe acts as governor.

The provisions are nearly exhausted, and Captain Smith, with six men, goes in a boat to purchase corn from the Indians; but the red men, knowing the wants of the whites, ask a round price, and will only sell a basketful. The man who cut off the heads of the three Turks is not to be trifled with. He orders the soldiers to fire a volley, to intimidate the savages. The guns flash, and the Indians flee in terror. The captain follows them, and finds a great store of corn; but the Indians, seeing that no harm has come to them, rally, and let fly their arrows. The soldiers fire once more, this time taking aim, and three of the Indians are killed or wounded, while the rest flee in terror, astounded at the effect of the guns. Captain Smith seizes their medicine, or idol, knowing that they will be greatly troubled at its loss. The medicine-man comes to beg him to give it up.

"Fill the boat with corn, and I will restore it."

The Indian is glad to comply, and his followers bring not only corn, but turkeys, ducks, and venison.

Smith ascends the Chickahominy as far as he can go with a large boat, and then, with two soldiers, in a canoe, goes on many miles. The soldiers left with the boat quarrel with the Indians; one is killed, the remainder flee, leaving Smith and his companions to whatever fate may await them. His two companions are killed, and he is taken prisoner. His captors lead him to their chief. He is promised his liberty if he will join in exterminating the colony. He feigns friendship, but informs them that the colonists have terrible weapons, and will destroy them all. "Send and see if it is not so." He writes a note to the colonists to fire their cannon.

The Indians arrive at Jamestown with the letter, and are amazed to see that everything happens just as Smith said it would. Their captive must be a supernatural being, for he can make paper talk. They bring back some gunpowder, which they intend to sow in the spring, and so raise their own powder.

Captain Smith is taken before the great chief, Powhatan, who wears a dress made of raccoon skins, with a crown of red feathers. He sits upon

THE FIRST FIGHT.

a platform, with his two daughters by his side — the oldest fifteen, the youngest thirteen years of age. They bring a bowl of water, that he may wash his face, and a bunch of feathers for a towel. Then he has his trial, and is condemned to die. An Indian rolls a stone into the wig-wam, and the captain's head is laid upon it. Two warriors raise their

POCAHONTAS SHIELDS HIM FROM THEIR CLUBS.

clubs to beat out his brains. His time has come; yet he does not trem-
ble. The Indians shall see that the white man can die without a sign
of fear.

The youngest girl by the side of the great chief gazes upon the scene.

Her heart is in commotion. A bound, and she is bending over him, shielding him from the clubs ready to descend upon his skull.

"Do not kill him! do not kill him!"

The chief loves his daughter, and for her sake spares the captain's life, and sends twelve warriors to conduct him in safety to Jamestown. Captain Smith sends back a handsome present to the chief and his daughter. He finds the colony divided. There are forty persons in all, but half of them have seized the vessel in the James, and are abandoning the place, intending to sail to England.

Captain Smith loads a cannon, and aims it at the vessel. "Return, or I will sink you."

The conspirators, awed by the command, return to the shore; and at the last moment the colony is saved from dissolution. Pocahontas is their friend. She comes often to the town, bringing provisions. The Indians who come with her respect the man who had no fear of death, and who can make paper talk.

"In a short time a great boat filled with white people will come from the sea," he says to them, and a few weeks later Captain Newport sails up the James, with one hundred and twenty emigrants. Now the brave man is a prophet; he can tell what is going to happen, and they stand in fear of him. The new-comers are nearly all "gentlemen," who despise labor, but they have come expecting to find gold as plentiful as in Peru, and are a burden rather than a help.

Captain Smith starts on a grand exploring expedition—up the Potomac, up Chesapeake Bay to the Susquehanna, and up that stream till he comes to a tribe of Indians who use copper hatchets, which they obtain from the far-distant north. Upon his return, he makes a treaty with the Rappahannocks, the chief giving up his arrows in token of friendship, and Captain Smith hanging strings of beads around the necks of three of the women of the tribe. After this there is a great feast and much dancing. From the Rappahannock River Captain Smith sails for Craney Island, near Norfolk, where the Indians attack him; but he fires a volley at them, burns their wigwams, and so humiliates them that they bring four hundred baskets full of corn to purchase peace.

At sunset, September 7th, 1608, the party reach Jamestown, after an absence of three months and a journey of nearly three thousand miles.

Another ship arrives with emigrants, among whom are two women—the first in the colony. Two years have passed since the colonists landed at Jamestown; but as yet little has been done toward making a permanent settlement. The gentlemen are idlers, but Captain Smith compels them

SUBMISSION OF THE RAPPAHANNOCKS.

to work. Some of them are terribly profane, and he makes a law that
for every oath they utter they shall have a canful of cold water poured
down their backs. He discovers that the chief Powhatan, though pro-
fessing friendship, is conspiring against the colony, and resolves to seize
him; but two worthless fellows flee to Powhatan with information of his
intentions. And now Pocahontas comes with the counter-information
that her father intends to kill all the English. Captain Smith holds a
parley with the chief of the Pamunkeys, who profess to be friendly.
While he is talking with the chief in his wigwam, a soldier rushes in.

We are surrounded by a great crowd of savages," he says, pale with fear.

"Never mind. Look to your guns," is the quiet reply of the dauntless man; then seizing the chief by the hair with his left hand, presents a pistol to his head, accuses him of treachery, threatens to blow out his

CAPTAIN SMITH SUBDUING THE CHIEF.

brains if he does not kneel and ask forgiveness. The chief kneels, promises submission, and also agrees to fill the captain's boats with corn.

"If you do not, I will fill them with the dead bodies of your warriors."

The Indians bring corn and provisions in abundance, standing in fear
of such a man.

King James appoints Lord De la Ware (Delaware) governor, who sails
from England with nine ships and five hundred emigrants. Two of the
ships are wrecked in the West Indies, where De la Ware himself remains

RUINS AT JAMESTOWN.

to refit them. The others reach Jamestown. The emigrants are a worthless set — spendthrifts for the most part, scapegraces, sons of nobles and
lords, so wild and reckless that their fathers are glad of an opportunity
of sending them out of the country.

Captain Smith has been in Virginia three years. Had it not been for
him, the colony would have perished. He is terribly burned by an explosion of gunpowder, and resolves to return to England. He bids farewell
to the colonists, some of whom are glad to be rid of a man who has compelled them to labor, while others cannot keep back the tears when they
remember how his wisdom, endurance, and bravery more than once have

saved them from destruction. He returns to England, draws a map of his explorations, which he presents to King James, who holds him in high esteem.

The colony numbers five hundred when he sets sail, but there is no controlling mind, no government. The new state founded on American soil in a few days is in anarchy. The idlers eat the provisions of the colony, but do no work. Winter comes, and provisions fail. Fever sets in. Starvation is before them. The Indians see how weak they are, and those who go to the wigwams of the savages for food are cruelly murdered. Spring opens, and of the five hundred only sixty remain ; the four hundred and more have perished. The survivors, disheartened, abandon the colony, embark on their vessel, and reach Chesapeake Bay. On the morrow they will bid farewell to the shores where disaster and failure have been their portion. What do they see ? Two ships. Lord De la Ware has obtained new vessels in the West Indies, and here he is with provisions. Sad the morning, joyful the night. With fresh courage they go back to Jamestown, take possession of their old homes, to begin once more the work of laying the foundations of an empire in the Western world.

CHAPTER XXX.

THE "HALF-MOON."

THE storks are building their nests on the chimney-tops in Amsterdam. The spring has come in its beauty. William Brewster and his fellow-pilgrims, in this year of 1609, are hard at work; but quite likely they have time to stop for a few moments, on this 25th day of March, to

OFF CAPE NORTH.

take a look at a vessel, the *Half-moon*, which is just starting for a long voyage, in search of a new route to China. Hendrick Hudson, an Englishman, Captain John Smith's friend, is skipper. He stands upon the

THE "HALF-MOON" IN CHESAPEAKE BAY.

deck issuing his orders. He has already been two voyages to the North, sailing amidst the icebergs; and now he is going to try to reach China by the way of Nova Zembla. The East India Company and the Amsterdam burghers have fitted out the ship. The sailors bid good-bye to their friends, and the *Half-moon* slowly moves away. The winds are fair, and in less than a month Captain Hudson is at Cape North; but there he encounters terrible storms. The air is thick with mist. There are dense fogs, and ice-fields block his way. He is not a man, however, to turn back at once to Amsterdam; but turns westward, loses his foremast in a fearful storm, but reaches the Banks of Newfoundland, where the crew catch a great supply of fish, and on July 17th drops anchor in Penobscot Bay. There are tall pines on the shore, and the sailors soon have a new mast in its place. They traffic with the Indians, and then Captain Hudson sails south, coasts along Cape Cod, and on August 18th drops anchor in Chesapeake Bay. From there he turns north, and discovers Delaware Bay. Still farther north, coasting along a sandy shore, he discovers a long, low point of land curved like a hook, and names it Sandy Hook. A little farther, and he drops anchor at the mouth of "the great North River of New Netherlands"—the Hudson. The Indians put out in their canoes

THE " HALF-MOON " IN THE HUD-
SON.

from the shores, come on
board the ship, bringing tobacco, corn, and bear-skins,
which they gladly exchange
for knives and trinkets.
The next day Captain Hud-
son sends a party of sailors
on shore, where they find a
great company of Indians,
who give them tobacco and
dried currants.   The next
day Captain Hudson sails
through the " Narrows," and finds himself in a beautiful and spacious harbor.   He sends a boat to the shore; but suddenly the Indians let their
arrows fly, and John Coleman, one of the sailors, is killed.   His comrades
bury the body on a point of land, which they call Coleman's Point.

On the 12th of September, the *Half-moon* begins her voyage up the great river. The Indians, astonished at the sight, come around the ship in great numbers, bringing corn and tobacco, and making signs for knives and beads. Two days later the ship is amidst the Highlands, and the sailors look out upon the lofty mountains that remind them of the Rhine.

On September 18th, Captain Hudson goes ashore, near the present village of Castleton, to visit the great chief of the region, who has seventeen wives, and who has corn and beans enough to load three ships like the *Half-moon*. The chief gives him a dinner of baked dog, and a dish of pigeons, which the squaws place before them in wooden bowls painted red. The chief would like to have him stay on shore overnight; and when he discovers that the captain is about to return to the ship, he orders his warriors to break their arrows and throw them into the fire, to let him know that no harm shall come to him. For supper they have pumpkins, grapes, and plums.

The *Half-moon* makes her way nearly to Albany, where, finding that the ship can go no farther, Captain Hudson sends a party in boats, to explore the river. He makes a feast to the Indian chiefs on board the ship, giving them brandy. One drinks so much that he becomes intoxicated, and rolls upon the deck; the others, not knowing what to make of it, leap into their canoes and hasten ashore; but return, bringing presents, and are much pleased to find the chief has come to life again, and who is anxious to stay with the white men, who have such strong water.

Little does Captain Hudson think that at that moment Samuel Champlain is only a few miles distant, exploring the shores of the lake which bears his name, and that, after a century has rolled away, the great battle for supremacy between France and England — between the old religion and the new—will be fiercely waged along its peaceful shores.

Retracing his course, Captain Hudson, October 1st, drops anchor in Haverstraw Bay, where an Indian, running his canoe under the stern of the vessel, climbs into the cabin window, and steals Captain Hudson's clothes; but the mate, seeing him, seizes a musket and shoots him. The Indians on the ship, amazed at the lightning, the smoke, and the roar of the gun, leap like frogs into the water, and swim for their boats.

Captain Hudson sends a boat filled with sailors to recover the stolen goods. One of the Indians in the water lays hold of the boat to upset it, but a sailor chops off his hand, and the Indian sinks to rise no more. The next day hundreds of Indians come in their canoes to attack the ship, but Captain Hudson brings a cannon to bear upon them. There is a flash, a roar, a boat is smashed, and those in it killed or wounded. The others flee in consternation before the white man's thunder and lightning. After a little while two canoes filled with savages put off from the shore and approach the ship rapidly; but there comes a second flash, and a rattle of musketry. One of the boats is riddled by the shot, and the poor creatures go down one by one, while those in the other canoe pull for the shore. They are powerless before the strangers. The *Half-moon* reaches the sea, spreads her sails, and on November 7th casts anchor in Dartmouth harbor, England, from whence Captain Hudson sends an account of his voyage to Holland; but King James will not permit him to sail thither. The king is jealous of the Dutch. Henry Hudson is an Englishman, and no Englishman shall be permitted to aid them in making new discoveries in the Western world.

CHAPTER XXXI.

STRANGERS AND PILGRIMS.

THOSE poor people from Scrooby and Austerfield, when they reached Holland, were in a sad condition. Their property was nearly all destroyed. They found themselves in a strange land. They could not speak a word of the language of Holland. They found the country intersected by canals, and that the people carried their cabbages and cheeses to market

A HIGHWAY IN HOLLAND.

by water. The canals were the highways. Women, and children, and dogs tugged at the boats. A boy or girl and a dog made a little team, a woman and a donkey a big team.

The fugitives find friends in Amsterdam—people from London who have sought refuge there. Some of them have queer ideas in regard to dress, and say that no person should wear a collar or a ruff, or any ornament upon the person, and are greatly troubled because Mrs. Johnson, their minister's wife, wears whalebone in her stays, and high-heeled cork-soled shoes. The fugitives from Scrooby and Austerfield are not in a condition to indulge in any superfluity of dress, for they are very poor. They remain at Amsterdam a short time, and then remove to Leyden—the town that made such a brave resistance to the Spaniards.

William Brewster, who used to entertain them in the old manor-house, is so poor that he has to teach school for a living, and while teaching he

ST. PETER'S CHURCH.

learns to set type, and establishes a printing-office. William Bradford becomes a weaver, and makes fustian cloth. One man learns to lay brick; another is a carpenter, another a blacksmith. In England they were all farmers, and it is hard work for them, while learning their trades, to keep the wolf from the door.

On Sunday, instead of carousing in the beer-houses and going out to have a dance in the fields, they meet at the house which they have purchased for their pastor, John Robinson, which stands just across the street from St. Peter's Church, which has been standing there for five hundred years, and from the top of which the people looked with longing eyes to see if the sea were coming in to drown out the Spaniards when the Silent Man cut the dikes. They sing and pray, and listen to the reading of the Bible; and after John Robinson has finished his sermon, they eat dinner together. They call themselves Strangers and Pilgrims in the land, hoping that ere long times will change in England, and that then they can go back. They live in peace and quietness with their Dutch neighbors, who, though they think the English are odd in dress, and rather peculiar in regard to keeping Sunday, yet like them because they are honest and truthful, and are very particular about paying their debts.

As the years go by, the Pilgrims are troubled about their children. There are no English schools, and they are too poor to educate them. They are disturbed at the thought of their becoming like the Dutch. They love the dear old land that gave them birth, even though they are exiles. What shall they do ? The men who have made such sacrifices for liberty talk over the great question, and, after much deliberation, resolve to find a home beyond the sea, where they can train their children to love and reverence those truths and principles which are dearer than life. Perhaps, now that they are out of England, James will permit them to go. John Carver and Robert Cushman visit London, where they confer with the merchants who have aided in settling the colony at James-town. The merchants obtain permission ; but the king stipulates that they must conform to all the articles of the Church creed. That they will not do. Having left all in England for the sake of their principles, will they now surrender them ? Not they.

Two years pass, and the exiles go on working at their trades. They have, by their industry, driven the wolf from their doors, and are better-ing their condition. They are still thinking of the home in that far-off land, when Thomas Weston, a merchant of London, comes to see them. A new company of speculators has been formed in England, called the Plymouth Company. Earls and lords belong to it, and they have induced James to give them all the land which Captain John Smith called New England. They are anxious to send out a colony. William Brewster and two others go to London to see what the adventurers, as the speculators call themselves, will do. They are influential enough to get the king to promise not to molest the Pilgrims. An agreement is made, and a company formed. The shares of the company are fixed at fifty dollars. Every settler sixteen years of age shall be considered as equal to one share ; every man who furnishes an outfit worth fifty dollars shall be entitled to an additional share ; children between ten and sixteen years of age shall be counted as half a share. All the settlers bind themselves to work to-gether for seven years, during which time all shall be supported from the common fund, and all their labor shall go into it. At the end of the seven years, the property shall be divided according to the shares. These are hard conditions. For seven years not a penny of their earnings can they claim ; they must endure all the hardships, encounter at, the dangers, do all the work—putting life, labor, health, on an equality with the dollars advanced by Weston and his fellow-speculators. Yell for the sake of being free, for the sake of bringing up their children in the principles that are so dear to them, they accept the conditions. The merchants obtain two vessels — the *Mayflower*, of one hundred and eighty tons, and the *Speedwell*, of sixty. All of the company at Leyden cannot go, but those who can make preparations for their departure. They are to sail across the Channel to Southampton, where once more they may look upon the green fields of their native land.

On July 21st they meet for the last time at the house of their pastor, John Robinson, who will stay with those who remain. They spend the morning in fasting and prayer, and the good minister preaches a solemn

DELFTSHAVEN.

sermon. After the fasting, they sit down to a frugal feast, and sing once more, with the tears streaming down their cheeks, the psalms they used to sing in the manor-house at Scrooby, and which are sweeter and dearer than ever, now that they are about to take leave of their friends forever.

The *Speedwell* lies at Delftshaven, fourteen miles from Leyden. In the morning they go on board the canal-boats with their friends, who accompany them to the ship. Some come all the way from Amsterdam to bid them farewell. They spend the night in conversing with their friends, who provide a feast for them. The last hour has come, the wind is fair, and the captain in haste to be away. The beloved pastor is with them.

THE FAREWELL MEETING.

They kneel upon the deck, and he offers once more a prayer. With tears upon their cheeks, they bid each other farewell. The vessel swings from the quay, the wind fills the sails. But there is joy in their sorrow; they are departing in obedience to their profoundest convictions of duty. Little know they of what is before them, or what they are about to do. God knows what will come of it, and in him they trust. They fire a parting salute with their muskets and their three pieces of cannon.

At Southampton they join the *Mayflower*, on board of which are those who have come from England. Some of them are from London, hired by the speculators. One is John Billington, a graceless fellow, so wild and reckless that his friends are rejoiced to ship him to a distant land. Thomas Weston is there. He wants the original plan changed, so that the conditions will be better for himself, and of course harder to the Pilgrims; but no change will they make, whereupon the grasping man claps his purse in his pocket, refusing to discharge an obligation of one hundred pounds, which, according to the agreement, he ought to pay. "I'll let you stand on your own legs," he says, and returns

THE "MAYFLOWER."

to London. To pay their bills, they sell what they sorely need, but which they can best spare—eighty firkins of butter. They will eat their bread without any butter, rather than be beholden to Thomas Weston, or in debt to any man.

All is ready. They chose a governor for each ship, and one or two to assist him. Let us not forget this: *they chose them.* They are not appointed by James, or anybody else, but are elected by votes. It is the beginning of a new order of things. The Governor of Jamestown holds his commission from King James; but John Carver, governor on board the *Mayflower*, is elected by the *people*.

The ships leave the port, but are hardly out of the harbor when the captain of the *Speedwell* discovers that the vessel is leaking, and both ships put into Dartmouth for repairs. Two weeks pass, and they sail once more; but they are hardly on their way when the captain of the *Speedwell* declares that they must return, or go to the bottom, and the vessels put into Plymouth. Some of the Pilgrims are discouraged; but there are others who have not yet lost heart. There is no time to get another vessel, nor have they the means to obtain one. Those who are still anxious to go are crowded into the *Mayflower*, with such goods as they can carry. They are one hundred and two.

On the 16th of September, the sails are spread once more, and the *Mayflower*, with the rights of the people and the destiny of a new world for a cargo, glides out upon the broad Atlantic. Fierce storms arise, and the vessel is tossed like an egg-shell upon the waves. The main beam is wrenched from its place, and the ship is in danger of breaking in pieces. One of the Pilgrims has a great iron screw, which he brought from Leyden—why, he does not know—but now it is just what they need; the beam is forced back into its place, and the vessel is saved. One passenger falls overboard, and is lost; but a child is born, and the parents name him Oceanus.

Land! land! The joyful cry rings through the ship on November 19th. There it is—a long reach of sandy shore, with dark forest trees in the background. They sail along the coast, steering south, but soon find themselves among shoals. They dare not sail in that direction, and so bear north-west, running along a strip of land curved as one may curve his finger, double a sandy headland, and on November 21st drop anchor in the calm waters of the harbor of Cape Cod.

That wild fellow, John Billington, and the others from London, have been obliged to behave themselves on shipboard; but, now that they are about to land, declare that they will do as they please. John Carver will have no authority on shore; they will be in the king's domain, for John Carver holds no commission from the king, nor have the Pilgrims any charter. The Pilgrims will see about that. They are men who respect law and order, and intend to have order in their community. It is their *right*, not derived from the king, but a *natural* right. In the cabin of the ship they sign their names to a solemn covenant. Thus it reads:

"In the name of God, Amen. We, whose names are underwritten, * * * by these presents, solemnly and mutually, in the presence of God and one another, covenant and combine ourselves together into a civil body politic, for our better ordering and preservation, and furtherance of the ends aforesaid, and by virtue hereof to enact, constitute, and form such just and equal laws, ordinances, acts, constitutions, and offices, from time to time, as shall be thought most meet and convenient for the general good of the colony, unto which we promise all due submission and obedience."

The world never before has seen such a paper. That writing given in the green meadows of Runnymede by John Lackland was a compact

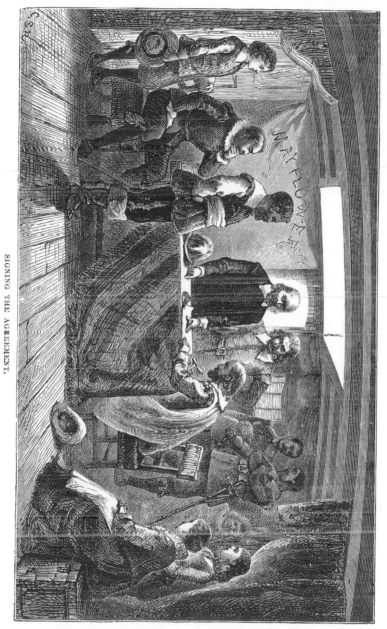

SIGNING THE AGREEMENT.

between two parties—the king and the barons; but here is only one party —the *people*. The paper is a *constitution*. It is fundamental—a new beginning—the founding of a state on a written law, emanating not from the king, but from themselves. John Billington's name is not down upon the paper; but the *majority* have signed it, and thenceforth and forever the *majority* shall rule.

Having established a government with a written constitution, the Pilgrims organize an army. It consists of only sixteen men; but they have a brave commander, Miles Standish, who has fought against the Spaniards in Holland. He was not a Pilgrim originally—did not come from Scrooby, but from the country west of that place. He has a lovely wife, Rose, as beautiful in person and character as the name she bears. The army of sixteen make a landing, and march into the forest. They cut down the trees, kindle a fire of cedar wood, and warm themselves by its cheerful blaze, and inhale the fragrant odor of the wood, sweet and refreshing after their long confinement on shipboard. It is Saturday, and when night comes all repair to the ship to keep the Sabbath as they ever have kept it. On Monday they are early astir. The men carry their pots and kettles on shore, the women land, carrying great bundles of dirty clothes. It is their washing day. While they rub and scrub the clothes, Captain Standish and his soldiers are standing guard in the forest, and the carpenter is repairing their boat. On Wednesday Captain Standish marches along the coast with his army, each soldier carrying his gun, sword, and corslet. They come upon a party of Indians, who flee so swiftly that the soldiers cannot overtake them. They find fertile places, where the Indians in other days have planted corn. They discover an iron kettle, and other indications that sailors have been cast away upon the shore. They are fortunate in finding a store of corn, and bring away all they can carry, resolving, if they ever find the owners, to pay them for what they have taken.

On December 7th, the great boat, large enough to carry twenty-four persons, is ready for use. The captain of the *Mayflower* is ready with the long boat, and they leave the ship, and row southward inside the cape: but the waves are tempestuous; so they sail into a creek, and wait for calmer weather. The next day they come to the place where Captain Standish discovered the corn, and find much more. Captain Jones fills his boat, and returns to the ship. They discover two wigwams, but the Indians have fled.

On Wednesday, December 16th, eighteen men in the large boat bid their friends farewell, and sail along the shore. They are bound for a harbor across the bay, twenty-four miles west of where the *Mayflower* is

CAPTAIN STANDISH ATTACKED BY THE INDIANS.

lying. The mate of the vessel has been there in a former voyage; but the waves are so high they do not dare to sail straight across the bay. The air is piercing cold. The spray dashes over them, and freezes on their clothing. At night they land, kindle a fire, eat their frugal fare, post their sentinels, and sleep as best they can. The next day half of the party march through the woods, and half creep along with the boat, and rest at night as before. The wolves howl around the men, who fire their guns to put the beasts to flight. They are astir before daylight, cooking their breakfast. Suddenly they hear a strange cry, and arrows fall around them. Captain Standish quickly has his army marshalled. Crack go the muskets, and one of the Indians is wounded at the first fire; the rest flee, carrying away the wounded man. Captain Standish follows them far enough to let them know that they are not afraid, nor in any way dis·couraged. The Pilgrims gather the arrows, in order to send them to Eng·land, to let their friends see what weapons the savages use. The wind is favorable; they hoist their sail, and glide along the shore northward now; but suddenly the wind changes to north-east, and the waves come rolling in. When they are highest their rudder breaks, and two men, with their oars, are hardly able to steer the boat.

"Be of good cheer; I see the harbor," shouts Robert Copping, mate of the *Mayflower*.

It is almost night, and they hasten to reach the harbor before darkness comes on. They hoist the sail; but the mast breaks, and the sail falls into the sea, and the boat heels over on one side: they are in danger of capsizing, but gather the sail on board, and the tide carries them into a cove. The breakers are rolling upon the beach. They can see the white foam through the darkness tossed high in the air.

"The Lord be merciful! My eyes never saw this place before. We must run the boat ashore," cries the mate.

But a sailor sees that the boat will be swamped. "About with her!" he shouts. The rowers bend to their oars, and the boat heads from the shore. They turn a sandy point, and find themselves in smooth water. Shall they go ashore? They are weary, hungry, chilled, and wet to the skin. It will be twelve hours to dawn. Will they not perish before morning? They will land, trusting, if In-

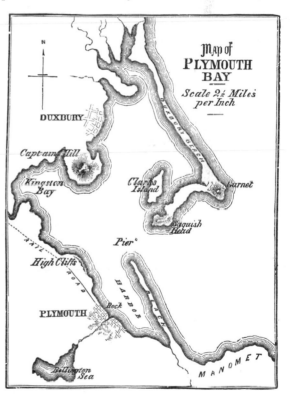

dians assail them, to defend themselves. They reach the shore, kindle a fire, and dry their clothes, keeping watch the while for Indians. In the morning they find that they are on an island, which they name Clark's Island, for Edward Clark, one of their number. The sun is shining once more; but they are weak and exhausted. Time is precious; but they will rest there through the day—Saturday—and prepare themselves to keep the Sabbath.

On Monday, rested and refreshed, they sound the harbor, and find it

PLYMOUTH HARBOR, DECEMBER, 1620.

safe and good. They pull westward to the main-land, where they find Indian-corn fields and a river of fresh water. They climb a high hill, view the landscape, and are pleased with the prospect. Under the brow of the hill, near a brook, and near springs of pure water, they will rear their homes. They return to the ship, and report their discoveries; and the *Mayflower* spreads her sails once more, and glides across the bay.

Winter has set in. The winds are chill, snow lies upon the hills. The spray freezes upon the shrouds of the vessel. The scene is cheerless—ice-bound shores, a dense forest, an unexplored wilderness, before them; a savage foe lurking beneath the pines; no homes, no welcome hearth-stone; forebodings of sickness and starvation.

On Sunday Elder Brewster preaches to them on shipboard for the last time. On Monday they examine once more the ground where they propose to rear their homes; and on Tuesday, after asking God to direct them in all that they are about to do, they take a vote as to where they shall build their houses. It is the first *town-meeting* ever held in America, and the majority decide. The new State—the new order of things—has begun. That which the human race has struggled for through all the ages has come at last—the right of the people to rule. Old George Buchanan, Mary of Scotland's tutor, enunciated the right to the world; but that which was theory to him has become a fact. *Self-government has begun.* Take note of it, ye lords, nobles, kings, and emperors, for of this beginning there will come a new order of things in human affairs!

The *Mayflower* is riding at anchor. The long-boat, filled with men and women, glides over the waves to the shore. They step from the boat to a rock. The new State is in possession of its future domain. January 1st, 1621, is a gloomy day, for death begins his ravages, taking one of the citizens, Degory Priest. Captain Standish goes out, with four or five soldiers, to make explorations. They find Indian wigwams, but none of the savages. The citizens are hard at work building a common house, in which they can store their goods. The boat plies between the ship and the shore, bringing boxes, and bales, and furniture—chairs, chests, pots, and pans. They build their houses of logs, and cover them with thatch; for they have not yet learned to peel the bark from the trees, or to rive the pines into shingles, for roofing. On Sunday, January 14th, they barely escape a terrible disaster, for the thatch on the common house takes fire, and they have hard work to put it out.

On the 29th of January, a great grief comes to Captain Standish. His beautiful wife, Rose, has been fading day by day. The hardships have

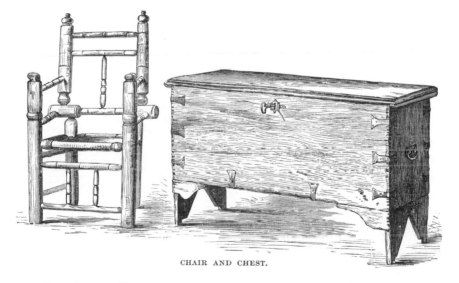

CHAIR AND CHEST.

worn her down. Possibly she pines for the green fields and the cheerful homes of Old England, which she never more will see. Heaven is nearer than the old home. With tearful eyes and swelling hearts, the living carry her up to the burial-place upon the top of the hill. This is the entry in their journal, mournful in its briefness: "*Jan.* 29. *Dies Rose, wife of Captain Standish.*"

Two days later the Pilgrims see two Indians lurking beneath the pines,

"WELCOME, ENGLISHMEN!"

but they quickly disappear. They see no other savages till March 16th, when they are greatly surprised to see an Indian march boldly into the settlement, and to hear him say, "*Welcome, Englishmen!*" His name is Samoset. He has been down the coast of Maine in other years, and has seen the Englishmen which have been in Sir Fernando Gorges' fishing establishment. He is kindly treated. He goes away, but soon returns with another Indian, Squanto, who was kidnapped years before by a villain named Hunt, who landed and seized twenty Indians, and carried them to Spain. Squanto has been in London, and can speak English. Samoset brings three more, who have skins for sale. He informs the Pilgrims that their great chief, Massasoit, is near by. In a few minutes the chief makes his appearance with sixty Indians. This is the account which the Pilgrims give of the interview:

"After an hour the king comes to the top of an hill over against us, with a train of sixty men. We send Squanto to him, who brings word we should send one to parley with him. We send Mr. Edward Winslow to know his mind, and signify that our governor desires to see him, and truck (trade), and confirm a peace. Upon this the king leaves Mr. Winslow in the custody of Quadequina, and comes over the brook with a train of twenty men, leaving their bows and arrows behind them. Captain Standish and Master Williamson, with six musketeers, meet him at the brook, where they salute each other; conduct him to a house, wherein they place a green rug and three or four cushions; then instantly comes our governor, with drum, trumpet, and musketeers. After salutations, the governor kissing his hand and the king kissing his, they sit down. The governor entertains him with some refreshments, and then they agree on a league of friendship.

MASSASOIT'S VISIT TO THE PILGRIMS.

THE PALACE OF KING MASSASOIT.

"After this the governor conducts him to the brook, where they embrace and part, we keeping six or seven hostages for our messenger. But Quadequina coming with his troop, we entertain and convey him back, receive our messenger, and return the hostages."

Massasoit's palace is not so gorgeous as that at Hampton, in which King James lives: it is a hut in the woods; but the Pilgrims soon discover that the chief is a better friend than the King of England. He is a true man, and the treaty which he makes with them is faithfully kept. James has persecuted them, but Massasoit befriends them. Archbishop Whitgift has driven them from their homes, but Massasoit bids them welcome. Their Christian brothers of England are their bitterest foes; the heathen savages of the wilderness their best friends.

But a foe whom they cannot fight is upon them. Spring comes. The trailing arbutus fills the air with its fragrance; the birds returning from

SUNDAY AT PLYMOUTH.

the distant South are singing in the forest; the sun sends down its cheerful beams upon the little settlement; but flowers, bird-songs, and the genial warmth of spring can never fill the void of aching hearts. Forty-six of the one hundred and one Pilgrims have finished their pilgrimage, and are at rest in the burial-ground on the top of the hill. They level the earth, that the Indians may not know how many have died. But the living have brave hearts. They go on with their work. On Sunday, William Brewster preaches in the common house, where their goods are piled. No bishop has licensed him to preach; he has *assumed* the right to use such gifts as he may be endowed with, and his hearers respect him as their religious teacher. He has no other authority over them. The members of the Church decide all questions that arise. William Brewster is their bishop, yet his vote counts but one. Theirs is a democratic State, and a democratic Church. Men are equals. Never before has the world seen such a community.

There comes a sad day. Through the winter the *Mayflower* has been swinging at her anchor in the harbor, but now she is about to depart for England. The last words are spoken, the sails are spread, and the ship sails away. They who stand upon the shore see it fade in the dim distance. The last tie that bound them to their old home is severed. While the vessel remained, they had the means of returning; but now their destiny is fixed. Well for the world that it is so. Such heroic souls as they are not afraid of destiny, no matter what it may be—prosperity or privation, success or failure, life or death. They may die, but Truth and Liberty are eternal; for these they will live, or, if God so will it, die.

Death takes them one by one. On the very day that the *Mayflower* sails, their beloved governor, Carver, is seized with sudden sickness, which ends in death. It is a sore stroke, for he was wise and prudent in council, brave of heart, and a righteous man.

Though the governor is dead, the State lives. "*The people are the only legitimate source of power.*" George Buchanan wrote it. The people elected John Carver, and the same people—those that are left—elect his successor, William Bradford—he who was baptized in the little old stone church in Austerfield. So the new State perpetuates its life. *The State cannot die.* A new truth dawns upon the world. As long as there is an individual, there will be a State.

At last, after ages of persecution and suffering, Liberty has found her home. The seed-corn of a great empire has been planted—an empire in which the lowest shall be equal with the highest; where he alone shall be king who does kingly deeds.

The contest is not yet ended between royal authority and the rights of men, between priestly prerogative and the consciences of individuals. King James will still persecute them; King George will attempt to exercise arbitrary authority; there will be persecutions, imprisonments, and banishments for conscience' sake: men cannot at once be emancipated from the ideas of the ages. The intolerance and bigotry of the Old World, like noxious weeds, will take root in the New, and many years must go by before men can be wholly free.

The little company—there are only fifty of them now—have no code of laws. In the Old World, kings, barons, nobles, archbishops, and bishops have made the laws; but these untitled, unlettered men assemble in town meeting and make their laws—each man voting. No edict from King James could add to the validity of their statutes; no archbishop or noble could frame laws more wise and just; no high constable of the kingdom could make them more effective, as John Billington finds out. He speaks words disrespectful of the new governor, and the citizens condemn him to be tied neck and heels, and fed on bread and water till he begs pardon.

The new State, composed of fifty individuals, elects its governor, frames its laws, and enforces them. Can a king do more? So the subject becomes king, ruling himself in his own God-given right. From the beginning of time kings have assumed the right to rule; but in the wilderness of the Western world the exiles from Scrooby and Austerfield take the sceptre into their own hands, and inaugurate a new era in human affairs.

Liberty is in her new home. Strong hands will subdue the wilderness, and brave hearts will establish an empire extending from the frozen regions of the North to the sunny climes of the South, from the stormy Atlantic to the peaceful Pacific. Through hardship, suffering, and sacrifice the great republic of the Western world shall rise to become a peer among the nations. Its starry flag shall be the emblem of the world's best hope; for to it the oppressed of all the earth shall turn with longing eyes, and beneath it there shall be peace and plenty, and the recognition of the rights of men.

INDEX.

THE END

The Story of Liberty

The secular humanists have edited God out of history! Now you can read what they cut out. Reprinted from the original 1879 edition, *The Story of Liberty* tells you the price that was paid for our freedom and how it was won. An excellent historical resource for your library. Quickly becoming a best seller among home schools and Christian educators.

415 page paperback, illustrated.
ISBN # 0-938558-20-X
$ 14.95

The Story of Liberty Study Guide

Steve Dawson's study guide for Charles Coffin's *The Story of Liberty* contains three main features designed to provide a comprehensive moral understanding of the people, main events and ideas contained inside Coffin's valuable book. Each chapter of the 98 page guide contains fill-in-the-blank questions to help facilitate personal and group study sessions or home schooling classes. The 8-1/2" x 11" guide comes with a separate answer booklet.

ISBN # 0-938558-27-7
$ 10.95   98 Pages

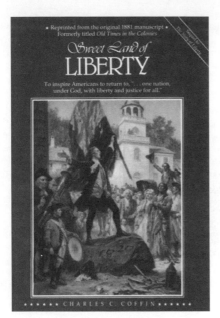

Sweet Land of Liberty

Sweet Land of Liberty, the sequel to *The Story of Liberty*, tells the historical highlights of colonial America with a Providential view. Written by civil war correspondent and children's author Charles Coffin, *Sweet Land of Liberty* has now been faithfully reproduced exactly as it was originally printed in 1881.

458 page paperback, illustrated.
ISBN # 0-938558-48-X
$ 14.95

The Boys of '76

"In this modern era of historical dishonesty, the work of Charles Coffin stands strong. His fear of God, his love for his country and his respect for historical truth all combine to give us a faithful, passionate, and accurate story of our nation's fight for liberty. I pray that everyone, young and old alike, will read and remember *The Boys of '76*."
Gregg Harris, Noble Institute

423 page paperback, illustrated.
ISBN # 0-938558-82-X
$ 16.95

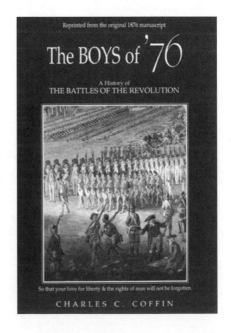

Life Changing Books
& Bible Studies
from Maranatha Publications

Bible Studies Series

Firm Foundation	Overcoming Life	Lovers of God	Preparation of the Bride	Life of Excellence
This study is our best seller. Covers the foundational truths in Scripture. It Includes repentance, baptism, healing, faith, and other studies. Paperback, 132 pages. $ 11.95 ISBN # 0-938558-005	Takes you a step further than the basics. Includes a series on brokenness, as well as righteousness, faith, and the work of the ministry. Paperback, 113 pages. $ 11.95 ISBN # 0-938558-01-3	Life changing truths from Philippians. The all-sufficiency of God, living in joy, victory over trials, having the mind of Christ, and fruitfulness in ministry. Paperback, 44 pages. $ 9.95 ISBN # 0-938558-03-X	Explains metaphors and hidden truths in the Song of Solomon. This study reveals the beauty of the union between Jesus and His Bride. Paperback, 234 pages. $ 16.95 ISBN # 0-88270-471-0	Help for building character in your Christian life... bridling the tongue, Godly Wisdom, our attitude toward sinners, living in the last days, and more. Paperback, 60 pages. $ 9.95 ISBN # 0-938558-04-8

Estudios Biblicos para un Fundamento Firmé

Firm Foundation also available in Spanish.

An interactive Bible Study that challenges the reader to utilize their Bible and seek out truths in Scripture. This top selling Bible Study is used around the world.
Paperback, 132 Pages
$ 11.95
ISBN # 0-938558-22-6

COUPON

COUPON

Receive $5.00 OFF

your next order of

$10 or more

with this coupon!

Good only with orders directly through **Maranatha Publications** (just include this coupon with your next order).

MARANATHA PUBLICATIONS, INC.

P.O. BOX 1799 • GAINESVILLE, FL 32602 • 904-645-3965 • FAX 904-645-3966

visit our website at www.mpi2000.net

Bible Study Books - *by Bob and Rose Weiner*

BOOK NAME	PRICE	QUANTITY	TOTAL
Firm Foundation	$ 11.95		
Overcoming Life	$ 11.95		
Lovers of God	$ 9.95		
Life of Excellence	$ 9.95		
Preparation of the Bride	$ 16.95		
One Set of Above Studies (Set of 5)	$ 55.75		
Jesus Brings New Life	$ 5.95		
Spanish *Firm Foundation*	$ 11.95		

Christian History Books

BOOK NAME	PRICE	QUANTITY	TOTAL
The Story of Liberty (A Christian History Text)	$ 14.95		
Story of Liberty Study Guide by Steve Dawson	$ 10.95		
Sweet Land of Liberty (Sequel to *Story of Liberty*)	$ 14.95		
The Boys of '76 (Sequel to *Sweet Land of Liberty*)	$ 16.95		

Booklets

BOOK NAME	PRICE	QUANTITY	TOTAL
Books by Bob and Rose Weiner			
How to Become a Dynamic Speaker	$ 2.50		
Mightier Than The Sword	$ 2.50		
The Bed Is Too Short	$ 2.50		
Christian Dominion	$ 2.50		
Books by Lee Grady			
Defending Christian Economics	$ 2.50		
A Vision For World Dominion	$ 2.50		
War of the Words	$ 2.50		

Sub Total	
Shipping	
Add FL sales tax	
TOTAL US Dollars	

VISA and MasterCard Accepted

Ship To:

Name _____

Address _____

City _____ State _____ Zip _____

Phone (_____) _____

Check Enclosed, payable to Maranatha Publications, Inc.

Charge to my:　❑ VISA　❑ MasterCard

Card No. _____ Expires _____/_____

Shipping & Handling:

Less than $10.00	$ 3.50
$10.00 - $24.99	$ 4.50
$25.00 - $49.99	$ 5.50
$50.00 or more	9%

Mail Order To: Maranatha Publications, Inc., P.O. Box 1799, Gainesville, FL 32602